Standards of Excellence in Budget Presentation

Denny G. Bolton

T. Gary Harmer

Association of School Business Officials International

ISBN 978-0-910170-75-8

Published by
Association of School Business Officials International
11401 North Shore Drive, Reston, VA 20190-4232

© 2000, ASBO International

Meritorious Budget Awards Committee

Janice R. Klein, RSBA, Chair
Director of Fiscal Services
Mt. Lebanon School District
Pittsburgh, PA

E. Danny Cash, RSBA
Assistant Superintendent Finance and Operations
Community Consolidated School District 21
Wheeling, IL

Brian D. Greene, CGA
Executive Superintendent of Business and Treasurer
Thames Valley District School Board
London, ON

James R. Graham, RSBA
Assistant Superintendent for Business and Finance
South Lyon Community Schools
South Lyon, MI

Wilson H. Hatcher, CPA
Executive Director of Budget and Planning
Colorado Springs School District No. 11
Colorado Springs, CO

John P. Welch
Director of Business and Financial Services
Federal Way Public Schools
Federal Way, WA

William R. Fellmy, Ph.D., RSBA, Board Liaison
Deputy Superintendent
Washington Township Metropolitan School District
Indianapolis, IN

Don I. Tharpe, Ed.D., Staff Liaison
Executive Director
ASBO International
Reston, VA

Linda K. Prevatte, Staff Liaison
Director of Professional Development
ASBO International
Reston, VA

ASBO International wishes to thank the following school districts for their contributions to this book:

Alpine School District, American Fork, UT

Broward County Public Schools, Ft. Lauderdale, FL

Colorado Springs School District, Colorado Springs, CO

Desoto Parish School Board, Mansfield, LA

Horry County Schools, Conway, SC

Jordan School District, Sandy, UT

Metropolitan School District of Washington Township, Indianapolis, IN

Mount Lebanon School District, Pittsburgh, PA

Owen J. Roberts School District, Pottstown, PA

Prince William County Public Schools, Manassas, VA

Richland Community College, Community College District #537, Decatur, IL

Salt Lake City School District, Salt Lake City, UT

San Carlos Unified School District, San Carlos, AZ

School District of Kettle Moraine, Wales, WI

Souderton Area School District, Souderton, PA

South Lyon Community Schools, South Lyon, MI

Tredyffrin/Easttown School District, Berwyn, PA

CONTENTS

CONTENTS *(continued)*

About the Authors

Denny G. Bolton, Ph.D., RSBA is the Chief Business Official (CBO) in the Owen J. Roberts School District, Pottstown, PA. Dr. Bolton has served as president of both the Pennsylvania Association of School Business Officials (PASBO) and the Association of School Business Officials (ASBO) International. He was Chair of the Task Force that designed the Meritorious Budget Awards (MBA) Program.

W. Gary Harmer, CPA, is the Assistant Superintendent for Business Services in the Salt Lake City School District, Salt Lake City, UT. Mr. Harmer has been president of the Utah ASBO, chair of ASBO International's Accounting Auditing and Budgeting committee and is currently the chair of the MBA committee. He was appointed a member of the Governmental Accounting Standards Board at its inception in 1984. He was also a recipient of an ASBO Eagle Service Award in 1992.

Author of the first edition of *Standards of Excellence in Budget Presentations*:

Dennis Strachota is the Strategic Policy Analyst for the Regional Environmental Management department at Metro, the nation's only elected regional government. Mr. Strachota is also an instructor in public policy and budgeting for The Mark O. Hatfield School of Government at Portand State University in Portland, Oregon.

Preface

ASBO International inaugurated the Meritorious Budget Awards Program (MBA) in July 1995 and the program has grown steadily, both in participation and stature in the education arena. *Standards of Excellence in Budget Presentations* is a hands-on practical guide to the MBA Program in particular and effective school budgeting in general. This second edition was commissioned to provide more and better examples of outstanding budget presentations meeting the MBA Program criteria. In addition, it reflects the minor changes made in the criteria for the 1998 program year.

Like its predecessor, this edition is divided into five chapters. Chapter 1 provides background on the program and offers tips on how to prepare a successful document and award submission. Chapter 1 concludes with an explanation of the program's general requirements. The remaining four chapters are devoted to each of the four major groupings of award criteria. Each chapter is followed by a checklist and examples from actual budget documents that satisfy those specific criteria.

Special thanks go to Denny G. Bolton, Ph.D., RSBA, Business Administrator, Owen J. Roberts School District, Pottstown, PA; and W. Gary Harmer, CPA, Business Administrator, Salt Lake City School District, Salt Lake City, UT, both pioneers who helped build the MBA Program and who added to the foundation laid by Dennis R. Strachota to create this second edition. Thanks also go to the Meritorious Budget Awards Committee, listed on a preceding page, for their outstanding work not only reviewing this book but administering the MBA Program. Finally, I would like to thank the school districts that have participated in the MBA Program, especially those featured in exhibits on the following pages. This book is a tribute to the hard work of all school systems that provide strong, useful school budget documents and will make an excellent resource for those seeking excellence in budget presentation.

Don I. Tharpe, Ed.D.
Executive Director
Association of School Business Officials International

CHAPTER 1
Background and General Requirements

This section of the guide to the Meritorious Budget Awards (MBA) Program serves dual purposes. One is to explain what ASBO International's MBA Program is and the benefits it provides to school business officials and two, provide some background on the awards program: its origin, purpose, eligibility requirements and application procedures.

This section also discusses the "General Requirements" that school budgets must satisfy to receive the Meritorious Budget Award.

BACKGROUND

The Meritorious Budget Awards Program was established in 1995 to encourage and recognize excellence in school system budgeting. It is an international awards program created by the Association of School Business Officials (ASBO) International to help school business administrators achieve a very high standard of excellence in budget presentation. The program sets minimum presentation standards for a school system's annual budget document. The program evaluates budget documents against specific criteria or minimum standards. Budgets that meet or exceed these criteria receive the prestigious Meritorious Budget Award.

Any school entity, including local school districts, educational services agencies (BOCES), private schools, intermediate units, and colleges and universities, is eligible to participate in the MBA program. The school entity does not have to be a member of ASBO International to participate.

School entities participating in this program cite the following benefits from their participation in the program:

■ Provides clear budget presentation guidelines;
■ Defines state-of-the-art budget practices;
■ Encourages both short and long range budget goals;
■ Promotes sound fiscal management practices;
■ Promotes effective use of educational resources;
■ Facilitates professional growth and development for the budget staff; and
■ Helps build solid skills in developing, analyzing, and presenting school entity budgets.

Those who receive the Meritorious Budget Award are recognized with:

■ A handsome plaque and certificate;
■ Recognition of their achievement published in ASBO Accents, School Business Affairs and their state or provincial ASBO Affiliate's newsletter;
■ News releases sent to their local media;
■ Letters of accomplishment sent to their Superintendent and School Board;
■ Comprehensive feedback about their budget from peers trained in up-to-date school budgeting techniques; and
■ Continuing education credits in ASBO's Professional Registration Program.

Until the development of the MBA criteria, practitioners had no guidelines to follow when attempting to explain the financial plan of the school entity to the public. The MBA format encourages budget developers to present a single document organized in a user-friendly way that translates plans for providing educational services into an easy-to-understand financial story.

In 1993 the ASBO Board of Directors made a decision to develop a school entity budget awards program and directed the ASBO president to appoint a task force. The task force was charged with developing a budget recognition program which would promote state-of-the-art practices for the development and presentation of school budgets. The task force was appointed and spent many hours researching what constituted state-of-the-art budget practices. The task force also developed and sent out a membership survey to assess member interest in such a program. The results of the survey confirmed that ASBO members would enthusiastically support the program. The following year, the task force finished their research and developed the program standards currently used as the MBA criteria.

School entities from representative states and provinces were asked to field-test the criteria by preparing budgets according to the requirements for a test review. Reviewer training workshops were developed, where school business officials were trained to serve as reviewers. A reviewer accreditation workshop was held in conjunction with ASBO's 1994 Annual Meeting in Seattle and also a Super Session at this meeting further acquainted ASBO members with the program's standards and benefits.

In 1995, the field-test budget reviews were completed, the criteria were refined, and the program began its first year July 1st. Applicants were invited to submit their 1995–96 budgets for review and consideration for the Meritorious Budget Award. During 1995, the MBA Task Force became one of the standing committees of ASBO officially known as the MBA Committee. The committee is comprised of school business officials who are experts in the field of budgeting. The committee oversees all aspects of the program, provides technical expertise, continuously reviews and updates the program criteria and presents MBA-related workshops.

Growth and Success of the MBA Program

During the first year of the program, 28 school entities submitted their budgets for review and 16 received the award. In the second program year, 33 school entities submitted their budgets and 21 received the award. Program year 1997–98, which was the third year of operation, was far more successful than the first two years with 51 school entities from 25 states submitting budgets for review and 33 school entities receiving the award. It is expected that the program will continue to experience this same kind of growth for many years into the future.

Since 1995, more than 100 dedicated school business officials and accounting professionals have been trained and certified as MBA Program reviewers. Becoming a reviewer is a professional development opportunity that gives an individual a chance to "give back" to the profession. Reviewers lend their expertise to the program by providing feedback to submitting school entities that enables them to create better and more effective budgets in the future.

In 1996, MetLife Resources joined forces with ASBO International to promote the MBA Program. MetLife understands how critical budgeting is for every school system's financial operations and is dedicated to helping ASBO in its endeavor to raise the standards of school system budgeting. Their sponsorship of the MBA Program supports ASBO's efforts to educate school business officials about the MBA criteria and to market and expand the program.

Application Process

Budgets should be submitted in the same form in which they are prepared. Participants will want to pay close attention to the MBA criteria as they develop their budgets. As applicant school systems develop their budgets, they will want to check their budgets against the criteria using the "The Criteria Location Checklist" before final printing. If minor adjustments are needed, participants can incorporate changes into the final document. This guidebook explains the criteria and offers examples of presentations that satisfy the MBA requirements.

The document must be submitted to ASBO within 90 days after the budget's legal adoption by the school entity's governing body. The submission should include:

- A completed MBA application form;
- A letter explaining criteria that are not relevant to the school entity (see "General Requirements" for more information);
- A response to any previous review team comments and recommendations;
- Four copies of the school system's budget;
- Four copies of a completed Criteria Location Checklist; and
- Payment of the application fee.

If any of the above items are missing from the application packet, processing of the submission will be delayed.

The application form requests information on:

- The school entity applying for the award;
- The school official responsible for the application;
- Beginning and ending dates of the budget year;
- The date the budget was legally adopted;
- The size of the budget; and
- The names and addresses of officials who should be notified of the review results.

Four copies of the approved budget document must be submitted. Applicants are discouraged from submitting supplemental information such as budget manuals and budgets-in-brief. ASBO sends a copy of the budget to each of the three reviewers and retains one copy for its program files.

The applicant must also complete and submit four copies of the Criteria Location Checklist. On the checklist, the applicant simply lists the page numbers in the document where individual criteria are satisfied. Budget reviewers rely on this checklist to help them locate specific examples of where in the budget document the MBA criteria are met.

Lastly, the applicant submits payment of an application fee, which helps defray the cost of the program. The fee is graduated by the size of the budget; applicants with smaller budgets pay a smaller application fee. Applicants also pay a lower fee if they are a member of ASBO International or join at the time of budget submission.

The Review and Notification Process

Once ASBO receives a complete application packet and processes the paperwork, a copy of the budget document and application materials are forwarded to each member of a three-member review team.

To qualify as member of a MBA review team, a reviewer must work in the school business field, be a member of ASBO International and adhere to certain program requirements, including participation in a reviewer accreditation-training program.

Independently the reviewers evaluate the assigned budget document. The reviewer rates the document against each of the MBA criteria using the following rating categories:

- Exceeds criteria
- Meets criteria
- Does not meet criteria

Applicants are expected to satisfy all of the criteria. The reviewers determine whether the failure to meet any one criterion has a substantial effect on the budget document taken as a whole and is sufficient reason to deny the award.

The reviewer also prepares written comments on criteria that may not be properly implemented in the budget document, how well the budget satisfies the criteria as well as suggestions on how to improve the document. Based upon an overall assessment of whether or not the document meets or exceeds all of the criteria, each reviewer recommends the budget for approval or denial of the Meritorious Budget Award. When the chair of the review team receives the rating sheets and comments from the other members of the review team, the results are compiled and a final decision to award or deny the Meritorious Budget Award is made.

Notification of results is sent to the school entity within 12 to 16 weeks of receipt of the budget submission. The time required to complete an evaluation will vary depending upon the availability of reviewers. During peak submission times, turnaround of reviews may take longer if sufficient reviewers are not available.

When the Meritorious Budget Award is awarded, the school system receives several important forms of recognition. The school administrator who submitted the document receives notification of the award and confidential comments prepared by the reviewers. In addition, the administrator earns continuing education units for ASBO's Professional Registration Program.

Notification of the award is also sent to the school superintendent/director and school board. The school system receives a personalized plaque and official recognition in ASBO's membership directory, *ASBO Accents*, and the Affiliate's newsletter. ASBO also provides a news release that the school system can distribute to its local news media.

If the MBA is denied, a letter of notification is sent only to the school administrator who submitted the budget. In addition, the school administrator receives confidential comments from the review team on how to improve the document.

The Appeals Process

A school system can choose to appeal a denial. Within 30 days of receipt of a denial letter, the school system should resubmit three copies of its budget and the original Criteria Location Checklist as well as a letter requesting an appeal and explaining why it believes the denial was inappropriate.

ASBO will send the resubmitted budget and letter to a separate appeal review team. The appeal team will review the budget and decide to award or deny the Meritorious Budget Award within 90 days. The decision of the appeal review team is final.

Continued Participation

Receipt of the Meritorious Budget Award is a special distinction received by few school entities. Because the award is granted for only one year, ASBO encourages school systems to apply for the award every year. Neither budget documents nor the MBA criteria are static. A school system can demonstrate how well its budget document adapts to changing conditions and standards through perennial participation in the MBA Program.

Participate as a Budget Reviewer

Another way to participate in the MBA Program is as a budget reviewer. Reviewers not only perform a valuable service for the program but also receive valuable information in return. Through the MBA Program, reviewers gain insight into effective budget presentation through the budget documents they evaluate each year. It is not unusual for reviewers to acquire new techniques and formats they can apply to their own documents.

GENERAL REQUIREMENTS

The MBA criteria are divided into five areas: General Requirements, Introductory Section, Organizational Section, Financial Section and Informational Section. All but the General Requirements criteria apply to specific sections of the budget document. For example, the criteria under the Introductory Section are ones that should be satisfied within the Introductory Section of a school entity's budget.

The General Requirements relate to the overall budget document but do not necessarily apply to a specific section of a document. They set criteria concerning the document cover page, the sectional division and table of contents, page numbering, information not included in the budget document, response to previous review team comments, use of graphs and charts, and the technical preparation of the document.

The Cover Page (Criterion A-1)

The budget cover page should contain the title "Budget", and include the full name of the school entity, the city/county and state/province in which the entity is located, and the budget year covered. Often the school entity's boundaries will include an area in more than one city or county. The city or county that is to appear on the cover page is the one used in the entity's formal address. See Exhibit 1-1 for an example of a cover page.

Document should be divided by major sections (Criterion A-2)

This criterion specifies that the budget document should be divided by major sections with consecutive page numbers. Unless a school system chooses to add other sections to its document, the major sections should include those sections delineated by MBA criteria: Introductory, Organizational, Financial and Informational Sections. These and other sections could be divided within the document by divider pages or tabs. Whatever method of division is used, page numbering should run consecutively rather than starting over with each major section.

This criterion also requires that the document include a table of contents. The table should, at a minimum, identify all major sections and precede the Introductory Section. Because the table of contents helps readers to locate specific sections of the document, school entities may also want to list subsections within the table. School systems are given wide latitude regarding the makeup and design of this element of the document.

Information not relevant to the school entity and other information required (Criterion A-3)

If there is any information required by MBA criteria that is not relevant to the school entity and, therefore, is not presented in its budget document, it should be identified and explained by the school entity official submitting the budget document in a cover letter accompanying the application form. For example, information on assessed and market value of taxable property and tax rates required by the Informational Section criteria may not be relevant to school systems which are dependent on a unit of general government for financial support or to an intermediate school unit. If the school system explains what information is not included and why it is not relevant to the school entity, then it will not be counted by reviewers as an omission of required criteria.

Relevance is the only factor, however, that can exempt a school system from meeting specific criteria. Applicants are expected to satisfy all of the MBA criteria. It is expected that a school system can include all the information required by the criteria in its budget document and still conform to legal requirements. The school entity may want to include additional information not required by the MBA criteria in order to meet legal requirements or to provide information required by their governing body, administration or citizens.

In some states, school entities report budget information to state education departments or other governmental agencies, which have oversight responsibilities for the school entity. These state education departments or other agencies have their own form for submitting this information. It is expected in these circumstances that the budget will be prepared according to the MBA criteria and used to communicate to citizens, bond rating agencies, and others with an interest in the budget story, and the budget information will also be reported to these oversight agencies according to their required form and format.

The MBA review team alone decides whether a school system has met all of the criteria and whether its failure to meet any one criterion is reason to deny the award.

Response to Previous Review Teams (Criterion A-4)

If the school entity has applied for the Meritorious Budget Award previously, a response to the previous MBA review team comments and recommendations by the school official responsible for the school entity submission is required.

Use of Graphs and Charts (Criterion A-5)

Graphs and charts should be an integral part of every budget. This MBA criterion encourages their use in all sections of the document. They are particularly helpful in stimulating readers' interest and aiding their understanding of budget information. The charts and graphs most frequently used in budgets are bar charts, line graphs and pie charts.

Bar charts can depict trends or how different variables change relative to one another over time. For example, the "sources of revenue" bar chart in Exhibit 1-2 shows how the percentage of revenue varies with the source (i.e., local, state and federal). If a few additional years of data for each revenue source were added to this graph, the reader could see how these percentages change over time. The same page in this exhibit also illustrates how bar graphs can be displayed either vertically or horizontally.

Line graphs are plotted on lines, with a horizontal axis and vertical axis. They are particularly useful in depicting financial projections or trends. When creating line graphs, those who prepare budgets should remember to label each axis and provide the proper scale for plotted data. Those who prepare budgets should also use different line patterns to display different variables and multiple lines to show the relationship between three or more variables. Exhibit 1-3 is an example of a simple line graph showing how enrollment in this school system has changed through the years. It presents a visual picture of what has happened over the space of many years at a glance.

The third most common type of chart is the pie chart. Pie charts are nothing more than circles divided into sections to show the relationship of the parts to a whole. They are useful for general comparisons of relative size, and often used to depict sources and uses of "money" within budget documents. Exhibit 1-4 makes effective use of pie charts to display the results of a survey.

Those preparing budgets can use a wide array of charts and graphs to clarify and reinforce budget data and narratives. Graphics and spreadsheet computer software make it particularly easy to prepare effective and attractive budget graphs and charts. Other visuals, such as photographs and maps, can serve the same purpose. Whatever visual device is chosen, it should be used properly. Graphs and charts are best used throughout the document rather than grouped together within a single section.

Technically Well Prepared (Criterion A-6)

The budget document should be technically well prepared, be easy to read and flow in logical sequence. The narration should be clear and understandable and free from spelling and grammar errors.

The Cover Page

(Criterion A-1)

Exhibit 1-1

Exhibit 1-1—The Cover Page

Mt. Lebanon School District

Adopted by the Board
of School Directors
May 19, 1997

Budget 97-98

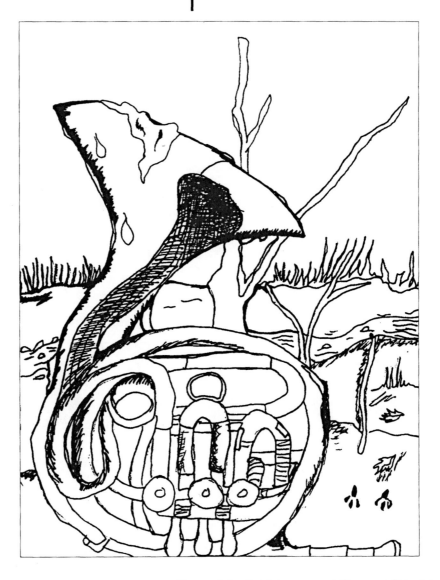

Artist: Melissa Arndell

Use of Graphs and Charts

(Criterion A-5)

Exhibit 1-2 through 1-4

Exhibit 1-2—"Source of Revenue" Bar Chart

graph below presents the sources of revenue to support the proposed operating budget.

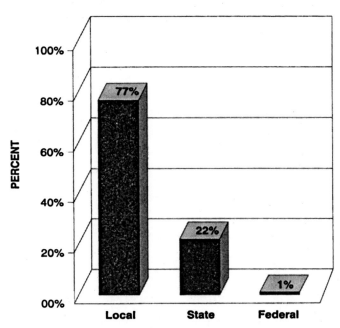

SOURCES OF REVENUE

The local sources of revenue to support the operations budget represents almost four-fifths (4/5) of total available sources of funds. Of this amount, the largest source of revenue available to the District is the property tax that is derived from current, interim, and delinquent real estate tax payments. Below is a graph that presents the various sources of local revenue included in the proposed budget to support General Fund operations for the 1995-96 fiscal year.

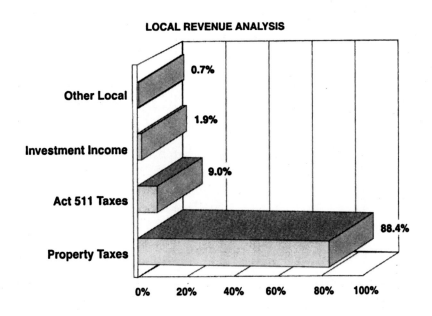

LOCAL REVENUE ANALYSIS

Exhibit 1-3—Simple Line Graph

SALT LAKE CITY SCHOOL DISTRICT

District Enrollment Trends
Years Ended 1965 to 1997 Actual with Projections from 1998 to 2002

These projections are made using multiple-year cohort survival analysis. In simple language, this means that students enrolled are projected to remain in schools but are moved up in grade as they become older. Each year, for many years, historical information has been kept relative to the number of students who leave our schools each year for various reasons and the number of students who enter the schools in each age group. From this data base, giving greatest weight to the most recent experience and making adjustments for observed changes in some neighborhoods, implied estimates of inmigration and outmigration are made. Birth data is also projected forward adjusted by the implied estimates of in and outmigration as described above. These projections of enrollment and average daily membership have been very accurate in the past; 1996-97 actual ADM of 25,400 was within 415 students of the projected 24,985 ADM for that year. Since the 1997-98 year is not yet complete, we do not have actual ADM for that year, but currently it appears actual ADM will be 25,221 students, which is approximately a 1.37-percent variance from the 24,880 projection included in the 1997-98 budget document.

Fiscal Year	ADM	Fiscal Year	ADM	Fiscal Year	ADM	Fiscal Year	ADM	Fiscal Year	ADM
1964-65	39,416	1972-73	30,411	1980-81	23,426	1988-89	24,338	1995-96	25,309
1965-66	38,652	1973-74	28,777	1981-82	23,909	1989-90	24,401	1996-97	25,400
1966-67	36,937	1974-75	27,611	1982-83	24,641	1990-91	24,897	1997-98	25,221
1967-68	36,027	1975-76	26,524	1983-84	24,579	1991-92	25,249	1998-99	25,190
1968-69	35,308	1976-77	25,832	1984-85	24,764	1992-93	25,261	1999-2000	25,172
1969-70	34,568	1978-79	23,830	1985-86	24,769	1993-94	25,410	2000-01	25,132
1970-71	33,531	1978-79	23,830	1986-87	24,581	1994-95	25,083	2001-02	25,121
1971-72	32,334	1979-80	23,201	1987-88	24,474			Projected	

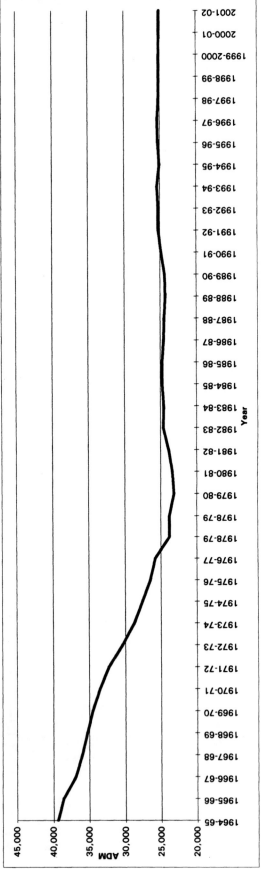

Exhibit 1-4—Pie Charts

Describe your individual course of study during high school.

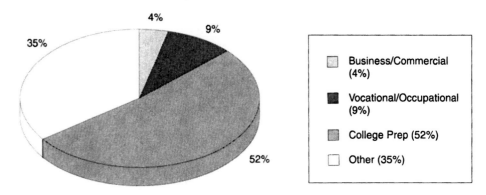

- Business/Commercial (4%)
- Vocational/Occupational (9%)
- College Prep (52%)
- Other (35%)

How well did high school prepare you for continuing your education?

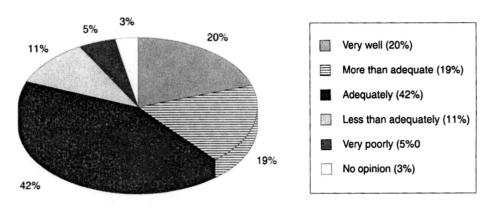

- Very well (20%)
- More than adequate (19%)
- Adequately (42%)
- Less than adequately (11%)
- Very poorly (5%0
- No opinion (3%)

How well did high school prepare you for your present occupation?

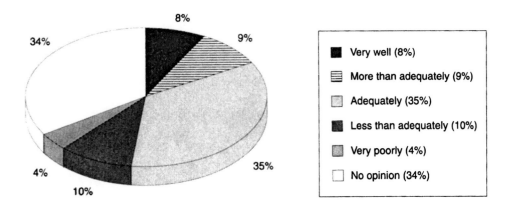

- Very well (8%)
- More than adequately (9%)
- Adequately (35%)
- Less than adequately (10%)
- Very poorly (4%)
- No opinion (34%)

CHAPTER 2
Introductory Section

The Introductory Section is the first major section of a school budget under the MBA criteria. As its name implies, this section introduces readers to the document as a whole. It highlights important information contained in the budget. Users rely on the Introductory Section to give an overview. They want a quick overview — a snapshot of what they can expect to find in the rest of the document.

Therefore, it is crucial that this section provide principally summary information, including data, graphs and narrative.

CONTENTS

At a minimum, the MBA criteria require applicants to include the following items:

- A liftable executive summary (liftable is explained later)
- A copy of the MBA certificate (if awarded in the preceding year)
- A listing of school board members and top level administrative personnel

Executive Summary (Criterion B-1)

A budget document's executive summary serves much the same purpose as a summary in any other important document. Its presents an abridged version of critical information contained in the document as a whole. Summaries, including graphs, are essential for readers who need to review major points without reading the entire document.

The MBA criteria establish guidelines concerning the format of executive summaries. The criteria require a summary that is "liftable" and which presents the budget in narrative, numeric and graphic form. A "liftable" summary is

one that can stand-alone. Like a budget-in-brief, an executive summary should require no further explanation if it were to be issued as a separate document. In addition, the summary should use a combination of narrative, data and graphs to convey information. The objective is to use a mix of interpretative devices to sustain reader interest, highlight major points and explain budget decisions or recommendations.

The criteria also set guidelines for the content of executive summaries. The summary should include a summary of the Organizational, Financial and Informational Sections of the budget document presented in an integrated fashion.

Organizational Component (Criterion B1a)

This part of the executive summary is a distillation of the information contained in the budget's Organizational Section. It focuses on issues of particular significance to the proposed budget, including:

- Statement of the mission of the entity
- Discussion of major goals and objectives
- Brief summary of the budget process, including public involvement
- Description of significant changes in budget process and/or policies
- Explanation of how human/financial resources are allocated to achieve significant goals and objectives

Financial Component (Criterion B1b)

This part of the summary extracts information from the Financial Section of the budget, including the following:

- Overview of revenues and expenditures/expenses for all funds

- Budget comparisons of at least the current year to the budget year
- Discussion of significant trends, events and initiatives
- Explanation of significant financial and demographic changes

Because they serve the interpretation of financial data well, charts and graphs are encouraged to enhance the presentation of the preceding.

Informational Component (Criterion B1c)

Information in which there is a high-level of public interest should be drawn from the Informational Section and included within the executive summary.

Exhibit 2-1 offers a good example of an executive summary that satisfies the above requirements. This summary examines both the financial and program make-up of the budget and focuses on major changes from the current year. This summary also makes good use of tables and graphs to highlight important financial data. Note that the tables and graphs are integrated with text and are used sparingly. This example is from a medium size school district. Exhibit 2-2 is from a very large school system and its Executive Summary is more complicated. This executive summary does a very good job of summarizing the financial and informational sections of the budget but needs to give more attention to summarizing the budget process, changes in budget process and budget policies. Exhibit 2-3 analyzes the proposed budgeted expenditures compared to prior years noting trends in the proportion of the expenditures devoted to each major function and object of expenditure.

MBA Certificate (Criterion B-2)

If a school has received the Meritorious Budget Award for the preceding budget, the Introductory Section should include a copy of the MBA certificate. Exhibit 2-4 shows what this certificate looks like. Schools may choose to accent the certificate with a border or other graphical device but the certificate itself should not be altered. The award certificate relates to only one budget year and the certificate for the immediately preceding year is the only certificate that can be displayed in a subsequent budget document.

School Board and Administrators (Criterion B-3)

The third requirement for the Introductory Section of the budget is a listing of school board members and first-level administrative personnel (administrators who report directly to the school entity's top administrator).

This information can be displayed in a number of ways. Exhibit 2-5 is an example of a simple listing of board members and administrators. Exhibit 2-6 is more elaborate and includes photographs and terms of school board members as well as a district map showing the geographical area of the school district represented by each school board member. Although not shown here, this last exhibit is supplemented with a listing of first-level administrators. A variety of formats would work well for this requirement and might be supplemented with other information.

CHECKLIST

The Introductory Section is the first section of your budget following the table of contents.

- ○ An executive summary is included in this section.
- ○ The executive summary is "liftable" and summarizes the budget in narrative, graphic and numeric form.
- ○ The summary discusses information from the Organizational, Financial and Informational sections of the document.
- ○ A discussion of major goals and objectives is provided in the executive summary.
- ○ The executive summary provides an overview of the budget process.
- ○ Significant changes in the budget process and/or budget policies are described.
- ○ The summary explains how human/financial resources are allocated to achieve significant goals and objectives.
- ○ An overview of revenues and expenses/expenditures for all funds is presented.
- ○ Budget comparisons of at least the current year to the budget year are provided.
- ○ Significant trends, events and initiatives are discussed.
- ○ Significant financial and demographic changes are explained.
- ○ The budget includes a copy of the Meritorious Budget Award certificate if it was received for the prior year.
- ○ A listing of school board members and first-level administrative personnel is provided in this section.

Executive Summary

(Criterion B-1)

Exhibit 2-1

Exhibit 2-2

Exhibit 2-3

Exhibit 2-1—Executive Summary

Owen J. Roberts School District

Administration Building
901 Ridge Road, Pottstown, Pennsylvania 19465
Telephone (610) 469-6261
Fax (610) 469-0748

The Honorable Board of Education
Owen J. Roberts School District
901 Ridge Road
Pottstown, Pennsylvania 19465-9314

Dear School Directors:

The budget for the fiscal year 1997-98 for the Owen J. Roberts School District is attached. The District Superintendent and the Business Administrator assume responsibility for data accuracy and completeness. This budget presents the District's finance and operations plan, and all necessary disclosures.

BUDGET PRESENTATION

The development, review, and consideration of the 1997-98 Governmental Fund Budgets (the General Fund Budget, the Debt Service Fund Budget, and the Special Revenue Fund Budgets - the Capital Reserve Fund and the Athletic Fund) and the Proprietary Fund Budget (the Food Service Budget) were completed with a detailed and exhaustive review of every revenue and expenditure item within the context of the District's mission, goals, and financial policies. Information on each of the fund budgets is provided in the budget document.

We are proud to publish and disseminate budget information to the Board of School Directors and to our community. We welcome the opportunity to present and discuss operational plans and related financial impact with all interested parties. Interaction among interested groups consistently leads to operational and educational improvements which become available to students of the Owen J. Roberts School District.

The budget document and the year-end Comprehensive Annual Financial Report (CAFR) are the primary vehicles to present the financial plan and the results of operations of the District. The information included in the budget document is structured to meet the requirements of the Meritorious Budget Award (MBA) of the Association of School Business Officials International (ASBO).

Exhibit 2-1— (continued)

To receive the MBA, a school entity must publish a budget document as a policy document, as an operations guide, as a financial plan and as a communications medium. We believe our current budget conforms to the requirements of the Meritorious Budget Awards (MBA) Program and we are submitting this document to the Association of School Business Officials International to determine its eligibility for the award.

The Meritorious Budget Award (MBA) is the highest form of recognition in budgeting for school entities. Its attainment represents a significant accomplishment by a school entity and its management. The award is made after comprehensive review by a panel of independent budget professionals. Using extensive criteria, the reviewers not only evaluate the effectiveness of the budget in meeting the MBA program criteria, but provide commentary and feedback to the submitting entity as a basis to improve the presentation of the District's financial and operations plan.

The budget of the School District has been awarded the Meritorious Budget Award for the fiscal years 1995-96 and 1996-97 from the Association of School Business Officials International (ASBO). The Owen J. Roberts School District was the first school entity in the nation to receive the Meritorious Budget Award.

However, our most important concern in the presentation of the budget data is to improve the quality of information to our community about the District's educational programs and services for the 1997-98 fiscal year which have been translated into a financial support plan. The material in the budget document includes information that has been suggested by the Directors of the School District, community members, and staff.

GOALS AND THEMES

Each year the Board of School Directors adopts goals as a vehicle to improve the education program. The human and financial resources are allocated in the budget to achieve the adopted goals of the District. The budget thus reflects the allocation of revenue and expenditures to support educational programs and services defined by the District's mission and goals articulated through financial and operating policies. It is a delicate balance of policy choices. It also represents a delicate balance between the educational needs of students and the ability of the community to provide the necessary financial support.

The Board of Directors has also adopted themes as a means to integrate and improve instruction. The first theme designated by the District is: "Owen J. Roberts - A Journey of Service and Justice." The theme emanated from the namesake of the Owen J. Roberts School District whose life was dedicated to justice, as a profession, and to community service, as a passion. The District has adopted a second District-wide theme - "People and their Environment," around which to organize instruction.

Exhibit 2-1— (continued)

BUDGET PROCESS AND SIGNIFICANT CHANGES

The budget process is comprised of five phases - planning, preparation, adoption, implementation, and evaluation. The preparation of the budget commenced in September with the development of the forecast of student enrollments for the 1997-98 fiscal year. In October, the Board gave approval to the forecast of pupil enrollments that projects an increase of forty-two (42) students. The forecast of enrollments provides the assumption on which allocations for building budgets are formulated and staff resources are determined.

Given the essentially stable enrollment and the objective to limit budget increases, the Board approved appropriations to educational units in December at the same levels as budgeted for the 1996-97 fiscal year. However, the budget does include appropriations for 4.4 additional staff positions primarily due to the increase in student enrollment. Building budgets and staffing allocations are based on board policy that has not been changed from prior years. In addition, the Board has not instituted changes in the delivery of educational programs and services that have materially affected the financial or operating policies of the District on which the budget has been constructed.

The following schedules present a comparison of the proposed expenditures for all Governmental and Proprietary Funds with the budgets for the current year.

TOTAL BUDGETS FOR ALL GOVERNMENTAL FUNDS

Fund	Budget 1996-97	Budget 1997-98	% Change
General Fund	$32,500,000	$33,500,000	3.08%
Debt Service Fund	1,468,365	1,276,222	(13.09%)
Capital Reserve Fund	2,432,500	1,431,000	(41.17%)
Athletic Fund	117,000	136,150	16.37%
Total Governmental Fund Expenditures	$36,517,865	$36,343,372	(0.48%)

Exhibit 2-1— (continued)

TOTAL BUDGET FOR PROPRIETARY FUND

Fund	Budget 1996-97	Budget 1997-98	% Change
Food Service Fund	$1,031,582	$1,074,948	4.20%

ANALYSIS OF PROPOSED BUDGETS

The education of students is a labor intensive enterprise that is reflected in the personnel costs. The workforce of the District is determined by the staffing policies and guidelines of the Board on the basis of projected student enrollment and curriculum requirements. Personnel costs are based on conditions of employment established by collective bargaining agreements. For the 1997-98 fiscal year, salaries and fringe benefits are budgeted to consume 73.7% of the expenditures in the General (Operating) Fund. However, the increase in personnel costs ($157,026) accounts for only 15.7% of the total increase in operating expenditures.

Other major increases in the budget for the fiscal year 1997-98 include the allocation of the equivalent of four mills of real estate taxes ($375,008) as the second installment payment for debt service for the renovation and expansion of the high school. This allocation accounts for 37.5% of the total increase in operating expenditures. The other major increases in the General Fund budget reflect additional costs for contracted housekeeping services in the amount of $30,000 (3.0%) and for the contracted transportation of students in the amount of $112,000 (11.2%). Most other budgeted expenditures for the 1997-98 fiscal year have been held at or below levels for the current year. A summary schedule of operating expenditures by object (expenditure category) are presented below.

Object	Budget 1996-97	Budget 1997-98	% Change
Salaries	$18,425,167	$18,894,682	2.55%
Benefits	6,114,107	5,801,618	(5.11%)
Professional and Purchased Services	5,441,173	5,739,394	5.48%
Supplies/Equipment	982,186	1,033,183	5.19%
Other Objects and Financing Uses	1,537,367	2,031,123	32.12%
Total General Fund Expenditures	$32,500,000	$33,500,000	3.08%

Exhibit 2-1 (continued)

The following graphs provide a comparison of expenditures by object (expenditure category) for the current and proposed General Fund Budgets in terms of the percentage of total budgets.

GENERAL FUND EXPENDITURES
BY OBJECT
(COMPARISON OF TOTAL EXPENDITURES OF CURRENT AND PROPOSED BUDGETS)

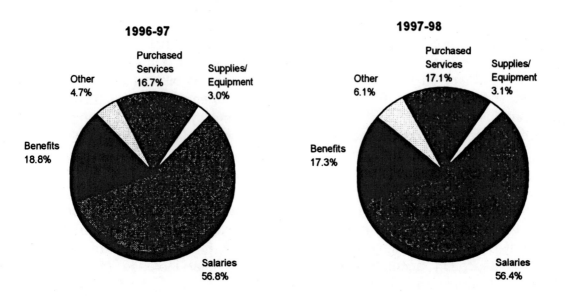

1996-97

Purchased Services 16.7%
Supplies/ Equipment 3.0%
Other 4.7%
Benefits 18.8%
Salaries 56.8%

1997-98

Purchased Services 17.1%
Supplies/ Equipment 3.1%
Other 6.1%
Benefits 17.3%
Salaries 56.4%

Included in the General Fund are allocations for transfer to the Debt Service Fund and the Special Revenue Funds - the Capital Reserve Fund and the Athletic Fund. The transfer of monies are provided to support the specified purposes for which the Debt Service Fund and the Special Revenue Funds are maintained. Budgeted fund transfers from the General Fund include $1,423,838 to the Debt Service Fund for principal and interest on outstanding debt, $93,000 to the Capital Reserve Fund for capital expenditures and $106,150 to the Athletic Fund for athletic programs and services.

The District has a Debt Service Fund to provide for principal and interest payments for outstanding debt in accord with generally accepted accounting principals for governmental entities. Funds in the Debt Service Fund will be used for principal and interest payments on General Obligation Bonds, Series 1995, Series 1996, and Series 1997 as well as interest payments on revenue bonds from the Emmaus General Authority (Bond Pool Program).

The major expenditure ($1,000,000) from the Capital Reserve Fund budget for the fiscal year 1997-98 is to provide for cost for the initial planning and construction of a new elementary school in the North Coventry attendance area. Other expenditures

Exhibit 2-1 (continued)

from the Capital Reserve Fund are in accord with the District's five year capital expenditure plan. There is an increase of $19,150 in the proposed Athletic Fund budget with an increase of $16,150 in the amount of monies transferred from the General Fund Budget to support athletic programs and services over the current fiscal year.

The increase in the budget of the Proprietary Fund (Food Service Fund) reflects increased labor and food costs based on collectively bargained conditions of employment, projected increases in the costs of food products, and the increase in student enrollment. Revenue to support the food service program is principally derived from operating revenues from the sale of food products to the students and faculty of the District during breakfast and lunch. The food service program also currently receives state and federal support in the form of cash and commodities. Food service operations are not projected to be self supporting and will, therefore, require a contribution from the General Fund in the 1997-98 fiscal year in the amount of $75,000 to maintain the program.

RESOURCES TO SUPPORT OPERATIONS

Programs and services included in the General Fund Budget are primarily supported by local and state sources of revenue. A comparison of revenue sources to support operations for the current and proposed General Fund budgets are presented below.

Revenue Sources	Budget 1996-97	Budget 1997-98	% Change
Local Sources	$25,226,142	$26,132,100	3.59%
State Sources	7,068,658	7,162,700	1.33%
Federal Sources	205,200	205,200	0.00%
Total General Fund Revenue	$32,500,000	$33,500,000	3.08%

The financial support for District operated programs and services is substantially and increasingly derived from local sources of revenue, primarily the property tax. The property tax is a regressive tax system that disadvantages senior citizens, farmers and low income households. The District continues to urge the State Legislature to provide more flexibility in the manner in which school systems are required to fund educational programs, many of which are mandated but not funded by State Government. The following graph presents the sources of revenue to support the proposed operating budget.

Exhibit 2-1 (continued)

SOURCES OF REVENUE

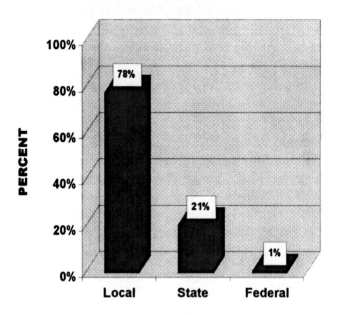

The local sources of revenue to support the operations budget represent almost four-fifths (4/5) of total available sources of funds. Of this amount, the largest source of revenue available to the District is the property tax that is derived from current, interim, and delinquent real estate tax payments. Below is a graph that presents the various sources of local revenue included in the proposed budget to support General Fund operations for the 1997-98 fiscal year.

LOCAL REVENUE ANALYSIS

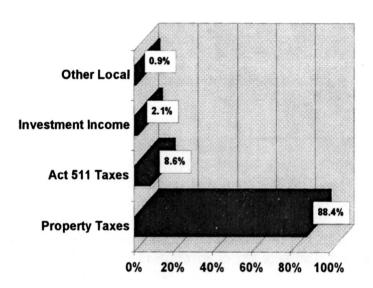

Exhibit 2-1 (continued)

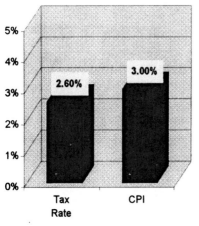

Comparative Annual Increase

In order to support the programs and services in the proposed General Fund budget, a tax increase of six (6) mills or an increase in the tax rate of 2.6% will be required. This translates into an increase of $42.00 for the median taxpayer in the District (assessed value = $7000). The proposed increase in the tax rate represents an increase that is less than the current inflation rate and continues a several year trend of increasingly smaller percentage tax rate changes.

During the past decade, there has been a substantial shift in the burden of funding local educational programs and services from the State to the local level. This shift in burden abrogates the historical partnership between the local community and State government for the education of students in the Commonwealth. The trend has also been accompanied by a number of unfunded State mandates, the most recent of which is the requirement to place an instructional support teacher (IST) in every elementary and middle school in the District at a cost of more than $294,000 or the equivalent of three (3) mills of real estate taxes.

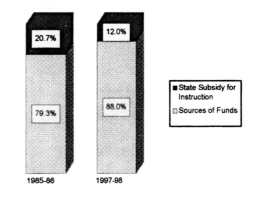

The bar charts illustrate the shift for the support of educational programs by a comparison of the State support for instruction provided to the District in the 1985-86 fiscal year and the amount of State subsidy for instruction anticipated in the proposed budget. If the State continued to provide the same level of support to the District for instruction as provided a decade ago, the District would receive two million seven hundred forty-eight thousand dollars ($2,921,250) more in additional State support than included in the proposed budget. This would permit a reduction in property taxes of thirty (30) mills or a reduction in taxes of $217.00 for the median taxpayer.

The Governor's proposed budget does include a minimal increase (1%) in funds for basic instruction in the amount of $37,430. The District does, however, expect to receive additional funds for retirement and social security payments in the amount of

Exhibit 2-1 (continued)

$55,600. In sum, the net increase in state funds is only projected to fund 9.4% of the increase in the General Fund Budget.

Federal sources of revenue do not represent a significant revenue source to the District for the operating fund and are projected to remain at the same level for the next year. However, the District anticipates that there will be a substantial decline in federal sources of revenue in future years, primarily for programs operated for disadvantaged students.

The District also receives both state and federal financial support for the Proprietary Fund (Food Service Fund). Despite the uncertainty of this funding source given the discussions at the national level, the District has not changed assumptions about the operation of the School Lunch program. Accordingly, federal sources of revenue to support the operation of the School Lunch program are included in the proposed Proprietary Fund budget. Should the Congress substantially change or modify the School Lunch program that would result in a loss of funds to the District, lunch prices will need to be raised or General Fund support increased to compensate for the reduction of funds.

ACKNOWLEDGMENTS

We appreciate the fiscal support provided by the Owen J. Roberts Board of School Directors and the Community for development, implementation, and maintenance of an excellent educational program for children of the District.

Terrance L. Furin, Ph. D.
District Superintendent

Denny G. Bolton, Ph. D.
Business Administrator

Exhibit 2-2—Executive Summary

Prince William County Public Schools
FY 1998 Approved Budget
Executive Summary

School Board	**Lucy S. Beauchamp, Chairman** *At-Large*
	Charles J. Colgan, III, Vice-Chairman *Gainesville Magisterial District*
	John David Allen, Sr. *Coles Magisterial District*
	Lyle G. Beefelt *Brentsville Magisterial District*
	Joan R. Ferlazzo *Dumfries Magisterial District*
	John Harper, Jr. *Neabsco Magisterial District*
	Steven Keen *Woodbridge Magisterial District*
	Linda H. Lutes *Occoquan Magisterial District*
Administration	**Edward L. Kelly** *Superintendent*
	Pamela K. Gauch *Associate Superintendent, Instruction*
	Robert Ferrebee *Associate Superintendent, Management*
	David Miller *Associate Superintendent, Services*
	Keith Lynch *Associate Superintendent, Area 1*
	Faye Patterson *Associate Superintendent, Area 2*
	Kris Pedersen *Associate Superintendent, Area 3*
	David Cline *Director of Finance*
	P. Stephen Partin *Supervisor of Budget*

Exhibit 2-2 (continued)

Executive Summary
Table Of Contents

Exhibit 2-2 (continued)

Budget at a Glance

- This budget is the first year of a five-year plan for addressing the needs of the school division.
- Student membership will increase by 1,035 students.
- None of the current instructional, support, or extracurricular programs are reduced or eliminated.
- The Operating Fund totals $304.9 million and the Debt Service Fund about $19.4 million.
- Operating revenue will increase by $14.6 million or 5.1 percent while inflation will increase an estimated 2.5 percent and student membership by 2.1 percent.
- The average salary increases by 4.6 percent including salary step and cost-of-living-adjustment.
- Health insurance premiums will increase by 21 percent and cost the School Board an additional $1.2 million.
- Funding is included for the debt payment on $19.9 million in bonds for the construction of two elementary schools to open in September 1998.
- Funding is included for bonds for the initial construction costs of a new high school to open in September 2000.
- Funding is included to purchase five additional classroom trailers.
- Cost containment initiatives have reduced compensation costs by $3.2 million.

Operating Fund
Fiscal Year 1998

Revenue Source	FY 1997	FY 1998	Change	Percent
Federal	$5,118,154	$5,915,727	$797,573	15.6%
State	$132,543,223	$140,212,006	$7,668,783	5.8%
County	$148,142,384	$153,255,105	$5,112,721	3.5%
Local	$1,369,448	$1,067,494	-$301,954	-22.0%
Undistributed	$600,000	$600,000	$0	0.0%
Beginning Balance	$2,500,000	$3,900,000	$1,400,000	56.0%
Total	$290,273,209	$304,950,332	$14,677,123	5.1%

Exhibit 2-2 (continued)

Vision Statement

In Prince William County Public Schools, all students will learn to their fullest potential. The education of each student will be individualized and developmentally appropriate. Student learning will be enhanced by national, global, and multicultural perspectives.

Students who graduate from Prince William County Public Schools will possess the basic knowledge and skills that will assure their proficiency in problem solving and the use of technology. Graduates will have a desire to learn and the skills to be life-long learners. They will be responsible citizens. All graduates will be competent to enter the work world and prepared to pursue advanced educational opportunities.

Mission Statement

Our Mission is to provide a high quality, comprehensive and meaningful education for all students. In our schools, each student will experience success. Students will be expected to succeed within the bounds of their abilities and chosen educational goals. Each student will be treated as an individual, given the tools to be a life-long learner, and taught to function effectively as a member of a group and as a productive member of society.

School Board Priorities

- To provide and maintain a comprehensive, high level curriculum which is followed by all schools and which can be documented.
- To foster effective and better discipline.
- To establish a new structure for schools.
- To create an awareness and use of technology by staff and students.
- To develop independent and effective political relations with various entities in the county.
- To develop a level of equity for all facilities and establish a plan for achieving this equity.
- To increase public participation in school division affairs.
- To exercise fiscal discipline.

Exhibit 2-2 (continued)

Achievements

- PWCPS students score significantly above state and national scores on standardized tests.

- The entire K-12 curriculum was revised and improved to raise student expectations and performance. This includes the expansion of staff development programs to support teachers in implementing the new curriculum.

- The development of local student assessments at benchmark years to determine the level of student learning based on the revised curriculum.

- The school division has made significant advances in the installation and use of technology in the instructional process and the management of the school division. Local-area computer networks connect all classrooms and offices in every school. All schools and support offices are also linked together through a wide-area computer network. Internet access is available to every classroom. Software applications have been implemented for management of instruction, student information, and administrative functions. By the end of the 1997-98 school year, over 75 percent of the classrooms will be equipped with a networked computer.

- During the past five years, the number of minority employees has increased by over fifty percent.

- PWCPS received the Meritorious Budget Award from the Association of School Business Officials International for the budget for Fiscal Year 1997.

- The energy management program has saved the school division over $350,000 each year for the past three years.

- The Retirement Opportunity Program and the combined salary scale have reduced compensation costs by over $3.2 million.

- Three years ago the school division worked with other agencies and jurisdictions to form a regional health insurance consortium. As a result, PWCPS and its employees have saved over $13 million in health insurance premiums during the three years.

- In order to improve efficiency and service, PWCPS has undergone an audit by a professional management firm and three reviews by citizen advisory committees during the past seven years.

Exhibit 2-2 (continued)

Executive Summary

Budget Calendar

February 5	The Superintendent submits the proposed budget to the School Board.
February 18	There is a public meeting on the budget at 7:30 P.M. at Osbourn Park High School.
February 20	There is a public meeting on the budget at 7:30 P.M. at Gar-Field High School.
February 21	Principals submit proposed school budgets to the Superintendent.
March 5	The Superintendent submits an addendum containing proposed school budgets.
March 31	The School Board must approve a proposed budget and submits it to the Board of County Supervisors by this date.
April 7	Board of County Supervisors holds a public meeting on the budget at 7:30 P.M. at Stonewall Jackson High School.
April 10	Board of County Supervisors holds a public meeting on the budget at 7:30 P.M. at Woodbridge High School.
April 30	The Board of County Supervisors approves the School Board budget.
June 9	Principals and central budget holders submit revised budgets according to the approved School Board budget.

Organization

Prince William County Public Schools (PWCPS) is organized to focus on meeting the needs of its 49,775 students while managing 66 schools and centers. It is an efficient and well managed organization.

PWCPS is governed by eight elected School Board members. The members are elected to four-year terms. One member represents each of the county's seven magisterial districts and the chairman serves at large. The School Board is charged by Virginia law and the regulations of the Virginia Board of Education to establish guidelines and rules that will ensure the proper administration of the county's school programs.

The Superintendent works closely with six associate superintendents to oversee the day-to-day operations of the schools and support services. Principals and support department heads report to the associate superintendents.

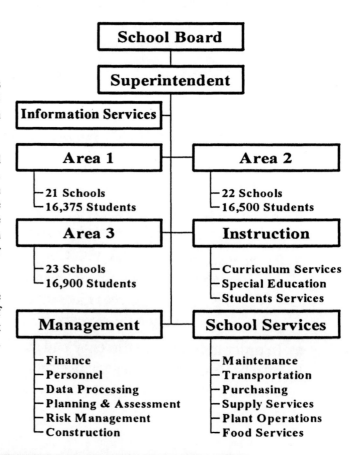

Exhibit 2-2 (continued)

Five-Year Budget Plan

Since FY 1991, the combined costs of student membership growth and the rate of inflation have exceeded the increase in revenues. As a result, the school division has reduced current programs and services by over $26 million and eliminated 57 central support positions. To maintain quality instructional programs, central support programs and facility renewal projects have absorbed most of these reductions. Many support programs can no longer effectively function with further budget reductions and some facilities are in need of critical repairs that cannot be deferred.

With assistance from a professional management audit and citizen advisory committees, the school division has implemented several successful cost containment initiatives to further reduce operating costs and improve efficiencies. The Retirement Opportunity Program combined with the new salary scale and placement policies reduced the funding needed for compensation by over $3.2 million this year. The health insurance consortium has saved the School Board and PWCPS employees over $13 million in health insurance premiums over the past three years. The energy management program has reduced utility costs by over $360,000 this year.

Due to these budget reductions, cost containment initiatives, and a slight increase in revenues, the financial situation has improved slightly. However, the projected revenues will still not be sufficient to meet all of the needs of the school division. The problem facing the school division has been, and still is, how to provide space for the increasing number of new students, repair and renew existing schools, maintain quality instructional programs with the necessary support programs and personnel, and maintain competitive salaries and benefits for employees.

Since it is difficult, if not impossible, to address all of these needs in a single year, a long-term approach was needed. Using recommendations from citizen advisory committees, external audits, and School Board priorities, a five-year budget plan was developed to address and manage these needs. The FY 1998 budget is the first year of this five-year plan.

While the five-year budget plan will not satisfactorily meet all of the needs, it will focus resources on the most critical needs and provide the framework to successfully manage the school division through the next five financially difficult years. While maintaining current programs and service levels, meeting minimum facility needs, and providing some increases in compensation, the plan may not adequately provide the needed compensation to remain competitive with other school divisions. If additional revenue becomes available, it should be used to provide additional salary increases for employees.

Five-Year Plan Objectives

- To maintain current instructional, support, and extracurricular programs and services.

- To provide services for 5,300 new students.

- To construct and operate the six new schools identified in the Capital Improvements Program.

- To complete all critical capital projects identified in the Capital Improvements Program.

- To fund and complete at least $37 million in priority school renewal projects.

- To maintain competitive salaries and benefits for all employees.

Aging School Buildings

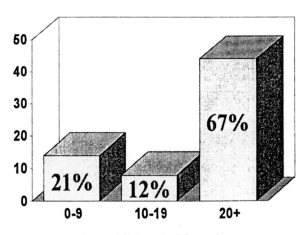

Age of Schools (Years)

Exhibit 2-2 (continued)

Executive Summary

This plan requires the sale of $137 million in bonds for the construction of new schools and renewal projects for current schools. The required debt service for these bonds will remove all flexibility for managing any unforeseen major expenditure requirement or any unanticipated loss of revenue.

The plan does not include enough funding to complete all of the school renewal projects identified in the Capital Improvements Program. There will still be over $40 million in renovations to current schools that will need to be done within the next 7-8 years. Also, the salary increases included in the plan may not be adequate to maintain competitive salaries.

In order for the plan to succeed, budget decisions for FY 1998 and subsequent years must be made with a view beyond a single year and be consistent with the revenue and expenditure assumptions used to develop the plan. Any significant expenditure increases without additional revenues to support them will jeopardize the success of the plan. It will require the understanding and support of the School Board, Board of County Supervisors, PWCPS employees, and the citizens of Prince William County.

Long-Range Revenue-Expenditure Assumptions

- Supplies and equipment costs will increase by 3.0% each year.
- Virginia Retirement System rates will continue to increase by 7.5 % each year through FY 2001.
- Health insurance premiums will increase by 20% in FY 1998-99 and 9% each year after FY 1999.
- The cost of providing services for new students will increase by 3.0% each year.
- Student membership will increase by an average of 2.2% or about 1,050 students each year.
- The funding for grants will remain constant.
- Construction costs will increase by an average of 4.5% each year.
- The interest rate on construction bonds will be 6.0%.
- Available revenues will increase by an average of 5.5% each year.
- The school division will receive 50% of additional available county revenues each year.
- No new programs nor major improvements to current programs will be implemented.

Revenue-Expenditure Projections
FY 1998 - FY 2002
($ in millions)

Description	FY 1998	FY 1999	FY 2000	FY 2001	FY 2002
Current Programs	$313.9	$327.3	$342.0	$359.2	$378.0
New Students	$5.2	$5.1	$5.6	$5.8	$6.1
New Schools	$3.2	$6.4	$10.7	$12.8	$11.1
School Renewals	$2.0	$8.0	$6.2	$11.4	$10.2
Total Expenditures	$324.4	$346.8	$364.5	$389.1	$405.3
Non-County Revenues	$152.8	$167.3	$173.7	$191.0	$198.2
County Transfer Needed	$171.5	$179.5	$190.8	$198.1	$207.2
Increase in County Transfer	$7.1	$8.0	$11.3	$7.4	$9.1
County Revenue Available	$14.1	$13.4	$16.8	$20.3	$20.1

Exhibit 2-2 (continued)

What is Included in the Five-Year Plan?

Current Programs & Services

- No reductions in current programs and services
- Annual adjustments for inflation in supplies and materials
- Annual 2.6% salary step increases for employees
- 1% cost-of-living-adjustments for employees in four of the five years
- Funding for the 5,300 new students expected during the next five years

"It costs about $4,900 to provide school-level services for each new student."

"PWCPS maintains about 6,000,000 square feet of space in 66 schools and centers."

Repairs and Renewals

Funding on a cash basis for $36 million for roof replacements, mechanical system renovations, and other critical repair projects

Funding for the debt service on $37 million in bonds for renewal projects at current schools
- Renewal of Brentsville District Middle & High School
- High school technology lab conversions
- Electrical upgrades to support technology
- Air-conditioning of middle school gymnasiums
- Middle school technology lab conversions
- First phase of the renewal of schools 30+ years old

New Schools

Funding for the debt service on $100.5 million in construction bonds, start-up costs, and operating costs for six new schools
- "Kingsbrooke" Elementary School (September 1998)
- "Queen Chapel" Elementary School (September 1998)
- Mid-County Middle School (September 2000)
- Eighth High School (September 2000)
- New Elementary School (September 2001)
- New Elementary School (September 2002)

"In the past ten years, PWCPS has built eleven elementary schools, two middle schools, and one high school."

Exhibit 2-2 (continued)

Executive Summary

Trends

Revenue & Expenditure Trends

Since FY 1991, expenditures for current programs and services, new students, and new schools have exceeded revenues resulting in the reduction of services and programs. Even though revenues are not expected to return to the 1990 levels, the latest projections show slow to moderate growth in revenues over the next five years. Total revenues are projected to increase by about six percent each year. If inflation remains low and student growth does not increase significantly more than projected, the financial situation should improve slightly.

The expenditure reductions and cost containment initiatives implemented during the past seven years have been successful in reducing current operating costs while maintaining educational programs. Even though revenues are expected to improve slightly, it will not be sufficient to meet all needs. The school division will need to continue seeking cost containment strategies and prioritizing expenditure needs.

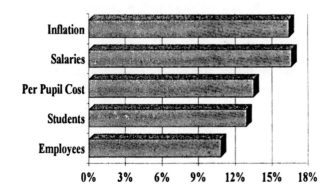

Five-Year Trends
1992 to 1997

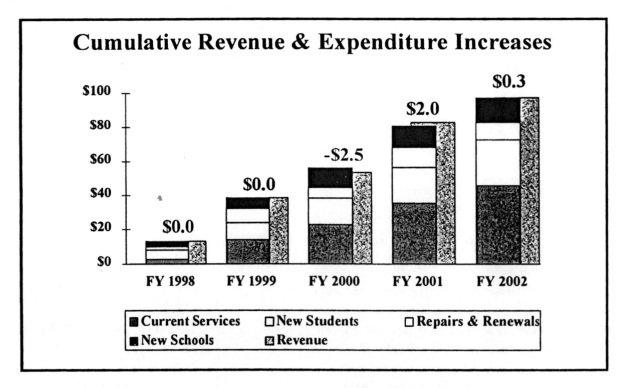

"By forming a consortium with other agencies, PWCPS and its employees have saved over $13 million in health insurance premiums over the past three years."

Exhibit 2-2 (continued)

Executive Summary

Enrollment Growth

PWCPS is the fourth largest of 138 school divisions in Virginia. In FY 1998, membership is expected to increase by 1,035 students. Almost half of the new students will be high school students. Student membership is projected to continue to increase at an annual rate of about 2 percent during the next five years. This will result in almost 5,300 additional students by the 2001-02 school year. In FY 1998, it will cost about $4,900 for personnel, employee benefits, and materials to provide school-level instructional and support services for each new student.

Student Membership

	FY 1997	FY 1998	Change	Percent
Pre-School	517	547	30	5.8%
Elementary School	22,852	23,173	321	1.4%
Middle School	10,807	10,949	142	1.3%
High School	14,376	14,852	476	3.3%
Special School	188	254	66	35.1%
Total	48,740	49,775	1,035	2.1%

In addition to the increased number of students, the composition of membership growth has added to the cost. In the past five years, increases in regular education students have been outdistanced by the increases of students enrolled in special education. Special education students require specialized instruction and smaller class sizes.

New schools are needed to meet student membership growth. An additional four elementary schools, one middle school, and one high school are needed during the next five years. The proposed budget for FY 1998 includes funding for two new elementary schools and funding for the initial construction work for a new high school. Over $100 million in construction bonds will need to be issued to fund the six new schools.

The funding to purchase and install five additional classroom trailers is also included in the budget. With these additional trailers, a total of 147 trailers will be used to provide classroom space. Based on the projected increase in student membership, the number of students for the 1997-98 school year will exceed the available permanent capacity by over 2,400 students.

Since over 70 percent of current schools are more than 20 years old, funding is also needed to renew and renovate these facilities. Over $78 million in renewal needs have been identified and need to be completed over the next 7-8 years.

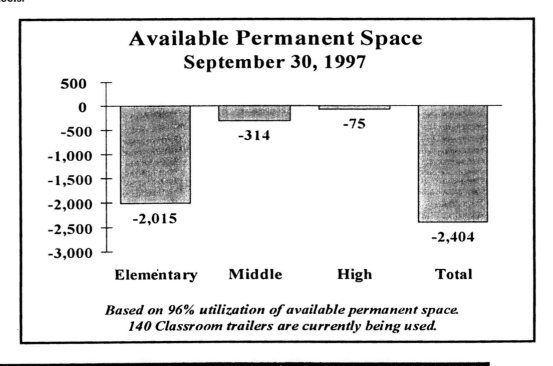

Available Permanent Space
September 30, 1997

Based on 96% utilization of available permanent space.
140 Classroom trailers are currently being used.

Exhibit 2-2 (continued)

Changing Demographics

In the past five years, minority student membership has increased by 55 percent, reaching over 34 percent of the total student membership in FY 1997. Minority student membership is projected to exceed 40 percent of the total membership by the year 2000. The greatest rate of increase will be Hispanic and African-American students.

The influx of language-minority students is expected to continue. During the past five years, students receiving English-for-Speakers-of-Other-Languages (ESOL) services increased by over 80 percent. This program is expected to continue to increase at the rate of 10-15 percent per year.

Students eligible for free or reduced lunch programs have increased by almost 90 percent during this same period. Almost 9,500 students are expected to be eligible for free or reduced lunches in FY 1998.

PWCPS has also actively worked to attract and hire more minority employees, especially minority teachers. During the past five years, the number of minority employees has increased by over fifty percent and the number of minority teachers by over sixty-five percent..

Inflation

We are all familiar with inflation and how it impacts our lives in the prices we pay for goods and services such as food, clothing, appliances, medical care, and utilities. Inflation has the same effect on the school division budget, as it does on household budgets, but on a much larger scale. It increases the costs for books, paper, supplies, utilities, and maintenance and repair costs for our 66 schools and centers. During the past five years, inflation has averaged more than 3.5 percent annually.

Due to the lack of sufficient revenue, salary increases for employees over the past six years have barely kept pace with the rate of inflation. The proposed salary increases in the five-year budget plan will not significantly improve this situation.

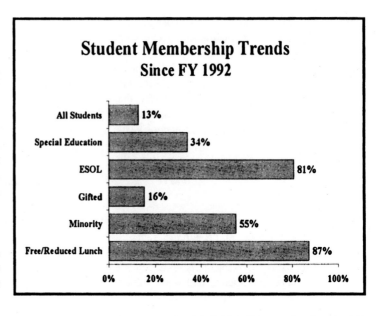

Student Membership Trends Since FY 1992

All Students	13%
Special Education	34%
ESOL	81%
Gifted	16%
Minority	55%
Free/Reduced Lunch	87%

Employee Salary Increases Compared to Inflation

	Salary	Inflation
FY 1993	3.2%	4.9%
FY 1994	2.5%	2.5%
FY 1995	2.5%	3.1%
FY 1996	5.8%	2.6%
FY 1997	2.6%	3.3%
FY 1998	3.6%	2.5%

(Inflation for FY 1997-98 are estimates)

A management review completed by Peat Marwick described PWCPS as "an exceptionally well run and cost-efficient system".

Exhibit 2-2 (continued)

Executive Summary

Revenues

PWCPS receives revenue to support the Operating and Debt Service Funds from three primary sources: funds transferred by the Board of County Supervisors, state aid, and federal aid. A small amount of revenue is also received from summer school, adult education, driver education fees, and non-resident tuition.

In FY 1998, PWCPS will receive about $324.4 million to support the school division's Operating and Debt Service Funds. This represents an increase of about $16.7 million more than budget estimates for FY 1997. This means that the school division must provide instructional and support services for a two percent increase in students, absorb an inflation rate of about 2.5 percent, and build new schools with only 4.2 percent in additional revenues. Total available revenue is expected to increase at the rate of about six percent per year over the next five years.

County Funds
$171.5 million

Real property, personal property, and local sales taxes are the primary revenue sources for Prince William County. The

Board of County Supervisors approves a transfer to PWCPS to finance most of the Operating Fund and the payment of debt service. Based on the school-division receiving last year's county transfer plus fifty percent of the additional revenue estimated for FY 1998, the county transfer is projected to be about $171.5 million. About $153.2 million will be used to support the Operating Fund. The remaining $18.3 million will be budgeted in the Debt Service Fund and used to pay debt service for previous and proposed school construction and capital improvement bonds.

The major source of county revenue is residential real property taxes. While the tax rate has remained constant since 1992, the assessed value of the 1992 residential base has decreased. Even with the small increase in assessed value for new homes, the revenue generated from each cent of the real estate tax has been relatively flat for the past two years. While the real property revenue from the new homes should have been available to provide school and county services for these new residents, the new revenue is not even enough to maintain current services for existing residents.

Operating & Debt Service Revenues
Fiscal Year 1998

	FY 1997	FY 1998	Change	Percent
County	$164,383,160	$171,520,105	$7,136,945	4.3%
State	$132,543,223	$140,212,006	$7,668,783	5.8%
Federal	$5,118,154	$5,915,727	$797,573	15.6%
Local	$2,369,448	$2,067,494	($301,954)	-12.7%
Undistributed Revenue	$600,000	$600,000	$0	0.0%
Beginning Balance	$2,650,000	$4,050,000	$1,400,000	52.8%
Total Revenues	$307,663,985	$324,365,332	$16,701,347	5.4%

Exhibit 2-2 (continued)

Executive Summary

State Aid
$140.2 million

State revenue includes two forms of funding: state aid and sales tax. State aid includes funding for basic aid to support the Standards of Quality (SOQ) and categorical aid for special programs and initiatives. Since the state operates under a biennial budget, state aid is generally fixed for a two-year period with adjustments limited to student membership changes during the second year. Since FY 1998 is the second year of the current biennial budget, it only includes the state's share of salaries and prevailing costs using state-wide averages for the 1995-96 school year.

PWCPS will receive about $140 million in state funding in FY 1998. About $26.3 million of this amount is the school division's share of the one percent sales tax collected to support public education.

Equalization

For years, the state has attempted to distribute aid to education equitably by recognizing that some localities are more able to fund education than are others. This approach, known as equalization, is achieved by applying a factor to adjust a locality's state aid reimbursement to reflect the locality's ability to pay for education. The factor, called the Local Composite Index (LCI), combines three separate measures of local fiscal capacity (assessed value of real property, adjusted gross income, and taxable retail sales) into a single index. Those school divisions with a low LCI receive the greatest amount of state aid per pupil while those with a high index receive less state support. The state minimum LCI is 0.2000 and the maximum is 0.8000. In FY 1998, the LCI for PWCPS is 0.4316. This means that Prince William County is required to pay about 43 percent of the cost of the minimum educational program set by the state Standards of Quality.

Since the current state funding methodology significantly underfunds the true cost of the mandated minimum instructional program, each school division in the state uses a greater share of its local revenues to cover the cost of education. A typical school division exceeds the funding requirements established by the state SOQ by 105 percent. Due primarily to the higher costs of doing business in northern Virginia, PWCPS exceeds the state required per pupil amount by 135 percent.

Cost-of-Competing

Based on well-documented proof that the prevailing costs of doing business are much greater in northern Virginia, the state has increased basic aid to education for these schools divisions by a cost-of-competing factor. Before FY 1995, PWCPS had received about 13 percent more in state aid based on these costs. This factor was arbitrarily reduced in FY 1995 to about 9 percent resulting in a reduction of about $2.4 million in state aid to PWCPS for FY 1998.

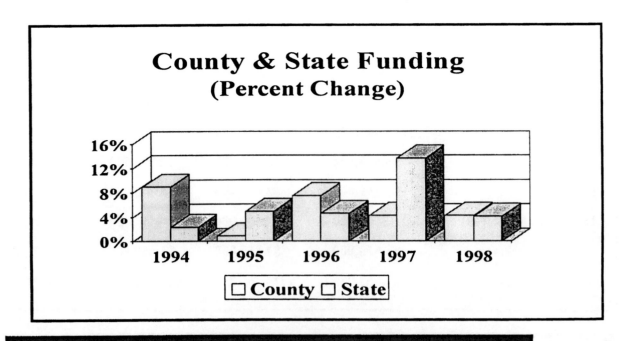

Exhibit 2-2 (continued)

Federal Aid
$5.9 million

Federal aid is usually derived from various entitled federal programs, specific grants, and Impact Aid. With the exception of Impact Aid, federal revenues are generally categorical and must be expended for specific purposes according to established statutes and regulations. Federal funds are provided to supplement the costs of providing instructional services for students in vocational, adult, special education, and programs for educationally and/or economically disadvantaged students. In FY 1998, PWCPS will receive about $5.9 million in federal funding.

Impact Aid partially compensates localities for the education of children whose parents live and/or work on federally owned property such as military bases. During the past three years, Impact Aid funding for PWCPS has decreased from about $1.8 million to about $500,000. Without the intervention and influence of our congressional representatives, PWCPS would have lost all of this revenue.

Other Revenue
$6.7 million

About $5.3 million in miscellaneous revenues from various sources is projected to be available in FY 1998. These include driver education fees, student parking fees, tuition for adult education classes, summer school, and revenue from small grants and awards.

Because of the time lapse between the sale of construction bonds and the actual expenditure of the proceeds from the sale, investment interest is earned on the bond proceeds and placed in a capital reserve fund. About $1,000,000 in interest from school construction bonds is available to offset the payment of debt service in FY 1998.

The budget also includes $600,000 in an undistributed revenue category. This provides budget capacity for revenue from various unbudgeted one-time grants that individual schools or the school division might receive during the next fiscal year.

During the past year, the School Board initiated a program to identify students who receive school division services that are reimbursable expenses under the federal Medicaid program. The proposed budget includes an estimated $160,000 in revenues from this program. This is a conservative estimate and the potential reimbursements from this program could reach several hundred thousand dollars in FY 1998.

For FY 1998, a beginning balance of $4,050,000 is budgeted. This includes $3,900,000 in the Operating Fund and $150,000 in the Debt Service Fund. As a result of cost-containment efforts, another $4 million in FY 1997 funds will be used for critical capital projects originally scheduled to be funded in FY 1998.

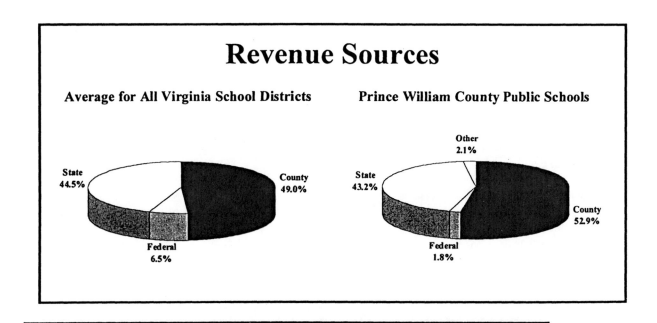

Revenue Sources

Average for All Virginia School Districts

State 44.5%
County 49.0%
Federal 6.5%

Prince William County Public Schools

Other 2.1%
State 43.2%
County 52.9%
Federal 1.8%

Exhibit 2-2 (continued)

Operating Fund Expenditures

The general revenues available to the school division are budgeted in the Operating and Debt Service Funds for the day-to-day operations and the payment of principal and interest on construction bonds. In FY 1998, expenditures in these two funds will increase by a total of $16.7 million.

The Operating Fund will increase by $14.7 million or 5.0 percent over the FY 1997 approved budget. The increase is primarily due to student membership growth, compensation increases, start-up costs for new schools, and inflation. The proposed budget only includes about $304,000 in new initiatives and resources.

The Debt Service Fund will increase by $2 million or 11.6 percent over the approved budget for FY 1997. The increase is needed to pay the debt service on $23.7 million in bonds for the construction of two new elementary schools and initial construction costs for a new high school.

Expenditure Adjustments
Fiscal Year 1998

Baseline Adjustments		**-$1,692,441**
Cost Containment in Compensation	-$3,128,676	
One-Time Costs	-$350,100	
Inflation in Selected Accounts	$1,511,046	
Increase in General Reserve Fund	$557,682	
Adjustments in Grants	-$282,393	
Compensation		**$14,079,723**
Salary Step Increase (2.6%)	$6,347,211	
Cost-of-Living-Adjustment (2.0%)	$4,920,918	
Increase in Substitute Teacher Pay	$216,377	
Restoration of Group Life Insurance Payment	$652,927	
Virginia Retirement System Rate Increase	$1,607,194	
Increase in Health Insurance Costs (21%)	$1,216,411	
Retirement Opportunity Program Savings	-$881,315	
New Students & Schools		**$6,181,427**
Funding for New Students (1,035)	$5,097,465	
Additional School Buses & Drivers (10)	$371,962	
Additional Classroom Trailers (5)	$150,000	
Start-up Costs for New Elementary Schools (2)	$562,000	
School Repairs & Renewals		**-$4,195,801**
Critical Repair Projects	-$4,000,382	
Renewal Projects (Classroom Computers)	-$195,419	
New Resources		**$304,215**
Middle School Security Specialists (11)	$136,648	
Equipment for Vehicle Emissions Testing	$13,800	
High School Writing Assessment	$70,450	
ESOL Curriculum Supervisor	$82,317	
Employee Recognition Program	$1,000	
Totals		**$14,677,123**

Exhibit 2-2 (continued)

Executive Summary

Baseline Adjustments
-$2.7 million

In this budget, baseline expenditures represent the costs of personnel, materials, equipment, and services to continue current programs and operations in FY 1998. Baseline adjustments will result in savings of about $2.7million.

Inflation

Selected accounts were increased for inflation, current market costs, and the projected costs of continuing existing services. An additional $1.5 million was budgeted in various central and school accounts to cover the increased costs for these services. A general inflation rate of 2.5 percent was used in adjusting most accounts.

During the past two years, the funding for custodial substitutes and homebound instruction has not been sufficient to meet needs. In order to adequately fund these two programs, each account was increased by about $85,000 for FY 1998.

Due to significant increases in vehicle fuels, these accounts were increased by 26 percent. This will require an additional $150,000 in FY 1998.

Maintenance service contracts for new computer software and hardware also increased greater than the rate of inflation. An additional $135,000 has been budgeted to cover these increases.

The budget includes an additional $131,000 to fund a projected 7.5 percent increase in workers' compensation, property, and liability insurance costs. This is based on rate increases in insurance premiums and increasing workers' compensation and self-insured claims.

Cost Containment Initiatives

During the past two years, a Retirement Opportunity Program and a new salary scale have been implemented in an effort to reduce compensation costs. In FY 1997, the savings from the Retirement Opportunity Program and salary policies which limit the salary credit for new employees were significantly greater than projected. As a result, compensation costs for FY 1997 will be about $3.2 less than originally projected. These savings also mean that compensation costs for FY 1998 can be reduced by a similar amount.

Other Adjustments

The approved budget for FY 1997 included funding for some supplies and equipment that can be eliminated in FY 1998. These include one-time costs associated with implementing new services or programs. The one-time costs eliminated for FY 1998 will save about $365,000.

Grants and other self-supporting programs are required to operate with the revenues available for these programs. Since revenues for these programs will be about $677,000 less in FY 1998, expenditures were adjusted by this amount. This includes a reduction in revenues and expenditures for the Summer School program of about $398,000 for FY 1998. This is due to reduced enrollments in high school summer programs and a reduction in state funding for summer school.

The budget includes funding for a new self-supporting program to manage the collection of Medicaid reimbursements for services provided by the school division to eligible students. These services include speech, occupational, and physical therapy. The cost of administering this program will be $111,000 with revenues for FY 1998 projected to be at least $160,000. The revenues collected above the operating costs for the program will be used as general revenue to offset the school division's cost of providing services to these students.

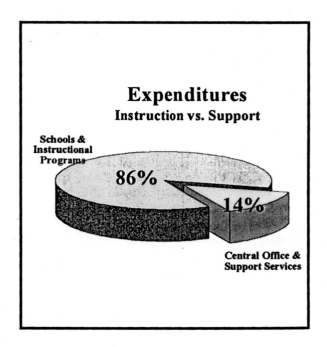

Expenditures
Instruction vs. Support

Schools & Instructional Programs — 86%

Central Office & Support Services — 14%

Exhibit 2-2 (continued)

Executive Summary

New Students & Schools
$6.2 million

The budget contains about $5.1 million for per pupil allocations to schools to provide programs and services for 1,035 new students. The average cost for providing direct instructional services and school-level support is about $4,900 per student. Other than transportation services, central support budgets have not been increased to support the indirect services for the additional students.

To transport the new students to and from school, ten additional school buses and related operating costs are required. The additional transportation costs are about $372,000. This includes the addition of ten bus drivers and four bus attendant positions.

The budget also includes $150,000 for the purchase and installation of five additional classroom trailers. The trailers are needed to house the additional students until new schools can be built.

Two new elementary schools are scheduled to open in September 1998. One of the schools will be located off Linton Hall Road and the other on Delaney Road. The budget includes $562,000 for library books, textbooks, supplies, and equipment needed to open these schools.

School Repairs & Renewals
-$4.2 million

The FY 1997 approved budget included $6.2 million for critical capital projects and matching funds for grants to upgrade school-level technology equipment. Critical capital projects include roof replacements, mechanical system renovations, and other repairs that must be completed within the next year.

The Capital Improvements Program identifies about $5.6 million in critical capital projects for FY 1998. By funding some of these projects with cost containment savings from the current year, the funding needed in FY 1998 has been reduced by $4 million.

The FY 1997 budget included $614,000 for the local matching funds required in order to receive the state Technology Grant of $1.8 million. The grant was used to purchase over 1,100 classroom computer systems. The grant has been continued in FY 1998 but the local matching funds

will be about $200,000 less. The grant and local matching funds should provide another 1,000 classroom computer systems next year.

Compensation
$14.1 million

The budget includes funding for a salary step increase and a two percent cost-of-living-adjustment (COLA) for all eligible employees. Half of the COLA is the advance payment of the scheduled one percent COLA contained in the five-year plan for FY 1999. It also includes adjustments in costs for other benefits and compensation programs.

Salaries

During the past five years, salary increases for most employees have barely kept pace with the inflation rate. For the 200 employees at the top of the salary scale, salary increases have averaged less than the rate of inflation. The step increases and two percent COLA will result in an average salary increase of about 3.6 percent; however, employees at the top of the scale will only receive the two percent COLA. The budget includes $11.4 million to fund these salary increases.

The Retirement Opportunity Program (ROP) implemented two years ago has been effective in reducing compensation costs. The program provides a financial incentive for eligible employees to retire. Since the difference between retiring senior employees and replacement employees averages about $22,000 in salary and benefits, the program reduces compensation costs for several years. In FY 1998, the net savings from the program will be about $881,000.

State Benefit Programs

In FY 1997, the state suspended the Group Life Insurance (GLI) payments for local jurisdictions. The payments have been restored for FY 1998 and will require about $653,000 for required GLI premiums.

In order to fully fund the annual three percent COLA for retirees participating in the Virginia Retirement System (VRS), increases in contribution rates for employers will increase by about 7.5 percent each year for five years. FY 1998 will be the second year of this phase-in of rates and will require an additional $1.6 million in VRS payments. VRS rates will increase by similar amounts during the next three years.

Exhibit 2-2 (continued)

Health Insurance

FY 1998 is the final year of the fully-insured health insurance plan with Trigon Blue Cross-Blue Shield through the health insurance consortium. Premiums for FY 1998 will increase by an average of 18 percent. Since Health Insurance Fund reserves were used to offset 10 percent of the premiums in FY 1997, the true rate increase will by about 28 percent. By using $700,000 of additional Health Insurance Fund reserves to offset premiums in FY 1998, the rate increase for employees and employer will be reduced to an average of 21 percent. The employer's share of the premiums will require an additional $1.2 million in FY 1998.

It is important to note that even though the increase in premiums for next year is significant, premiums are still about 11 percent lower than the premiums three years ago and the services provided are basically the same. Through the efforts of the consortium and Trigon's under-estimation of costs for the fully-insured program, the School Board and employees have saved over $13 million during the three years of the current program.

During FY 1998, the consortium will solicit competitive proposals for health insurance services and select a service provider. Based on the information available today, the recommendation will probably be to return to a self-insured plan beginning July 1, 1998. Since the school division has maintained the required reserve funds to support a self-insured program, this should be an easy transition.

New Resources
$0.3 million

The budget includes some funding for additional services and the expansion of current services. These primarily address needed improvements in instructional support and security programs.

Two years ago, the School Board approved funding to provide a security aide at every middle school. In order to better meet the needs of middle schools, these positions need to be reclassified to attract applicants with more experience and skills in safety and security. The budget includes $137,000 to upgrade these positions.

Due to the rapidly expanding enrollment in the English-for-Speakers-of-Other-Languages (ESOL) program, additional support is needed to coordinate and manage the program and curriculum. The budget includes $82,000 to fund the salary and benefits for a curriculum supervisor for this program.

The revised Quality Management Program includes a required writing assessment at the high school level. An additional $70,000 has been budgeted to develop materials, train teachers, and grade the writing projects.

Due to changes in requirements for conducting emission inspections on school buses, a one-time cost of $13,800 is needed to purchase the equipment. The testing equipment will be jointly purchased and operated by the school division and the county transportation department. This is much more cost-effective than contracting for the inspection services.

The budget has been increased by $1,000 to fund the implementation of an employee recognition program. The funds will be used to provide certificates and awards to outstanding employees.

New Elementary School Costs & Staffing	
Square Feet	70,000
Acres	20
Student Capacity	690
Construction Cost	$9,500,000
Start-Up Supplies	$281,000
Annual Utilities	$100,000
Annual Debt Payment	$1,045,000
Baseline Staffing	$350,000
Principal	
Librarian	
Guidance Counselor	
Custodians	
Secretarial/Clerical	

"The average teacher salary is $40,342".

Exhibit 2-2 (continued)

Expenditures By Category

The school operating budget is categorized by type of expenditure. In this budget, about 86 cents of each dollar will be spent for salaries and employee benefits.

Salaries ($205.5 million)
Regular salary costs related to personnel positions, overtime, temporary employees, and supplemental pay.

Employee Benefits ($52.8 million)
Health insurance, retirement plans, Social Security, life insurance, and workers' compensation.

Supplies & Materials ($11.5 million)
Textbooks, instructional supplies, office and custodial supplies, computer software, transportation and maintenance materials, and reference materials.

Equipment ($11.3 million)
Replacement and additional equipment and furniture, school buses, vehicles, computer equipment, and capital projects.

Contractual Services ($8.0 million)
Equipment service contracts, legal fees, advertising costs, tuition, rental of equipment, and insurance costs.

Utilities ($10.8 million)
Heating fuels, electricity, telephone service, sewer and water, refuse removal, and water service.

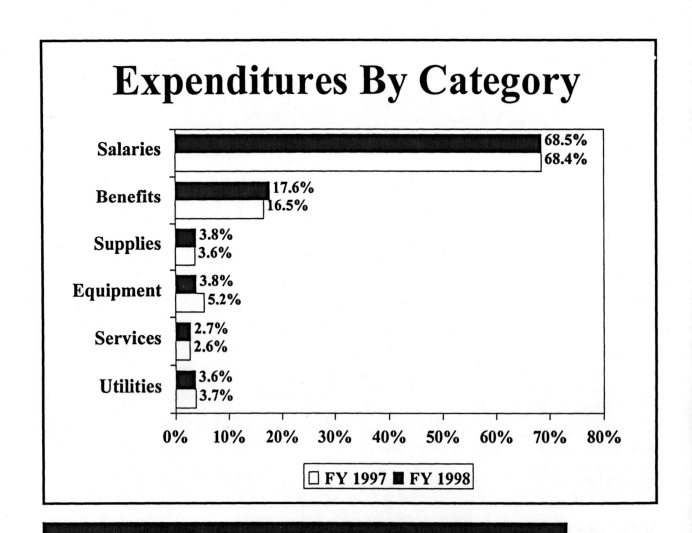

Exhibit 2-2 (continued)

Expenditures by Program

The Operating Fund has been divided into fifteen programs. Program budgets include costs due to new students, program requirements, and new resources. Program budgets do not include compensation adjustments nor benefits for salary increases. In FY 1998, program budgets at the school level have generally only been adjusted for current average salaries, benefit rate changes, inflation, and new students. Support budgets have generally only been increased for inflation and benefit rate changes.

Expenditures By Program
FY 1997 - FY 1998

	FY 1997	FY 1998	Change
Instructional Programs			
Elementary Schools	$86,716,504	$90,946,234	$4,229,730
Middle Schools	$46,839,093	$48,761,007	$1,921,914
High Schools	$60,493,004	$63,878,705	$3,385,701
Special Schools	$6,677,201	$7,438,031	$760,830
Other Programs	$6,565,111	$6,793,412	$228,301
Grants	$9,431,917	$9,548,435	$116,518
Support Programs			
Executive Administration	$2,224,374	$2,261,781	$37,407
Instructional Support	$8,179,170	$8,467,487	$288,317
Management Support	$6,397,471	$6,748,089	$350,618
Services Support	$26,848,231	$27,628,082	$779,851
Benefits & Salary Increase	$7,719,437	$13,540,188	$5,820,751
Capital Improvements	$6,219,551	$2,023,750	-$4,195,801
Utilities	$10,562,145	$10,826,199	$264,054
Property & Liability Insurance	$1,750,000	$1,881,250	$131,250
General Reserves	$3,650,000	$4,207,682	$557,682
Total	**$290,273,209**	**$304,950,332**	**$14,677,123**

Exhibit 2-2 (continued)

How Does the Typical Student Use $6,147?

Another way of looking at expenditures is to show how the operating budget relates to a typical student. In FY 1998, the budget will fund 49,775 students. This represents a cost of about $6,147 for each student. Using recent expenditure information, the graph below shows how the division's operating budget will be used to support this typical student.

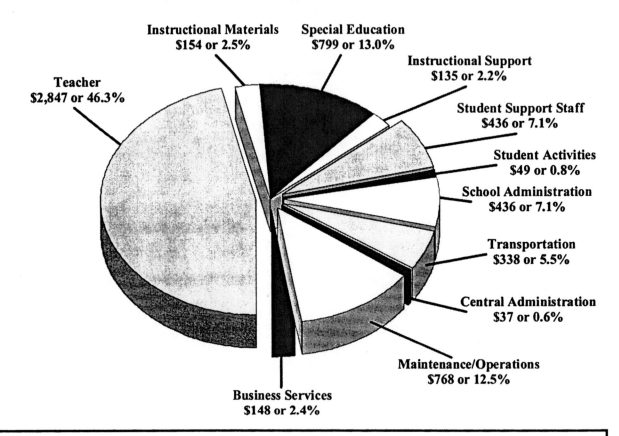

Instructional Materials
$154 or 2.5%

Special Education
$799 or 13.0%

Instructional Support
$135 or 2.2%

Teacher
$2,847 or 46.3%

Student Support Staff
$436 or 7.1%

Student Activities
$49 or 0.8%

School Administration
$436 or 7.1%

Transportation
$338 or 5.5%

Central Administration
$37 or 0.6%

Maintenance/Operations
$768 or 12.5%

Business Services
$148 or 2.4%

Description of Categories

Teacher: Salaries, benefits, and related expenses for regular classroom teachers, regular resource teachers, and regular teacher assistants

Instructional Materials: Textbooks, instructional materials, and instructional equipment

Special Education: Salaries, benefits, and related expenses for special education teachers and assistants

Instructional Support: Salaries and benefits for curriculum and staff development employees, testing materials, substitutes, and related expenses

Student Support Staff: Salaries and benefits for librarians, counselors, psychologists, visiting teachers, nurses, attendance personnel and related expenses

Student Activities: Extracurricular supplements, transportation for athletic programs, officials, and related expenses for these programs

School Administration: Salaries and benefits for school administrators, clerical staff, security staff, office supplies and equipment, and related expenses

Transportation: Salaries, benefits, and related expenses for transportation staff, and the operation of buses and vehicles

Central Administration: Salaries, benefits, and related expenses for the School Board, Superintendent, associate superintendents, and the support staff for these offices

Maintenance/Operations: Salaries and benefits for maintenance and custodial staff, utilities, repair and maintenance of facilities, and related expenses

Business Services: Salaries, benefits, and related expenses for Finance, Personnel, Data Processing, Planning, Risk Management, Purchasing, and Supply

Exhibit 2-2 (continued)

Cost Per Pupil

Cost per pupil amounts, both regular and special education, are calculated by identifying the costs directly associated with an instructional program and adding a proportionate share of the indirect school and central support costs. This total amount is then divided by the student membership for the program to determine the average cost per pupil. A cost per pupil is calculated for each regular and special education program. In FY 1998, the average per pupil cost will be about $6,147. This represents an increase of about 4.3 percent over the per pupil cost for the current fiscal year.

Cost per pupil figures provide a good perspective of the cost of instructional programs as well as a measure of comparison to previous years, state and federal averages, and surrounding jurisdictions. PWCPS has traditionally maintained a cost per pupil lower than many other school divisions. The chart below shows the cost per pupil for regular education as well as the incremental costs for special education and English for Speakers of Other Languages (ESOL) programs.

Cost Per Pupil Comparison FY 1997	
Falls Church City	$9,358
Arlington County	$9,305
Alexandria City	$8,999
Fairfax County	$7,120
Manassas City	$6,154
Loudoun County	$5,933
Prince William County	$5,894

Source: Metropolitan Area Boards of Education

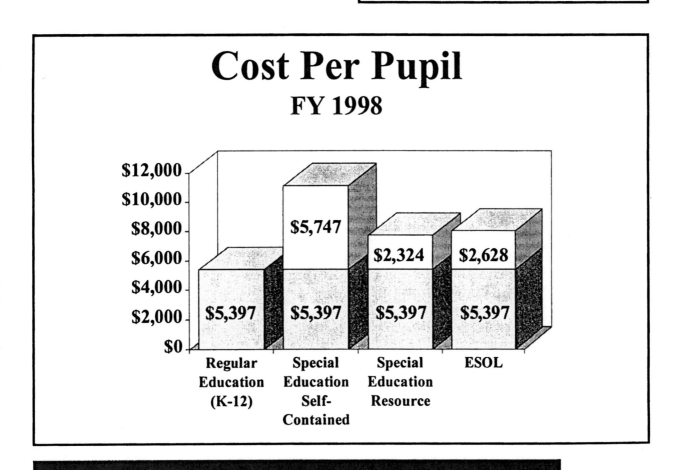

Cost Per Pupil FY 1998

Exhibit 2-2 (continued)

Executive Summary

The average special education cost per pupil is projected to be $11,144 for FY 1998. The cost per pupil for special education self-contained programs is significantly higher than the average cost per pupil. The higher costs are primarily due to the lower pupil-teacher ratios which average about 8 students per teacher. However, in recognition of the fact that a student not enrolled in a self-contained program would be in a regular education class, a net cost for special education self-contained is calculated. In FY 1998, the net cost per pupil for self-contained programs, compared to the average regular education cost, is $5,747.

Unlike self-contained classes, special education and ESOL resource programs augment a student's regular education. For FY 1998, the special education resource cost per pupil will be about $2,324 and the ESOL per pupil cost will be about $2,628.

National Comparison

The cost per pupil figures can also be used to compare the costs in PWCPS to other similar school divisions. Each year, Educational Research Services compiles a comparison of per pupil costs for PWCPS with other similar school divisions in the country. PWCPS is compared to other school divisions with at least 25,000 students and a per pupil cost of more than $5,000. Based on the final expenditure data for FY 1996, PWCPS spent $5,560 per pupil while comparable school divisions averaged expenditures of $6,252 per pupil. The chart below details this comparison.

Expenditure Comparison
ERS National Average vs. Prince William County Public Schools
Fiscal Year 1996

	National Average		Prince William	
	Per Pupil	Percent	Per Pupil	Percent
Total Per Pupil Expenditure	$6,252	100.0%	$5,560	$100.0%
Instructional Services	$4,042	64.7%	$3,873	$69.7%
Classroom instruction, guidance, library, curriculum development, textbooks, supplies				
School Site Leadership	$323	5.2%	$396	7.1%
Principals, assistant principals, clerical and support staff, related materials				
Student Services	$428	6.8%	$391	7.0%
Transportation, health and attendance, student activities				
School Board Services	$34	0.5%	$4	0.1%
School Board, clerical staff				
Executive Administration	$99	1.6%	$28	0.5%
Superintendent, associate superintendents, clerical and support staff				
Central & Business Services	$152	2.4%	$128	2.3%
Finance, Personnel, Community Relations, Planning, Data Processing, Purchasing				
Maintenance & Operations	$473	7.6%	$429	7.7%
Staff, equipment and supplies for care, upkeep and operation of facilities				
Utilities	$150	2.4%	$212	3.8%
Heating, cooling and other utilities				
Capital Outlay	$413	6.6%	$68	1.2%
New vehicles, major maintenance items, new facilities funded with operating				
Other Expenditures	$138	2.2%	$31	0.6%

Exhibit 2-2 (continued)

Executive Summary

Personnel Positions

As the largest employer in Prince William County, PWCPS employs 5,400 full-time and over 1,000 part-time employees. Almost 86 percent of these employees reside in Prince William County. Of these employees, about 85 percent are in classrooms and schools directly serving the needs of students.

In the past five years, more than 700 school-based positions were added to support student membership growth and program improvements. These improvements were made in part by redirecting resources from support services to instructional programs. Non-school based functions were reduced by 42 positions to redirect resources to maintain educational programs.

Transportation is the only central support department that has increased in personnel to accommodate the growth in student membership. In the past five years, a total of 45 bus drivers and bus aides were added to provide student transportation to and from school.

In FY 1998, the number of employees increase by about 150 full-time-equivalent positions.

Approved Positions
FY 1998

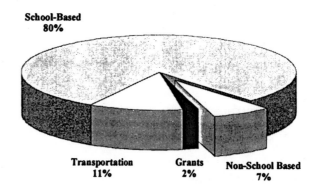

School-Based 80%

Transportation 11%

Grants 2%

Non-School Based 7%

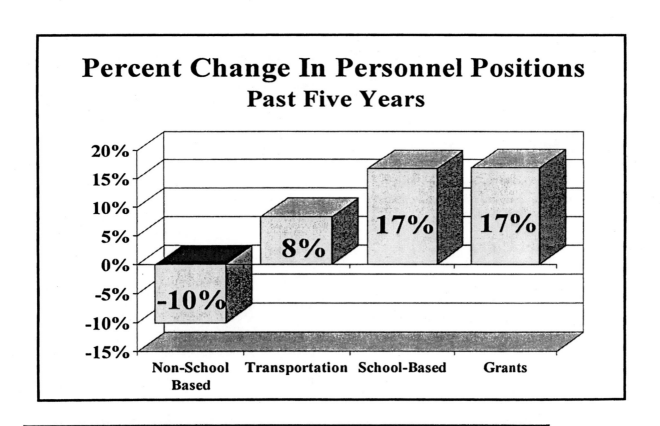

Exhibit 2-2 (continued)

Executive Summary

School Board Funds

Other than the Operating Fund, the budget includes funds for the management of special activities and functions. The FY 1998 budget consists of the ten major funds under the control of the School Board.

Operating Fund
$304,950,332
5,645.5 positions

This fund provides for the day-to-day operations and maintenance of the schools and is funded primarily by county, state, and federal funds.

Construction Fund
$81,957,000

This fund provides for all new facilities and most facility renovations and expansions. Funds are primarily from the sale of bonds.

Debt Service Fund
$19,415,000

This fund pays principal and interest on bonds and loans sold to finance capital projects in the Construction Fund. County funds almost entirely support this fund.

Food Services Fund
$11,124,207
456.0 positions

This fund provides for all food services' operating and administrative costs. The fund is supported primarily by food sales and federal/state subsidies.

Health Insurance Fund
$16,411,913
4.0 positions

This fund pays claims and related expenses for the health care program. The fund is supported by transfers from the Operating Fund and premium payments by employees.

Administrative Cafeteria Fund
$68,845
2.0 positions

This fund provides for the operating costs of the cafeteria in the Administration Building at the Independent Hill Complex. The fund is entirely supported by the sale of food in the cafeteria.

Facilities Use Fund
$230,000
2.0 positions

This fund pays claims and related expenses for workers' compensation and property losses for which the school division is self-insured and the premiums for general property and liability insurance coverage. The fund is supported by transfers from the Operating Fund.

Regional School Fund
$10,006,776
2.0 positions

This fund provides for the operation of the Northern Virginia Regional Program jointly operated by PWCPS, Manassas City Schools, and Manassas Park City Schools. The school provides certain special education services and is supported by transfers from the three school divisions.

Self-Insurance Fund
$3,713,265
3.0 positions

This fund pays claims and related expenses for workers' compensation and self-insured losses. The fund is supported by transfers from the Operating Fund.

Warehouse Fund
$2,000,000

This fund is used to track the purchase of warehouse stock items from vendors and the sale of issued items to schools and departments. It serves as the accounting mechanism for the warehouse function and does not require any revenue.

Exhibit 2-2 (continued)

Common Budget Questions

1. *What is the difference between the pupil-teacher ratio and average class size?*

   The pupil-teacher ratio is determined by dividing the number of students by all classroom and resource teachers. This includes regular classroom, reading, special education, gifted education, and other teachers involved with teaching students. The pupil-teacher ratio for PWCPS is 16.8 students per teacher.

   The average class size is determined by dividing the number of students in regular education programs by the number of regular education teachers. For example, the average class size for elementary school is determined by dividing the number of regular education students (excluding special education self-contained students) by the number of regular kindergarten through fifth grade teachers. PWCPS' average class sizes are 24.6 students per elementary class, 23.1 per middle school class, and 22.9 per high school class.

2. *What is the average cost per pupil and how is it determined?*

   The average per pupil cost is determined by dividing the total operating budget by the total number of students. For FY 1998, the total operating budget of about $305 million divided by the 49,775 students expected results in an average per pupil cost of $6,147. This is the lowest per pupil cost among all of the major school divisions in the Washington metropolitan area.

3. *What is the average teacher salary?*

   The average teacher salary for the current year is $40,342. In addition to salary, the school division will spend another $10,747 for the School Board's share of employee benefits for state retirement, Social Security, health insurance, supplemental retirement, and life insurance.

4. *How much of the budget is used for athletic and other extracurricular programs?*

   The budget includes about $1.5 million to support extracurricular and athletic programs. The School Board only funds the costs for salary supplements paid to coaches and sponsors, transportation costs, and officials for middle school athletic contests. All other costs are funded through gate receipts and revenue generated by the programs.

5. *How much more does it cost to operate the school division under school-based management?*

   No additional funding is needed to operate the school division under school-based management. School-based management allocates funds to schools using the same basic methodology as before, but allows the schools greater flexibility in how the funds are used to achieve the goals of the school division and the school.

6. *Under school-based management, are the schools responsible for the maintenance of building and equipment?*

   No. The repair and maintenance of facilities and equipment is a central responsibility. During the budget process each year, schools submit facility renewal projects which are prioritized in the division's capital improvements and major maintenance plans. Due to limited funding, not all projects are funded and some schools decide to fund some of these projects from their allocated funds.

7. *Does the state fully-fund all of the programs and services it mandates?*

   No. The complex formula used to determine costs of mandated programs significantly under-funds the state's share. This requires all school divisions in the state to spend additional local funds to make up the underfunding received from the state.

Exhibit 2-3—Executive Summary

Salt Lake City School District
440 East First South
Salt Lake City, Utah 84111-1898

May 19, 1998

The Honorable Board of Education
Salt Lake City, Utah

Dear Board Members:

GOVERNMENTAL FUND BUDGET TOTALS

I hereby submit and recommend to you a budget for the Salt Lake City School District for fiscal year 1998-99 and a revised budget for fiscal year 1997-98. The budget includes all Governmental and Proprietary Funds of the school district. The fund structure of the district is discussed in detail under the heading "The District Fund Structure" in the *Organizational Section* of this budget document. I am asking that you approve the proposed budget for fiscal year 1998-99, the revised budget for fiscal year 1997-98, and the proposed tax rate for the 1998 calendar year. The following schedule compares the proposed expenditures for all Governmental Funds with the revised estimate of expenditures for the current year.

TOTAL BUDGET FOR ALL GOVERNMENTAL FUNDS

	Revised 1997-98		Proposed 1998-99	
	Amount	% Change Prior year	Amount	% Change Prior year
Maintenance & Operation Fund	$ 116,299,455	10.43 %	$ 121,433,367	4.41 %
Special Programs Fund	13,412,254	5.07	13,270,747	-1.06
Capital & Debt Service Funds	16,710,372	-48.92	28,531,839	70.74
TOTAL	$ 146,422,081	-2.90 %	$ 163,235,953	11.48 %
Less Bond Proceeds			-10,000,000	
Net Governmental Fund Expenditures	$ 146,422,081	-2.90 %	$ 153,235,953	4.65 %

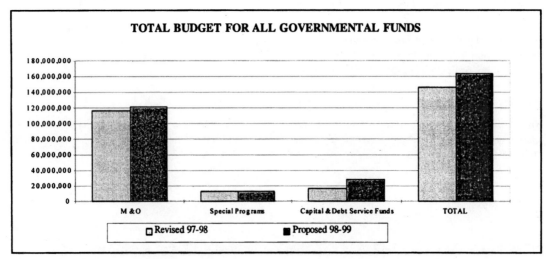

Exhibit 2-3 (continued)

SIGNIFICANT BUDGETARY TRENDS

The first questions asked about the budget are usually (a) what is the total budget amount ($163.2 million), and (b) how much has it changed from the previous year (increased $16.8 million or 11.48%). The schedule on the preceding page answers these questions. It is important to note, however, the totals for each fund. The Maintenance and Operation Fund expenditures are those for educational and support services provided to students in the K-12 regular day school program. The Special Programs Fund expenditures provide services to other than K-12 regular day school students and other services to students and the community that are not a part of the K-12 regular day school program. Examples of such services are the adult training services provided by the Columbus Community Center, Head Start services for pre-kindergarten students, and community school services. The other Governmental Funds (the Capital Outlay Fund, the Capital Reserve Fund, and the Debt Service Fund) are all involved in renovating or constructing physical facilities or the purchase of equipment. On this schedule, the bond proceeds are subtracted from the total expenditures of all Governmental Funds because if both the bond proceeds and Debt Service Fund expenditures are counted as expenditures, the proceeds from the bonds would be counted as expenditures twice. Once when the proceeds are spent to construct new buildings and again when the debt repayment is counted as expenditure. The net Governmental Fund expenditure ($153.2 million for fiscal year 1999 and $146.4 million for fiscal year 1998) represents the net amount spent that is financed by taxes and other Governmental Fund revenue.

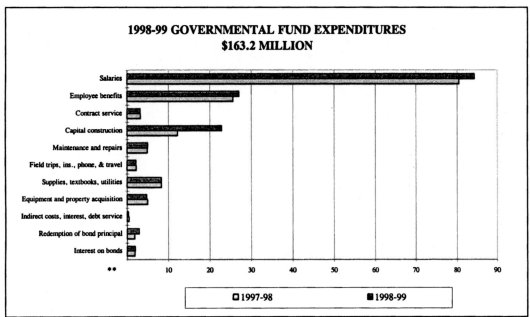

**in millions

The chart above breaks down the $163.2 million expenditures by object. The district spends the largest proportion of the 1998-99 budget on salaries (52%), which is an increase from the 1997-98 revised budget of 5%. Capital construction increased from 8% of the budget in 1997-98 to 14% of the budget in 1998-99, which is a 87% increase from the 1997-98 budget.

Exhibit 2-3 (continued)

PROPRIETARY FUND BUDGET TOTALS

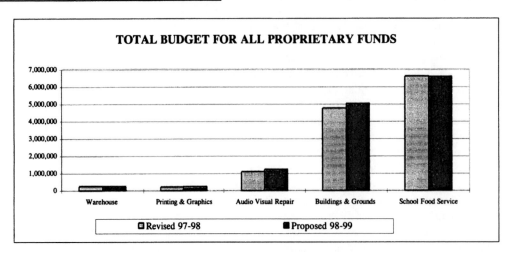

Presented above is a total for all Proprietary Funds, but since these funds are all self supporting and in the case of the Internal Service Funds, their revenue is already included as an expenditure in the Maintenance and Operation and other funds, they are not added into the total.

EXPENDITURES PER PUPIL

The Maintenance and Operation Fund expenditures are the expenditures that directly provide services to the students enrolled in K-12 regular day school programs. These expenditures are analyzed in the following schedule in order to see what the rate of increase is per pupil and also to identify any change in the portion of total current expenditure applied to each functional division of service such as instruction, media services and educational supervision, or general district administration.

Expenditures Per Pupil in Average Daily Membership (ADM) by Function

	1996-97 Actual		1997-98 Revised Budget		1998-99 Budget	
Expenditures and Encumbrances:	Amount Per ADM	% Current Expend.	Amount Per ADM	% Current Expend.	Amount Per ADM	% Current Expend.
Instruction	$2,947.40	71.08 %	$3,336.99	72.37 %	$3,488.08	72.36 %
Child accounting and counseling	120.90	2.92	136.63	2.96	145.10	3.01
Media serv. and educ. Supervision	277.45	6.69	313.94	6.81	320.87	6.65
General district administration	21.90	.53	24.73	.54	25.24	.52
General school administration	231.57	5.58	232.58	5.04	241.97	5.02
Accounting and purchasing services	35.48	.86	37.94	.82	38.90	.81
Operation and maintenance of school buildings	393.84	9.50	399.05	8.65	424.44	8.80
Student transportation	70.50	1.70	78.45	1.70	81.80	1.70
Personnel, information systems and volunteers	47.38	1.14	50.91	1.11	54.30	1.13
Total	$4,146.42	100.00 %	$4,611.22	100.00 %	$4,820.70	100.00 %
Increase in expenditures per pupil	6.79 %		11.21 %		4.54 %	
Pupils in ADM	25,400		25,221		25,190	

Exhibit 2-3 (continued)

There is only one significant change in the proportion of the budget allocated to the various functions. The portion of the budget spent on the instruction and school counselors function is increased due to action taken by the Board of Education in 1997 and previous years in allocating any discretionary resources to these areas. Each year, for eleven consecutive years, the district has increased the proportion of its total expenditures for instruction and counseling. The Salt Lake City School District takes pride in this record of eleven consecutive years in which the district has become more efficient and effective by allocating proportionately more of its resources to direct instructional services and counseling and fewer resources to support services.

The 1998-99 expenditure per pupil of $4,820.70 is an increase of 4.54% over the previous year and is primarily due to budgeted salary and benefit increases.

The next schedule analyzes the change in proportion of Maintenance and Operation Fund expenditures applied to each object of expenditure such as salaries, fringe benefits, contracted services, etc. The proportion of total expenditures consumed by salaries and employee benefits, as shown in the budget for 1998-99 is increasing while the proportion of the budget consumed by other items except equipment and building maintenance is decreasing. This budget does not include any major program increases or new initiatives. The legislative increase to public education allows for no more than a continuation of the district's programs other than a small decrease in class size in grades seven and eight.

Expenditures Per Pupil in Average Daily Membership (ADM) by Object

Expenditures and Encumbrances:	1996-97 Actual		1997-98 Revised Budget		1998-99 Budget	
	Amount Per ADM	% Current Expend.	Amount Per ADM	% Current Expend.	Amount Per ADM	% Current Expend.
Salaries	$2,616.33	63.10 %	$2,843.33	61.66 %	$2,995.16	62.13 %
Employee benefits	833.33	20.10	919.92	19.95	973.14	20.19
Contract services-professional and educational	55.53	1.34	118.43	2.57	118.12	2.45
Maintenance and repairs	149.43	3.60	169.66	3.68	172.42	3.58
Field trips, insurance, telephone, and travel	97.23	2.35	73.59	1.60	70.79	1.47
Supplies, textbooks, and utilities	270.39	6.52	302.73	6.56	304.23	6.31
Equipment building maintenance	124.18	2.99	183.56	3.98	186.84	3.87
Total	$4,146.42	100.00 %	$4,611.22	100.00 %	$4,820.70	100.00 %
Increase in expenditures per pupil	6.79 %		11.21 %		4.54 %	
Pupils in ADM	25,400		25.221		25,190	

The next questions to be answered are what is the proposed tax rate for this budget, how has it changed from the current year, and what is the tax impact of this budget on the average home owner in the district.

Exhibit 2-3 (continued)

PROPERTY TAX RATES

CHART 7 – SCHEDULE OF PROPERTY TAX RATES BY FUND

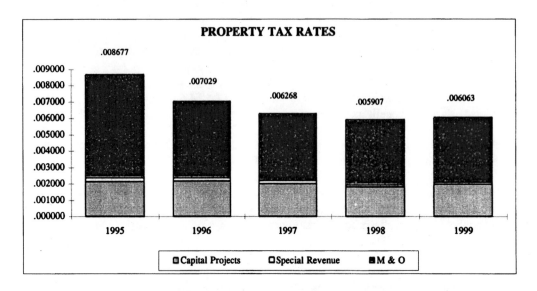

As can be seen from Chart 7 (which is presented here and in the *Informational Section* on page 114), the proposed tax rate for 1998 (fiscal 1998-99) is slightly increased from the current tax rate. The chief cause for this increase is a judgement levy assessed to recover a refund of back taxes to U.S. West.

TAX BURDEN ON HOME OWNER

Each year the district must determine a "certified tax rate" based on an assessed valuation estimate provided by the Salt Lake County Auditor. The certified tax rate is that rate which will provide the same property tax revenue as was collected for the current year, plus taxes on new growth in the city. I propose the district adopt the certified tax rate including the judgement tax rate calculated by the Salt Lake County Auditor, which rate is .006063. The district cannot maintain viable educational programs and let the tax rate drop below this level. The effect of the proposed tax rate on the owner of a $100,000 home would be as follows:

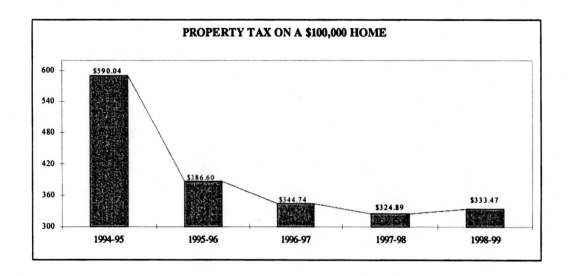

Exhibit 2-3 (continued)

You will note that the taxpayer ends up paying slightly more in 1998-99 on a $100,000 home. What this chart does not show is the tax impact resulting from any increase in the market value of a home during the past year. We do not expect any significant general increases in assessed value of homes in the city this year.

LAW, POLICY & ORGANIZATIONAL CHANGES

The *Organizational Section* of this budget includes an organizational chart for the district and a description of laws and policies that guide the development and administration of this budget. There are no significant changes in the organization currently, however, the district is planning to make significant changes during the budget year. As of now, though, decisions have not been made as to exactly what the new organization will look like. The law restricting any increases in tax rates beyond the calculated certified tax rate was changed in 1998. In recent years, this law had changed several times. First any tax rates beyond the certified tax rate could be approved by the Board of Education after meeting certain advertising and disclosure requirements and after holding a public hearing. Then the legislature changed that requirement and provided that in addition to the above, such a tax increase must also be approved by a majority vote of district citizens. The vote of citizens requirement expired at the end of 1996. For 1998, the legislature has now imposed this vote of citizens requirement for all tax rates other than the district's basic Capital Outlay tax rate. Also, the district has established a new long range strategic plan. The mission statement, vision statement, performance results, and parameters have not changed.

AVERAGE DAILY MEMBERSHIP AND DISTRICT STAFFING LEVELS

This budget anticipates a decrease in the total student average daily membership (ADM) of 31 students for 1998-99. This 31 student decrease is accounted for by an increase of 82 students in ADM in elementary schools; a decrease of 97 students in ADM in middle schools; a decrease of 84 high school students in ADM; and a 68 ADM increase in self-contained special education and youth in custody classes. Even though there is projected a decrease in ADM, there is anticipated an increase of one teacher in the regular school program. The number of teachers is slightly increased over last year because of some under staffing or filling permanent positions with temporary staff during 1997-98. Programs are both increasing and decreasing in number of staff. There is a net increase of 10 FTE in total staff projected by this budget *(see Informational Section, District Staffing Levels on page 130)*. The increase in staff is the result of eight additional teachers for class size reduction in grades seven and eight, one additional teacher as mentioned above, and one principal to organize the new school which will open in the West Point area in 1999-2000. This budget is primarily a maintenance of effort budget, there are no new programs or major initiatives included in this budget.

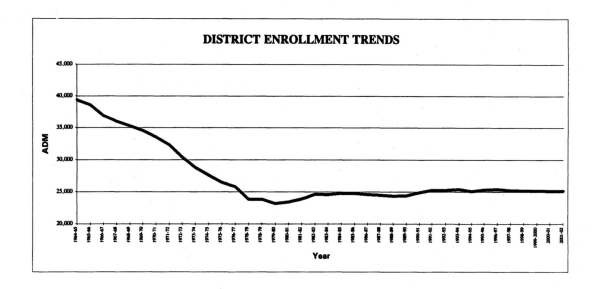

Exhibit 2-3 (continued)

CAPITAL BUDGET (NEW BUILDINGS, BUILDING RETROFIT, AND BUILDING REMODEL)

The Salt Lake City community is very much aware of the district's building retrofit program. The purpose of the program is to bring every building in the district up to current life safety building code requirements, including earthquake life safety building codes; and at the same time, improve all buildings to meet current building codes in regard to access for disabled persons, air condition all schools, and make other minor building improvements. The current plan will replace 20 buildings and retrofit 17 buildings over a ten year period and complete air conditioning of every school within an eight year period. The plan also includes the construction of one new elementary school in the West Point area and a new bus facility, which will be built in conjunction with a new city fleet facility.

Included in the 1998-99 budget are appropriations for the new school in the West Point area, the installation of air conditioning at East, Highland, and West high schools, and the design costs for the replacement of Whittier, Franklin, and Riley elementary schools, and the retrofit of Jackson Elementary School.

GENERAL OBLIGATION BONDS

This budget anticipates the sale of $10 million in general obligation bonds before the end of the 1998 calendar year. This will bring the total of bonds sold to $50 million out of the $70 million authorized by voters on November 2, 1993. All of the bonds sold have been rated "Aaa" by Moody's Investors Service. The district will need to hold a new bond election prior to the end of calendar year 2000 to accomplish its long range capital plan.

INFORMATIONAL SECTION SUMMARY – FUTURE PROSPECTS

The *Informational Section* of this budget has many charts, graphs, and schedules that illustrate trend factors important in the development of this budget and the financial management of the district such as revenue and expenditure trends, enrollment trends, staffing trends, taxable value and tax rate trends, etc. All of this is interesting and important information that helps us understand where we have been, and to some extent where we may be going.

Included in the *Informational Section* is a chart and schedule displaying the Maintenance and Operation Fund Revenue and Expenditures Growth History and a schedule projecting the Maintenance and Operation Fund Budget for fiscal years 1998-99 through 2001-2002 (see pages 120-123). It is encouraging to see that during the period beginning with the 1992-93 fiscal year and concluding with the 1993-94 fiscal year our current revenue and expenditures were almost perfectly matched. For 1994-95 and since that time our revenues have grown more than our expenditures. These are years that are closed and we have an accurate measure of actual and not estimated amounts. Projecting this trend through the year 2001-2002 is encouraging. It indicates the district has expenditure

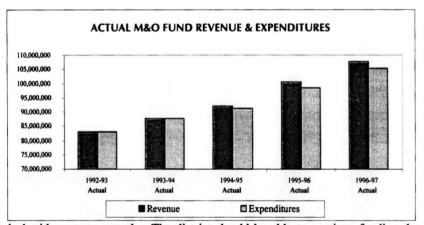

growth under control and matched with revenue growth. The district should be able to continue funding the current services to students throughout this period, and even enhance current services. This is not saying

Exhibit 2-3 (continued)

things will be easy. There will always be more demands for improved services, which are beyond the district's financial capacity. Keeping expenditures within the limits of available revenue will continue to be a challenge, but there appears to be no reason to believe that the district will have to reduce services because of shrinking resources.

EDUCATIONAL PROGRAM ACHIEVEMENTS & CHANGES

The major focus this year has been to work out and establish the Annenberg Process. This is a process for systemic reform for the entire district with the emphasis on student achievement. The Salt Lake City Board of Education vision statement affirms, "Each student is valued and nurtured to achieve his or her highest potential academically, physically, and socially, resulting in a principled contributor to society."

In accordance with the vision statement, an educational analysis of the district and each of the Salt Lake City School District's thirty-six schools was begun. This analysis involved the gathering of many kinds of information, which included academic, demographic, and socio-economic data on a district-wide basis, as well as for each individual school. The district also acquired much information about public perception of the Salt Lake City schools. More than fifteen thousand surveys were completed and returned by parents, teachers, students, administrators, and community members. Survey respondents were invited to reply to open-ended questions included in the survey. Responses were compiled, tabulated, and distributed for the district and for each of the district's thirty-six schools. Meetings were held for staff and parents where the data compilation was disseminated. Additional meetings were held for administrators, teachers, parents, and site teams for an explanation of the data. The central office is working to ensure the establishment of processes for public and school involvement. As information is analyzed by the individual school site teams, each will develop a school profile, which in turn will be used as a baseline of accountability for enhanced and continual student academic achievement.

We have continued our district performance assessments in reading and writing in grades 4-10. We have added end-of-level assessments in math for grade 6 and middle school pre-algebra classes.

During the 1997-98 school year, Student Education Plans (SEP's) were introduced at the elementary level. All elementary teachers held two conferences with parents and students during the year. At the secondary level, all schools continued to meet the state requirements for Student Education Occupation Planning (SEOP) conferences. A district committee was established and is presently seeking to develop a new SEOP form that will combine accountability for the district performance results and SEOP into one electronic document that is to be supported by individual student performance records and portfolios of student work and achievement.

The Salt Lake City School District and the Salt Lake Area Chamber of Commerce combined their efforts and applied for a Federal Urban/Rural Opportunities (Poverty Grant) which was awarded October 1, 1997. The funding allocation for the grant was $1.6 million over the next five years. The funding will be used to serve poverty students identified in targeted areas throughout the district.

It is always difficult to match scarce resources with the many needs of our educational system and there is never enough to satisfy all needs. However, I believe that this budget demonstrates reasonable progress in the effort to satisfy the many needs of the system, and I recommend to you this 1998-99 budget.

Sincerely,

Darline P. Robles
Superintendent

MBA Certificate

(Criterion B-2)

Exhibit 2-4

Exhibit 2-4—MBA Certificate

Association of School Business Officials International

This Meritorious Budget Award is presented to

Central School District

for excellence in the preparation and issuance

of its school system budget,

for the Fiscal Year 1995-1996.

The budget is judged to conform

to the principles and standards of the

ASBO International Meritorious Budget Awards Program.

President   Executive Director

School Board and Administrators

(Criterion B-3)

Exhibit 2-5

Exhibit 2-6

Exhibit 2-5—Simple Listing of Board Members and Administrators

Mt. Lebanon School District
1997-98 Budget

PROFILE OF OUR SCHOOL DISTRICT

BOARD OF SCHOOL DIRECTORS

Jean H. Palcho	President
Carol J. Walton	Vice President
Ronald R. Hoffman	Member
Henry J. Kasky	Member
Lori Humphreys	Member
Beverly A. Maurhoff	Member
Judith M. McVerry	Member
John W. Seltzer	Member
Templeton Smith	Member
Janice R. Klein	Board Secretary
Thomas A. Peterson	Solicitor
Mellon Bank, N. A.	Treasurer
Maher Duessel	Auditor

CENTRAL OFFICE ADMINISTRATORS

Glenn F. Smartschan	Superintendent
A. Richard Pitcock	Assistant Superintendent
David D. Disque	Director of Physical Plant Services
Janice R. Klein	Director of Fiscal Services
Deborah P. Allen	Director of Student Support Services
George E. Wilson	Director of Secondary Instruction

BUILDING PRINCIPALS

Pamela J. Boyd	Washington Elementary
Larry R. Snyder	Lincoln Elementary
Nancy A. Williamson	Markham Elementary
Kenneth W. Getkin	Howe Elementary
Barbara B. Float	Foster Elementary
Michael T. Schnirel	Jefferson Elementary
Robert C. Mallery	Hoover Elementary
J. Kevin Lordon	Junior High School
Otto L. Graf	Senior High School

The School Board generally meets monthly for a discussion session on the second Monday at 7:30 p.m. in various school buildings and for an action meeting on the third Monday at 7:30 p.m. in the Band Room of Jefferson School. The public is welcome to attend both meetings.

Exhibit 2-6—Elaborate Listing of Board Members and Administrators

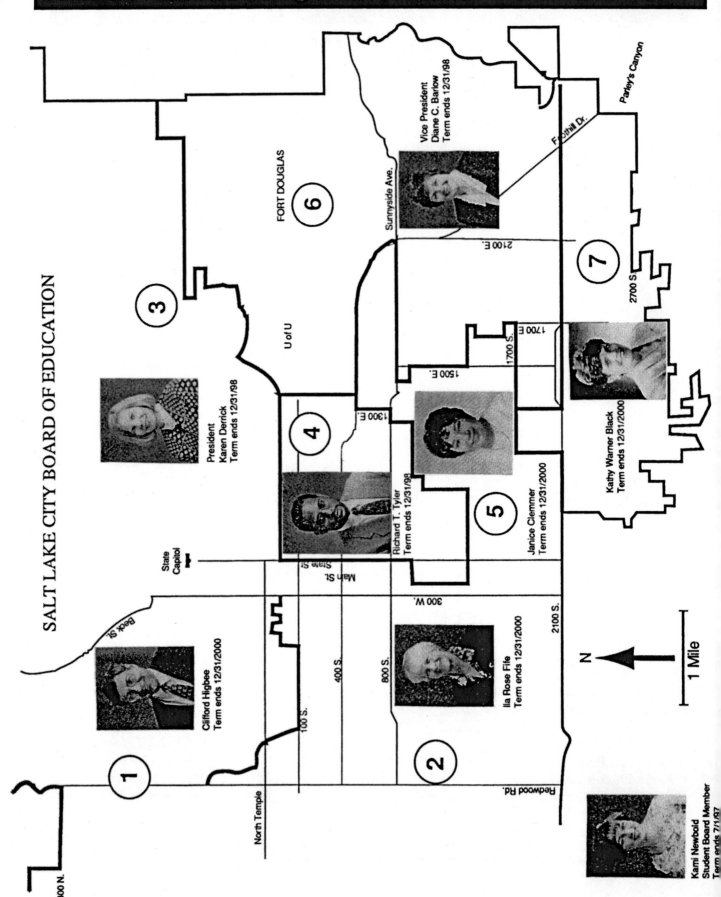

SALT LAKE CITY BOARD OF EDUCATION

President
Karen Derrick
Term ends 12/31/98

Vice President
Diane C. Barlow
Term ends 12/31/98

Clifford Higbee
Term ends 12/31/2000

Richard T. Tyler
Term ends 12/31/98

Janice Clemmer
Term ends 12/31/2000

Kathy Warner Black
Term ends 12/31/2000

Ila Rose Fife
Term ends 12/31/2000

Kami Newbold
Student Board Member
Term ends 7/1/97

FORT DOUGLAS

U of U

State Capitol

CHAPTER 3
Organizational Section

The Organizational Section provides the context and framework within which the budget is developed and managed. The context for the budget is substantially predicated on the type and level of service to be provided to the students of the community. This framework also includes the school entity's organizational and financial structure as well as the controls that direct and regulate the development and administration of the budget. Such controls consist of statutory requirements, board policies and administrative procedures that guide and govern the budget development and financial management processes within the school entity.

Within this framework and context, the Organizational Section sets forth the mission, goals and objectives of the school entity, which should drive the development of the budget. The mission defines the purpose of the organization while the goals describe the preferred future state.

Together, the mission and goals establish a general direction for the organization. They serve as the basis for the development of programs, including the type and level of services to be provided and the capital assets to be obtained. Goals should be developed after undertaking an assessment of community conditions and other external factors, and a review of internal operations of the school entity, including its services, capital assets, and management practices.

The mission and goals of the school entity are achieved through the identification of management strategies, or objectives, that are consistent with financial policies as well as program, operating, and capital policies and plans. The objectives should have measurable outcomes that permit an assessment of progress toward the achievement of the mission and goals of the school entity.

CONTENTS

At a minimum, the MBA criteria require the following information in this section:

1. Explanation of the school entity (Criterion C-1)
2. Significant budget and financial policies (Criterion C-2)
3. Organizational chart (Criterion C-3)
4. Statement of the mission (Criterion C-4)
5. Major goals and objectives (Criterion C-5)
6. The operating and capital budget development process (Criterion C-6)
7. The budget administration and management process (Criterion C-7)

Explanation of the School Entity (Criterion C-1)

The Organizational Section is intended to familiarize readers with the specifics of the organization's legal operating environment, the nature and scope of the services that the school entity provides, and the governmental accounting structure and policies used to present financial information.

School organizations are the most common type of special-purpose governments and are considered primary governmental entities if they meet all of the following criteria:

- The members of the governing board are chosen in a general election;
- The organization functions as a separate legal entity; and
- The school entity is fiscally independent.

A school organization is considered to be a separate legal entity (legally autonomous) if it enjoys the corporate rights typically associated with separate legal status. If a school entity is not legally separate, it is considered to be an integral part of whichever government does exercise those powers.

Fiscal independence exists when a school entity is not subject to arbitrary interference in establishing its budget, setting tax levies and charges, or issuing bonded debt. A school entity is fiscally dependent if it is unable to complete one or more of these procedures without the substantive approval of another government. Blanket limitations are not considered to impair a school entity's fiscal independence. Such blanket limitations include such statutory constraints as the issuance of bonded debt. Exhibit 3-1 provides an excellent example of the description of the legal and fiscal status of the school system.

A school entity is fundamentally defined by the type and level of service that it provides to the students and members of the community that it serves. A key element, therefore, that helps the reader understand the budget requirements includes the type of service. The type of service may be delimited as the level of education such as general programs with a range of kindergarten to twelfth grade (k-12) or specialized programs such as jointly operated vocational education schools with a range of nine to twelfth grade (9-12).

Budget requirements also are dependent on quantity of services to be provided. In large measure, resource demands are a reflection of the size and nature of the community as well as the number of students to be served. Key elements that help define the quantity of service include the geographic area of the community, which may include such description as the number of square miles and the number of residents as well as the nature of the community (rural, suburban or urban). Other essential information that helps to define the quantity of service includes the number of students to be served and the number of buildings in the organizational entity. Exhibits 3-1 and 3-2 provide good examples of the description of the type and level of service funded in the school budgets. The descriptions include the level of education and the kind of education programs as well as the size and scope of the school entities. The size and scope are defined in terms of the population and geography of the community along with the number of students and number of buildings in the school entity.

Finally, this item of the Organizational Section requires that the informational infrastructure for the presentation of accounting and financial data be defined. This description is essential given the unique environment in which governments, including school entities, operate. It is also important since the system of governmental accounting and financial reporting differs from that of the private sector and also differs among school entities based on local options.

Most important, school organizations use a variety of separate accounting entities known as "funds" to control and monitor the receipt and disbursement of resources for specified purposes. Without an understanding of the governmental accounting structure, which includes the conventions, rules and procedures for the presentation of budget data, the reader could not make sense of the financial information.

The accounting and financial informational infrastructure used by school entities is classified into seven "fund types" that are established as required by law and for sound financial administration. In describing the school entity, the Organizational Section should identify the governmental funds (general fund, special revenue funds, debt service funds, and capital projects funds), proprietary funds (enterprise funds and internal service funds) and fiduciary funds used to present budget information. Exhibit 3-3 sets forth an example of the funds included in the budget.

The description of the accounting and financial informational infrastructure should also include an explanation of the classification of revenues and expenditures as well as an explanation of the basis of accounting for budget revenues and expenditures. Exhibit 3-4 provides an example of the system used for the classification of revenues and expenditures for the school entity.

A typical school entity's annual appropriated budget provides estimates of revenues and authorizes expenditures. That is not to say, however, that all state and provincial governments define "revenues" and "expenditures" in the same way for this purpose. The system used by an individual school entity to determine when budgetary "revenues" have been realized and when budgetary "expenditures" have been incurred is known as its "budgetary basis of accounting."

Sometimes, the budgetary basis of accounting is the same basis of accounting used to prepare financial statements in conformity with GAAP. In many cases, however, some other basis of accounting is used for the budget. For example, some school entities recognize revenues and expenditures when cash is received or disbursed. This is characterized as a "cash basis of accounting." Other school entities recognize revenues and other financial resource increments such as proceeds from a bond issue when they become both "measurable" and "available" to finance expenditures of the current period. This is a modification of the accrual basis of accounting adapted to the governmental fund-type measurement focus referred to as the "modified accrual basis of accounting." Still other school entities use some other basis of accounting. Exhibit 3-5 describes the basis of accounting for the school entity.

Budget and Financial Policies (Criterion C-2)

There are many requirements that govern the operation of school entities including the adoption and management of budgets and financial resources. They include external requirements that are set forth in laws and regulations adopted at the state and province level. They also include internal requirements established in policies and procedures adopted at the board and administrative levels.

These laws, polices and procedures establish the constraints for resources allocation decisions. Because of their importance, all significant budget and financial policies should be described in the document since these policies set the parameters within which budgetary decisions and other actions can be made.

Exhibit 3-6 sets forth the legal requirements adopted by the state that include the definition of legal responsibilities for the preparation and presentation of the budget. The legal requirements in this example also establish the time frame for the adoption of the budget, limitations on fund balance, limitations on appropriations, interfund transfers, the payment of bills, emergency funds, and financial reporting.

Exhibit 3-7 provides an excellent example of the kind of organizational policies and procedures adopted by boards and administration that provide controls on the budget and financial management process. Such policies and procedures include the operating budget policy, capital budget policy, debt management policy, revenue estimation procedures, budget administration, fund balance management, encumbrance and expenditure control, and financial reporting.

Organizational Chart (Criterion C-3)

Organizational charts help users of budget documents to visualize the structure of an organization and the relationships within it. These charts typically show divisions or subdivisions of an organization, the hierarchy and relationship of groups to one another and lines of control.

The MBA criteria require an organizational chart, which includes administrative staff by position or title. Exhibit 3-8 shows administrative staff by title (e.g., divisions) and indicate lines of authority. The chart also provides the name of the individual in the position and also provides a phone number. Positions less than full time are also denoted on the chart. Exhibit 3-9 shows the organizational chart for a community college that delineates the structure also by division. The chart also provides the name of the person who serves in the position.

Exhibit 3-10 provides a more detailed presentation of the organization structure for the school entity. Chart 3-10A sets forth the organization chart for the school entity. Chart 3-10B, Chart 3-10C, and Chart 3-10D provide a further breakdown of the school organization by major divisions. Similar charts, not shown here, are presented for the other administrative units such as school buildings and the food service department. Each of the organization boxes is identified by a job position. The boxes also include the number of equivalent full time positions within the position classification for the division. The positions in the organizational chart are cross-referenced in the Financial and the Informational Sections of the budget document.

Mission Statement (Criterion C-4)

A mission statement defines an organization's fundamental purpose. It should guide the development of programs and services. It is the unifying theme that links an organization's many diverse functions and programs. Many organizations adopt a mission statement as part of their strategic planning process.

Regardless of its origin, a school entity's mission statement should be presented in the budget document. This is necessary because resource allocation decisions should be connected to the general direction of the organization as set forth in the mission statement. The mission of the entity should be the foundation for resources allocation decisions. The mission statement should be clear and coherent with linkage to organizational goals and objectives. Exhibits 3-11 and 3-12 provide examples of mission statements from two school entities that are linked to the goals of the organization in Exhibits 3-13 and 3-14 respectively.

Major Goals and Objectives (Criterion C-5)

If an organization's mission statement constitutes a vision of what it hopes to accomplish, then its goals and objectives are the action plans by which it can achieve that vision. Goals and objectives are terms often used interchangeably. For purposes of budgeting and financial planning, consistent use of these terms facilitates comparisons among programs and services and can help with the establishment of priorities and the evaluation of results. Two common definitions of goals and objectives are:

- Goals — An organization's long-term direction or target of what it wants to accomplish.
- Objectives — Measurable and time-bound activities that must be met for an organization to attain a goal.

Goals typically represent what an organization wants to accomplish over several years. Objectives generally relate to specific targets for the budget year. Goals and objectives can be established and presented at various levels of an organization.

Exhibit 3-13 presents a comprehensive framework for the attainment of the mission of the organization through the implementation of goals and objectives. The framework is referred to as the "Quality Management Plan (QMP)". The plan contains six specific and linked elements – vision statement, mission statement (see Exhibit 3-11), standards of quality, goals, performance standards (objectives), and implementation process. While goals have been established for the school entity as a whole, the QMP extends to the school and department levels in the organization. Each goal is implemented with several performance standards (objectives) that are measurable outcomes. The QMP also defines a control system and implementation schedule for assessment and resource allocation. This is an excellent example of the important linkage between strategic planning, resources allocations and performance measurement.

Exhibit 3-14 sets forth the objectives and strategies of the school entity to achieve its mission (see Exhibit 3-12). The school entity established objectives that are specific to each strategy. This framework is notable because it defines the resources required to achieve specific measurable outcomes. It also presents strategies, measurable outcomes and resource requirements in the same exhibit. Resource allocations are thereby tied directly to specific objectives.

School entities can use these and other formats to present their goals and objectives. The criteria suggest, but do not require, entities to include the cost of specific goals and objectives if the cost of a goal or objective is significant and measurable. Obviously, it would be much easier to estimate the cost of a new program or facility than it would be to estimate the cost of an educational goal, which cuts across programs and locations.

Budget Development Process (Criterion C-6)

The school entity must describe the process for the preparation and adoption of the budget in a timely manner. The process should include the capital budget development process. In some jurisdictions, the capital budget is prepared separately from the operating budget. In other jurisdictions, capital improvement planning is done as part of the operating budget. In either case, the operating budget should describe the process followed to budget both operating and capital expenditures.

The budget development process most typically would include a budget calendar; the preparation of budget guidelines and instructions; a mechanism for coordinating the budget preparation and review; procedures to facilitate budget review, discussion, modification, and adoption; and opportunities for stakeholder input.

Exhibits 3-15, 3-16 and 3-17 present timelines with specific tasks for the development of the budget. These timelines are presented in narrative form (Exhibit 3-15), chart form (Exhibit 3-16) and graphical form (Exhibit 3-17). The functions specified are typical tasks in the budget development process. Each describes the major steps in the process and the timeframe within which they are performed.

Exhibit 3-18 is a more comprehensive approach to the description of the budget process that includes specific narrative on the operating and capital budget processes. It also describes the budget process more broadly to include planning, preparation, adoption, implementation and evaluation. This narrative is supplemented with a description and flowchart of the stages in the financial planning process. The budget calendar supplements the narrative and charts. It lists detailed budget activities and expected completion dates with handy calendars for quick reference. Note that both the narrative and calendar identify

the opportunities for the public to obtain information and to comment on the proposed budgets.

Budget Administration and Management Process (Criterion C-7)

In addition to budget preparation and adoption, the MBA criteria require school budgets to describe the process used to administer and manage budgets. At the minimum, the document should describe the process used for budgetary control, budget modification and financial reporting — the most critical elements of budget accountability and disclosure. The budget administration and management process also includes the practices needed to monitor and assess progress in meeting the goals and objectives of the school entity.

Exhibits 3-19, 3-20, and 3-21 describe how three school entities handle such matters as expenditure control and approvals, encumbrance control, budget transfers and budgetary reporting. The exhibits also explain such other budget administration and financial management control processes as auditing and management information systems.

CHECKLIST

1. An explanation of the school entity which includes the following:
   a) Legal autonomy, fiscal independence/dependence
   b) Level of education provided
   c) Geographic area served
   d) Number of students and number of schools
   e) Number of funds and fund types and titles
   f) Explanation of the classification of revenues/expenditures
   g) Explanation of the measurement basis for budget revenues/expenditures
2) A discussion of significant budget and financial:
   a) Policies
   b) Procedures
   c) Regulations which govern the budget process
3) An organizational chart which includes the administrative staff by position or title.
4) A coherent statement of the mission of the school entity.
5) A description of the major goals and objectives for the school entity (If the cost of a goal or objective is significant and measurable, it is suggested that the cost be included).
6) A description of the budget development process (Include the capital budget development process).
7) A description of the budget administration and management process.

Explanation of the School Entity

(Criterion C-1)

Exhibit 3-1—Explanation of School Entity

FISCAL YEAR 1997-98   **THE DISTRICT ENTITY**

The District is Legally Autonomous

The legal name of the district is Horry County School District. To distinguish the district entity from the legislative body which governs the district, the name Horry County Schools is used to describe the district entity.

The boundaries of the district are coterminous with the boundaries of Horry County, South Carolina; however, the school district is an independent entity. The present boundaries of the school district and authority of its Board were established in 1952 by Act No. 754 of the Acts and Joint Resolution of the General Assembly of South Carolina which established a county-wide school district.

The District is Fiscally Independent

The district became fiscally independent on August 31, 1995 which fulfilled Strategy 11 of the district's Strategic Plan. In the order granting summary judgment signed by James E. Lockemy, the Circuit Judge ordered:

The Horry County School Board is legally empowered by Act 239 to determine the necessary millage for the operation of schools of the Horry County School District and the Horry County Auditor shall receive statements of such rates pursuant to S.C. Code Ann. §: 12-39-180 from the Horry County School Board.

District Size and Scope

Horry County Schools serves a county of 175,500 people along the Atlantic coastline of northeastern South Carolina. Encompassing approximately 1,134 square miles, the school district ranks first as the largest school district in the State in land area. Included in the school district is Conway, the County Seat of Horry County, with a population of 9,819 and the City of Myrtle Beach, the largest city in the County, with a population of 28,087.

The school district has eight attendance areas: Myrtle Beach, Conway, Socastee, North Myrtle Beach, Loris, Aynor and Green Sea Floyds and Carolina Forest. Each area consists of a high school and the elementary and middle schools that feed into it. The middle and high school for the Carolina Forest attendance area opened in August, 1997.

Horry County Schools

Exhibit 3-1 (continued)

District Size and Scope
(continued)

Number of Schools:

Primary/Elementary Schools	23
Middle Schools	7
High Schools	8
Career Centers/Laboratory Schools	3
Total	41

All schools in the district and the district itself are fully accredited by the South Carolina Department of Education and the Southern Association of Colleges and Schools. Horry County Schools is the fifth largest of the state's ninety-one (91) school districts and ranks second in the state in student enrollment growth during the past ten (10) years. For fiscal year 1997-98, the student enrollment is projected to be 27,242:

Primary/Elementary Schools	13,108
Middle Schools	4,783
High Schools	9,351
Total	27,242

The District provides a full range of programs and services for its students. These include elementary and secondary course offerings at the general, vocational and college preparatory levels. A broad range of co-curricular and extra-curricular activities to complement the students' curricular programs are also offered.

Horry County Schools

Exhibit 3-2—Explanation of School Entity

MSD Washington Township, Indianapolis, Indiana
Our Community and its Schools
1998 Annual Budget

Community Overview

Washington Township is a multi-ethnic community of over 130,000 residents with a variety of racial and religious groups and economic levels represented in the student population. While nearly all of Marion County is organized into a unified, city-county government, the eleven school districts are autonomous. The MSD of Washington Township is a public school district system located on the north side of Indianapolis, Indiana providing a comprehensive educational program to 10,025 students, grades kindergarten through twelve. The school district is characterized by a high degree of involvement and support for the schools as represented in parent/teacher organizations, specialized advisory committees, Parents' Council, and Presidents' Council (committee consisting of all parent/teacher organization presidents), and many parent volunteers. The school district covers 48 square miles and maintains 8 elementary schools, 3 middle schools, 1 high school, 1 alternative education school, and 1 vocational education school. The educational program offers regular instruction, special instruction, vocational instruction, gifted instruction, and necessary support programs.

Elementary Education - Grades K-5

Elementary schools enroll students in kindergarten through grade 5. A Limited Choice Program allows parents to apply to attend any elementary school. Enrollment is dependent upon available space and maintenance of racial balance. Major instructional topics composing the elementary student's day include language arts, handwriting, mathematics, science, health, and social studies. Each elementary school is staffed with a music, art and physical education teacher, a language arts and a media specialist, and a remedial mathematics teacher. Computers are also a part of the classroom environment with students using them as learning tools.

Middle School Education - Grades 6-8

Students in grades 6 through 8 are housed in three middle schools which provide programs especially designed for the young adolescent. Classes in the basics (reading, English, mathematics, science, and social studies) are usually scheduled in blocks. Students also have programs in exploratory arts (home economics, music, art, and industrial technology) and health/physical education.

Choir, band, orchestra, communication skills, and foreign language, which begins in grade 7, are among the electives available. Each school utilizes a microcomputer laboratory for the development of computer literacy and computer-assisted learning experiences. An interscholastic athletic program is available to seventh and eighth grade students, and an intramural program is available to students in all grades.

Counselors provide academic, social, and personal counseling to assist students through the years of early adolescence. In addition, they work with students and parents to plan schedules for grade nine and to facilitate the transition from middle school to high school.

All three middle schools are accredited by the North Central Association of Colleges and Secondary Schools and by the Indiana Department of Education.

High School Education - Grades 9-12

North Central High School, which is generally considered one of the finest comprehensive high schools in the Midwest, enrolls students in grades 9 through 12. North Central represents excellence in terms of staff, facilities, and programs. Over 200 curricular offerings with college prep, modified, and honors classes are provided. In 1995, nearly 75% of North Central graduates attended college or other advanced programs.

Exhibit 3-2 (continued)

North Central is the first Indiana high school to offer the International Baccalaureate (IB) program, an optional academic program requiring participants to take rigorous course work in English, science, mathematics, foreign language, and social studies and culminating in a series of examinations. Successful completion of the International Baccalaureate program enables students to gain entrance into a variety of prestigious universities abroad and offers advanced placement in American universities.

North Central High School is accredited by the North Central Association of Colleges and Secondary Schools and the Indiana Department of Education, and received the "Excellence in Education Award" from the U.S. Department of Education. North Central consistently ranks among the top public high schools in the United States in number of National Merit Scholarship Semifinalists. Redbook magazine recently identified North Central as the best high school in Indiana.

North Central students have a history of excellence in academic areas, the fine and performing arts, athletics, and extracurricular activities. Students consistently win high honors in mathematics, writing, academic competitions, and fine and performing arts contests. The North Central trophy case includes 41 trophies representing Indiana High School Athletic Association state team championships. Extensive opportunities are available for students to participate in student government, speech and forensic activities, dramatic events, musical groups, and athletics.

Alternative Education

The Metropolitan School District of Washington Township opened an alternative school for middle and high school aged students in the fall of 1994. The school was named Phoenix School and was composed of at-risk students. The goal of the program was to get the students to correct their problems and return to their regular school program renewed and ready for the challenges that the regular program presents.

The middle school program was a six-hour instructional program geared toward participatory, hands-on activities; extended instructional periods or large blocks of time; alternating schedules; high emphasis on experiential learning; and a period of physical education or organized recreation activity each day. The program included a counseling component. Each student was also given training in conflict resolution.

The high school program involved three components: instruction in the basics, counseling, and vocational training (each child had a job or a community service project). The students attended either the morning session for three hours or the afternoon session for three hours. The students either worked on their jobs in the morning and attended school in the afternoon or attended school in the morning and worked in the afternoon. Each student was given training in conflict resolution.

Effective with the 1997-98 school year, Phoenix School was closed due to budgetary constraints. An alternative education after-school component will be available to high school students only in 1997-98.

Special Education Services

Special Education Services provide programs for exceptional children ages 3 through 21. Psychological Services personnel evaluate students referred with specific learning difficulties. Case Conference Committees consider students' eligibility and placement for appropriate programs and services.

Programs include education of students considered:

> Mildly/Mentally Handicapped
> Moderately/Mentally Handicapped
> Severely/Profoundly Mentally Handicapped
> Emotionally Handicapped

Exhibit 3-2 (continued)

Programs include education of students considered: (continued)

Visually Handicapped
Physically Handicapped
Learning Disabled
Hearing Impaired
Multiply Handicapped
Communication Handicapped
Deaf/Blind
Autistic
Orthopedic Impaired
Other Health Impaired
Traumatic Brain Injury

Also provided are:

Occupational and Physical Therapy
Developmental Kindergarten for the Multiply Handicapped
Home/School Counseling Services
Homebound Instruction/Hospital Bound Instruction
Special Transportation
Augmentative/Assistive Communication Equipment

Special programs, procedures, and curriculum enable students to work toward their potential at their own pace while also having the opportunity for inclusion/integration into regular classrooms and neighborhood schools, when appropriate. The department is served by a Parent Advisory Council for students with special needs.

Vocational Education - Student and Adult

The J. Everett Light Career Center provides vocational training for high school students for entry-level positions in the job market. Programs for adults are also available. The Career Center is operated on a year-round basis. Programs for high school students are offered during morning and afternoon sessions; adult programs are offered during late afternoon and evening sessions. Counseling services are available to students enrolled at the Center, and a placement service is provided to assist students in obtaining employment. Vocational programs available to students include:

Administrative Support Services	Electronics
Auto Body	Health Occupations
Auto Mechanics	Heating Ventilation Air Conditioning
Child Care	Horticulture/Landscaping
Commercial Art	Interdisciplinary Cooperative Education
Computerized Accounting	Machine Trades
Computer Operations/Programming	Metal Fabrication
Construction Trades	Printing
Cosmetology	Radio/Television
Dental Assisting	Welding
Dental Occupations	

During the 1989-90 school year an Adult Basic Education program was instituted. This program is intended to provide educational services to adults, dealing with the basic studies of reading, writing and arithmetic, to prepare for successful completion of the GED test. The J. Everett Light Career Center became a test center for the GED in 1990.

Exhibit 3-2 (continued)

Title I

Title I programs are for students experiencing difficulty in language arts and mathematics. Staffed by three instructors and eleven aides, the elementary and middle school Title I mathematics program stresses realistic mathematical experiences through the use of manipulative and individualized instruction.

Gifted Education

Elementary gifted students in grades 3-5 are assigned to the Inquiry Program in one of the three cluster schools where they are served by a team of specially trained teachers. Approximately 10% of the elementary students in grades 3-5 are enrolled in gifted education classes.

Middle school gifted education students are usually grouped for two or three class periods to receive accelerated or enriched instruction in language arts and social studies. As in the elementary schools, approximately 8% of the middle school students are enrolled in these classes.

Gifted and talented students at the high school level are exposed to a comprehensive variety of classes and activities with the total high school offerings. The International Baccalaureate and Advanced Placement programs provide additional opportunities for academic stimulation and challenge.

An artistically talented program is available for students in grades 4-12 for art enrichment. Students are identified for this program through nominations by teachers, parents, and students, and an evaluation of their art work by the selection committee.

Media Services

Library Media Centers staffed by professional personnel have been established in all Washington Township Schools. The goal of the media program is to prepare students to be effective users of ideas and information. This is done by providing a variety of resources as well as the instruction necessary for students to locate, retrieve and use information to make informed decisions and to generate new ideas. School library media centers also provide reading, listening and viewing guidance.

Electronic technology is having a great effect upon the media program. The cataloging and processing of library materials for the district has been automated. North Central High School has installed an automated circulation system. An automated card catalog and circulation system has been installed in each school media center. All students have the ability to access information from remote databases electronically from the school media center.

The professional library located in the Administrative Services Center offers an extensive collection of books, periodicals and audiovisual materials to staff, parents and community members. The audiovisual center houses a large collection of video cassettes and video laser disks for classroom use. The library office provides centralized cataloging and classifying of all library materials.

Technology Education

Technology education in our school district has exhibited a level of growth which reflects the change technology has effected on contemporary society.

Technology has been integrated across the curriculum at every level within our district, and staff members receive on-going training in new hardware and software.

Each school in our district has a video, voice, and data network. There is a district wide network connecting all buildings.

Exhibit 3-2 (continued)

Professional Staff

The Metropolitan School District of Washington Township is proud of its highly professional staff of teachers and administrators. Seventy-eight percent of the 671 staff members have a masters degree; 53 percent have graduate studies beyond the masters degree.

A wide variety of colleges and universities throughout the United States is represented in the graduate and undergraduate programs of the staff which provide a rich and varied source of ideas and experiences.

Staff development and inservice training have a high priority in Washington Township. The staff participates regularly in numerous workshops, conferences, and seminars designed to improve knowledge and skills.

The staff's blend of knowledge, skills in teaching, and concern for students contribute significantly to the excellent education program in the district.

Exhibit 3-3—Explanation of School Entity

Prince William County Public Schools
FY 1998 Approved Budget

Basis of Presentation

The accounting system of the Prince William County School division is organized and operated on the basis of self-balancing accounts which comprise its assests, liabilities and fund balances, revenues and expenditures as appropriate. School division resources are allocated to and accounted for in individual funds based upon the purpose for which they are to be spent and the means by which spending activities are controlled. The various funds are as follows:

Governmental Funds

The *Operating Fund* is utilized to account for the revenues and expenditures necessary for the day-to-day operation of the school district. Revenues are received from federal, state, and county government sources. Tuitions and fees for some programs are collected to partially offset costs of those programs. Expenditures are tracked by agency (each central office and each school), function, and object code (description of the expense).

The *Debt Service Fund* is utilized to account for the transfers of funds for, and the payment of, general long-term debt principal and interest and appropriate costs arising from the administration of bonds by outside agencies as well as principal and interest payments to the State Literary Fund for funds borrowed for school building projects.

The *Construction Fund* is utilized to account for the financial resources to be used for the acquisition or construction of major capital facilities. This fund receives revenue from the sale of bonds and funds from the Literary Fund.

Fuduciary Funds

The *Self-Insurance Fund* is utilized to account for its financial resources to be used for the payment of claims and related expenses for workers' compensation and general liability losses for which the school division is self-insured. It is supported by transfers from the Operating Fund and interest earned on the fund balance.

The *Health Insurance Fund* is utilized to account for its financial resources to be used for the payment of claims and related expenses for the self-insured health care program. It is supported by transfers from the Operating Fund and by insurance premium payments by employees.

Proprietary Funds

The *Food Services Fund* is utilized to account for all revenues and expenditures relative to the operation of cafeteria services at schools. This fund is financed and operated in a manner similar to a private business enterprise in that its costs are financed through user charges. Some federal and state revenues are received in addition to receipts from the sale of meals to students.

The *Administration Building Cafeteria Fund* is utilized to account for its revenues and expenditures pertaining to its operations. Its costs, including the payment of required sales tax, are wholly financed through user charges.

The *Facilities Use Fund* is utilized to account for its revenues and expenditures pertaining to the operation of the school division's facilities rental program by non-school organizations. The revenues are used to fund the positions for managing the program.

Other Funds

The *Warehouse Fund* is utilized to account for the purchase of warehouse stock items from vendors and the sale of issued items to schools and departments. The fund serves as the accounting mechanism for the warehouse function.

The *Regional School Fund* is utilized to account for the revenues and expenditures for its operations. It is funded through tuition payments from Prince William County Public Schools, Manassas City Public Schools, and Manassas Park City Public Schools which provide special education services to students from these school divisions.

Exhibit 3-4—Explanation of School Entity

However, differences are minor and do not materially alter results published in the document.

Accounting for and reporting of financial transactions in the fiscal year when a cash receipt or payment is made is called cash basis accounting. Accrual basis accounting, on the other hand, recognizes revenues and expenditures when the event leading to the financial transaction takes place, rather than when cash is exchanged. The budget for all funds recognize revenues and expenditures on a an accrual basis. Property taxes are recognized in the school year they are levied because they become due and collectable within the fiscal year.

Encumbrances are commitments against a budget amount. Encumbrance amounts represent the value of purchase orders issued for goods or services. Kettle Moraine does not include encumbrances as expenditures in the fiscal year the purchase commitment is made. An expenditures is not accrued until goods or services have been delivered and accepted, which may occur in a fiscal year other than the year the purchase order is issued.

The district does not depreciate long term physical assets. Purchase of these assets are recorded in the year acquisition is made.

System of Classifying Revenues and Expenditures

Revenues for the district are classified by source within a fund. Revenues are grouped into major divisions. The divisions, with examples of major revenue sources, are:

- Property Tax.
- Local Sources - Investment Income, Student Fees and Fines.
- Intermediate Sources - Tuition paid to Kettle Moraine by other school districts or agencies.
- State Sources - General State Aid, Handicapped Education Aid, Transportation Aid, Library Aid, State Funded Projects.
- Federal Sources - Federal Handicapped Education Aid and other federally funded projects.
- Other

Expenditures are classified by fund, operating unit (location), object, function, program and purpose. The district does not present operating unit or program budgets in this document. The primary presentation for the General Fund is by purpose. Supplemental information by object and function are also presented for the General Fund. Expenditures for all other funds are presented by object.

Exhibit 3-5—Explanation of School Entity

Prince William County Public Schools
FY 1998 Approved Budget

Basis of Accounting

Basis of accounting refers to the timing of recognition of revenues and expenditures or expenses in the accounts and in the financial statements, regardless of the measurement focus.

The accounting and financial reporting treatment applied to a fund is determined by its measurement focus. All governmental funds and expendable fiduciary funds are accounted for using a current financial resources measurement focus; that is, only current assets and current liabilities generally are included on the balance sheets. Operating statements of these funds present increases (revenues and other financial sources) and decreases (expenditures and other financing uses) in net current assets.

The proprietary fund is accounted for on a flow of economic resources measurement focus. With this measurement focus, all assets and all liabilities associated with the operations of this fund are included on the balance sheet. Proprietary fund type operating statements present increases (revenues) and decreases (expenses) in fund equity (net total assets).

Modified Accural Basis of Accounting

The modified accrual basis of accounting is followed for all governmental type funds of the school division. Revenues are recognized in the accounting period in which they become susceptible to accrual, that is both measurable (the amount of the transaction can be determined) and available (the amount is collectible within the current period or soon enough thereafter to be used to pay liablilities of the current period). Expenditures, other than long-term debt and the long-term portion of accumulated sick and vacation pay, are recorded when the fund liability is incurred.

Accrual Basis of Accounting

The accrual basis of accoounting is utilized by the Proprietary Fund type and the Fiduciary Fund type. Revenues are recognized when earned, and expenses are recogniized when incurred.

Significant Budget and Financial Policies

(Criterion C-2)

Exhibit 3-6

Exhibit 3-7

Exhibit 3-6—Significant Budget and Financial Policies

III. Budget Preparation and Procedures

UTAH BUDGET CODE PROVISIONS

53A-19-101. Superintendent of school district as budget officer–School district budget.

(1) The superintendent of each school district is the budget officer of the district.

(2) Prior to June 1 of each year, the superintendent shall prepare and file with the local school board a tentative budget. The tentative budget and supporting documents shall include the following items:

    (a) the revenues and expenditures of the preceding fiscal year;

    (b) the estimated revenues and expenditures of the current fiscal year;

    (c) an estimate of the revenues for the succeeding fiscal year based upon the lowest tax levy that will raise the required revenue, using the current year's taxable value as the basis for this calculation;

    (d) a detailed estimate of the essential expenditures for all purposes for the next succeeding fiscal year; and

    (e) the estimated financial condition of the district by funds at the close of the current fiscal year.

(3) The tentative budget shall be filed with the district business administrator for public inspection at least 15 days prior to the date of its proposed adoption by the local school board.

53A-19-102. Local school boards budget procedures.

(1) Prior to June 22 of each year, each local school board shall adopt a budget and make appropriations for the next fiscal year. If the tax rate in the proposed budget exceeds the certified tax rate defined in Subsection 59-2-924(2), the board shall comply with the Tax Increase Disclosure Act in adopting the budget.

(2) Prior to the adoption of a budget containing a tax rate which does not exceed the certified tax rate, the board shall hold a public hearing on the proposed budget. In addition to complying with Chapter 4, Title 52, the Open and Public Meetings Act, in regards to the hearing, the board shall do the following:

    (a) publish the required newspaper notice at least one week prior to the hearing; and

    (b) file a copy of the proposed budget with the board's business administrator for public inspection at least ten days prior to the hearing.

(3) The board shall file a copy of the adopted budget with the state auditor and the State Board of Education.

53A-19-103 Undistributed reserve in school board budget.

(1) A local school board may adopt a budget with an undistributed reserve. The reserve may not exceed 5% of the maintenance and operation budget adopted by the board in accor-

Exhibit 3-6 (continued)

dance with a scale developed by the State Board of Education. The scale is based on the size of the school district's budget.

(2) The board may appropriate all or a part of the undistributed reserve made to any expenditure classification in the maintenance and operation budget by written resolution adopted by a majority vote of the board setting forth the reasons for the appropriation. The board shall file a copy of the resolution with the State Board of Education and the state auditor.

(3) The board may not use undistributed reserves in the negotiation or settlement of contract salaries for school district employees.

53A-19-104. Limits on appropriations—Estimated expendable revenue.

(1) A local school board may not make any appropriation in excess of its estimated expendable revenue, including undistributed reserves, for the following fiscal year.

(2) In determining the estimated expendable revenue, any existing deficits arising through excessive expenditures from former years are deducted from the estimated revenue for the ensuing year to the extent of at least 10% of the entire tax revenue of the district for the previous year.

(3) In the event of financial hardships, the board may deduct from the estimated expendable revenue for the ensuing year, by fund, at least 25% of the deficit amount.

(4) All estimated balances available for appropriations at the end of the fiscal year shall revert to the funds from which they were appropriated and shall be fund balances available for appropriation in the budget of the following year.

(5) A local school board may reduce a budget appropriation at its regular meeting if notice of the proposed action is given to all board members and the district superintendent at least one week prior to the Meeting.

(6) An increase in an appropriation may not be made by the board unless the following steps are taken:
 (a) the board receives a written request from the district superintendent that sets forth the reasons for the proposed increase;
 (b) notice of the request is published in a newspaper of general circulation within the school district at least one week prior to the board meeting at which the request will be considered; and
 (c) the board holds a public hearing prior to the board's acting on the request.

53A-19-105. School district interfund transfers.

(1) The State Board of Education may authorize school district interfund transfers for a financially distressed district if the board determines the following:
 (a) the district has a significant deficit in its maintenance and operations fund which has resulted from circumstances not subject to the administrative decisions of the district that cannot be reasonably reduced under Section 53A-19-104; and
 (b) without the transfer, the school district will not be capable of meeting statewide educational standards, adopted by the State Board of Education.

(2) The board shall develop standards for defining and aiding financially distressed school districts under this section.

53A-19-106. Warrants drawn by business administrator.

The business administrator of a local school board may not draw warrants on school dis-

Exhibit 3-6 (continued)

trict funds except in accordance with and within the limits of the budget passed by the local school board.

53A-19-107. Emergency expenditures.
This chapter does not apply to appropriations required because of emergencies involving loss of life or great loss of property.

53A-19-108. Monthly budget reports.
(1)   The business administrator of each local school board shall provide each board member with a report, on a monthly basis, that includes the following information:
        (a)   the amounts of all budget appropriations;
        (b)   the disbursements from the appropriations as of the date of the report; and
        (c)   the percentage of the disbursements as of the date of the report.
(2)   A copy of the report shall be available for public review.

Exhibit 3-7—Significant Budget and Financial Policies

FISCAL YEAR 1997-98

**BUDGET AND
ADMINISTRATIVE POLICIES**

The following budget and administrative policies of the Board of Education guide the preparation and administration of the 1997-98 budget.

*Budget
Operating
Policy*

The State Constitution provides that each school district shall prepare and maintain annual budgets with sufficient revenue to meet estimated expenditures for each year. Whenever ordinary expenditures of a school district for any year shall exceed the revenue, the governing body of the school district is required to provide for levying a tax in the ensuing year sufficient, with all other sources of revenue, to pay the deficiency in the preceding year, together with the estimated expenditures for the ensuing year.

State law provides that the fiscal year for school districts begin on July 1 of each year and end on June 30 of the following year. The Board is required to adopt annually a budget for the operation of the School District. The budgets must identify the sources of anticipated revenue including taxes necessary to meet the financial requirements of the budgets adopted.

The District's budget is prepared utilizing the zero-based budgeting philosophy. Additionally, the District employs intense involvement by school principals, staff, and community members in the budget development process. The Board shall expect the associate superintendents to work closely with the principals in their respective areas in studying the needs of the schools and in compiling a budget to meet those needs. The principals are expected to confer with teachers in obtaining budgetary requests and information on requirements.

Based upon school enrollments, schools were provided an allocation of funds with each principal making the ultimate decision on the best utilization of these funds. Each principal's decision was made after substantial input from his/her staff and parent advisory groups. Principals must continue to meet all local, state and federal requirements regarding the staffing levels of the school; however, each principal has the authority to utilize excess personnel funds to contract needed services or purchase other supplies or equipment. This process provides each principal with new flexibility regarding budgeting and financial management.

The Superintendent and administration shall submit a preliminary budget to the Board for its consideration on or before April 1 of each year. The Board is required by law to conduct a public hearing to receive input from its citizenry regarding the budget. The hearing must be advertised in the local newspapers at least fifteen (15) days prior to

Horry County Schools

Exhibit 3-7 (continued)

*Budget Operating
Policy (continued)*

the hearing. The Board shall determine the necessary millage and approve the budget for the operation of schools.

The Board expects its administrative staff to operate the school system within the budget established for the particular department or school. In the event that some unusual or extenuating circumstance occurs during the year and the principal overspends the budget for his/her school, that amount will be charged against the budget of that school for the ensuing year. If a surplus exists at the end of the year, this balance shall be carried over, subject to limitations, and added to the budget of that school for the next year. Refer to pages 26-27, *Fund Balance and Reserve Policy*, for limitations.

*Capital Projects
Budget Policies*

◊ The district will develop and administer a multi-year plan for capital improvements and update it annually.
◊ The district will budget for major capital projects in accordance with the priorities of the Board of Education.
◊ The district will coordinate development of the capital improvement budget with development of the operating budget. Future operating costs associated with new capital improvement will be projected and included in operating budgets.
◊ The district will identify the estimated costs and potential funding sources for each capital project proposal before it is submitted to the Board for approval.
◊ The district will determine the least costly financing method for all new projects.
◊ The district will monitor monthly the financial activity of the capital projects comparing the budgeted funds to reduce cost overruns.
◊ The district will maintain all assets at a level adequate to protect the district's capital investment and to minimize future maintenance and replacement costs.
◊ The district will restrict any new or replacement construction to be consistent with state guidelines for school building utilization.
◊ The district will continue its twelve (12) year replacement equipment allocation to address replacing aged or obsolete equipment.

*Debt
Management
Policies*

◊ The district will confine long-term borrowing to capital projects and purchases of equipment, as required by law.
◊ The district will try to keep the average maturity of general obligation bonds at or below fifteen years.
◊ The district will not use long-term debt for current operations.
◊ The district will meet all debt service obligations when due.

Horry County Schools

Exhibit 3-7 (continued)

*Debt
Management
Policies
(continued)*

◊ The district will maintain communication with bond rating agencies regarding its financial condition and seek to obtain the most favorable rating. The district will follow a policy of full disclosure in every financial report and official statement.

◊ The district will provide to the capital markets ongoing disclosure of annual financial information and material events that may affect the district's financial strength.

◊ The district will continually evaluate outstanding debt to determine if refunding of older issues would be more favorable.

*Revenue Estimation
Policies*

◊ The Assistant Superintendent for Finance will estimate annual revenues by an objective, analytical process. The district will not include revenue in the budget that cannot be verified with documentation of its source and amount.

◊ The district will set fees and user charges in its proprietary funds at a level that will ensure the program is self-sufficient.

*Fund Balance and
Reserve Policy*

◊ To maintain and protect the long-term financial capacity of the district, unreserved fund balance in the General Fund will be maintained in an amount which is acceptable and advisable by the Board of Education and its bond counsel and financial advisors.

The district reserves General Fund fund balance by an amount sufficient to cover inventory and prepaid expenses. In addition, a reserve for school budget carryover is provided as follows:

The schools are currently authorized to "carry-over" unexpended funds from one fiscal year to the next. The "carry-over" funds may not exceed 10% of the non-personnel allocation or $10,000, whichever is less. Based on this, each school is to plan to close the fiscal year with a balanced budget.

If a school closes the fiscal year with a deficit balance, the deficit will be carried over to the next fiscal year. The school will be required to submit a plan for the elimination of the deficit.

Any other reserves against fund balance must be specifically approved by the Board.

Horry County Schools

Exhibit 3-7 (continued)

**BUDGET AND
ADMINISTRATIVE POLICIES**

Encumbrances

The District maintains an encumbrance accounting system as one technique of accomplishing budgetary control. Encumbered amounts at year end lapse and are reappropriated. There is no reserve against fund balance for encumbrances.

*Budget
Management*

The principal is responsible for the proper budgeting and expenditure of all resources allocated to a school. This responsibility includes:
◊ Ensuring that adequate funds are available in a program and object code prior to expending funds against that account; and
◊ Ensuring that expenditures and transfers are recorded using the appropriate program and object codes.

The principal has some flexibility to transfer budgeted funds or expenditures to respond to changing program requirements. Budget transfers are the transfer of budgeted funds from one account code (function code, object code, location code, modifier code) to another. The primary reason for transferring budgeted funds is to ensure that sufficient funds are available in an account code prior to charging an expenditure to the account code. The principal must complete and submit a budget transfer form to the Division of Finance with adequate documentation attached.

Initiating a budget transfer is the responsibility of each department's administrator/designee. The budget transfer must be issued for approval as soon as the administrator becomes aware of a situation that will change the annual total of the approved appropriation.

Deficit budgets are not permitted. In addition, strict requirements necessitate timely budget transfers to permit account expenditure monitoring. It is the function of the Director of Accounting Services to assist each administrator in processing budget transfers through the appropriate administrative channels.

All financial commitments must have approved budgets prior to the issuance of purchase orders, contracts, etc.. If an item requires a budget transfer, the budget transfer must be approved <u>before</u> the financial commitment can be issued.

All budget transfers must be signed and dated by the initiator and Director of Accounting Services prior to posting in the general ledger. Written justification must be complete and supporting documentation attached before a budget transfer is approved.

Exhibit 3-7 (continued)

*Budget
Management
(continued)*

<u>*Procedures Recap by Responsibility*</u>

<u>*Initiator*</u>
◊ Determine need for budget appropriation adjustment.
◊ Prepare transfer using a Budget Transfer Form.
◊ Provide written justification/explanation for adjustment.
◊ Attach all documentation supporting the transfer.

<u>*Staff Accountants*</u>
◊ Review transfer request.
◊ If approval is recommended, sign and date the budget transfer form.
◊ Forward signed form to Director of Accounting Services.

<u>*Director of Accounting Services*</u>
◊ Reviews for compliance with procedures and verifies accuracy of data. Signs, if approved, dates, and forwards to Data Processing for entry in the general ledger system.

*Funding for
Student Population
Changes*

The non-personnel allocation to schools was based upon the prior year's 45-day ADM with a weighting factor applied to each student classification to provide for the relative cost differences. To provide adequate funding for student population changes (due to growth or transfers within the district), adjustments will be made based on the current year official 45-day ADM. An increase in student population of greater than or equal to 10 students will result in additional funding being provided based upon the weighted per pupil increase. Conversely a decrease in student population of greater than or equal to 10 students will result in a decrease in the original budget allocation based upon the weighted per pupil decrease. The following procedure will be used:

◊ Upon receipt of the official 45-day ADM, the Division of Finance will calculate the budget allocation adjustments and notify the respective schools.
◊ The school will complete the budget transfer form and specify the account numbers affected.
◊ This will then be returned to the Division of Finance to be posted on the school's budget report.

Horry County Schools

Exhibit 3-7 (continued)

Personnel Budget
Reallocations

The Division of Human Resources will provide school's with their school's personnel allocations based on the Board-approved personnel allocation formula. As a school-based manager, the principal will have the discretion to utilize these allocations in the best manner to accomplish his/her school's goals and objectives. If your staffing mix results in unexpended budgeted personnel allocations, then you will be able to utilize the unexpended FTE allocation times the average salary for that allocation plus related fringe benefits. On a personnel budget reallocation form complete the calculation of the unexpended funds available including fringe benefits, then specify the intended use of these funds (i.e., employ a .5 custodian, purchase computer equipment, etc.). Enter the account numbers affected by this reallocation. Forward the completed personnel budget reallocation form to the Division of Human Resources for verification and prior approval. Supporting documentation will need to be attached that validates the unexpended allocation. Division of Human Resources will then forward the approved request to the Division of Finance for inclusion in the school's budget.

Expenditure
Controls

In an effort to control the budgeted line item accounts as approved by the Board, the following expenditure control procedures have been established:

◊ Funds to cover the purchase orders should be in the budget under the appropriate category before the Procurement Office will authorize encumbering the order. If funds are short, a budget transfer must be prepared to transfer funding into the account. Upon signature approving the transfer, the purchase order will be authorized for encumbering.

◊ Purchase orders in excess of $1500 are to be reviewed by the Procurement Office for:
   ◊ verification of account code,
   ◊ verification of line item funding availability, and
   ◊ compliance with the District's Procurement Code.

◊ Department Managers are responsible for not exceeding the amount appropriated within their department during the fiscal year.

◊ The Finance Department is responsible for monitoring expenditures. Actual expenditure reports are distributed each month to the department managers. In the event a department appears to be experiencing an expenditure problem (exceeds the appropriate allocation limit), the Finance Department will work with the department to develop a solution. In the event errors are detected in account codes an expenditure transfer can be made to correct the error.

Horry County Schools

Exhibit 3-7 (continued)

*Accounting,
Auditing, and
Financial Reporting
Policies*

◊ The accounting system will report financial information on a basis consistent with Generally Accepted Accounting Principles as established by the Governmental Accounting Standards Board.

◊ The district will prepare monthly financial reports comparing actual revenues and expenditures to budgeted amounts.

◊ An independent certified public accounting firm will be selected by the Board of Education and will perform an annual audit, and will publicly issue their opinion on the district's financial statement.

◊ The district will seek to obtain and maintain a Certificate of Achievement for Excellence in Financial Reporting from the Association of School Business Officials International and the Government Finance Officers Association.

Organizational Chart

(Criterion C-3)

Exhibit 3-8—Organizational Chart

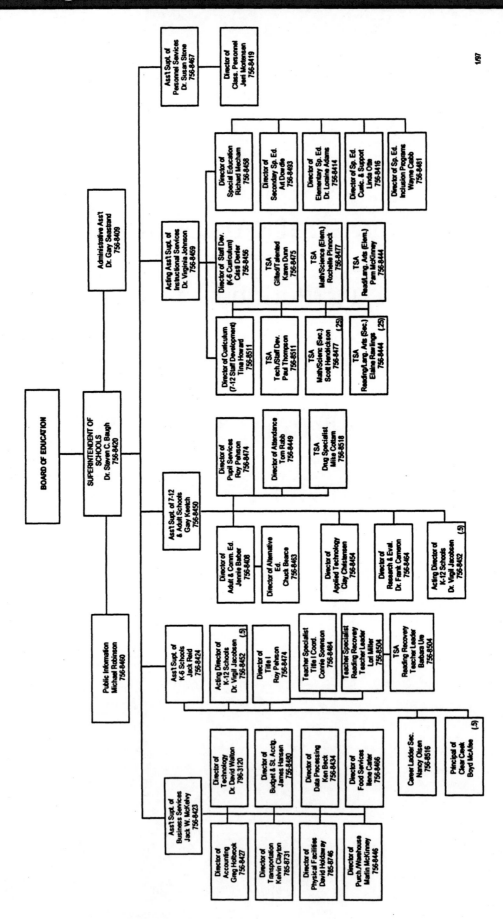

Exhibit 3-9—Organizational Chart

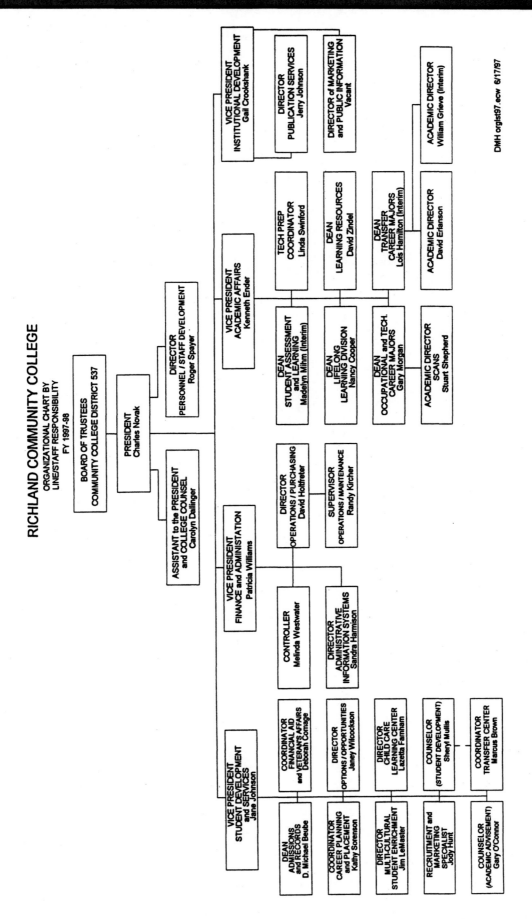

RICHLAND COMMUNITY COLLEGE
ORGANIZATIONAL CHART BY
LINE/STAFF RESPONSIBILITY
FY 1997-98

BOARD OF TRUSTEES
COMMUNITY COLLEGE DISTRICT 537

PRESIDENT
Charles Novak

ASSISTANT to the PRESIDENT
and COLLEGE COUNSEL
Carolyn Dallinger

DIRECTOR
PERSONNEL / STAFF DEVELOPMENT
Roger Speyer

VICE PRESIDENT
INSTITUTIONAL DEVELOPMENT
Gail Crookshank

DIRECTOR
PUBLICATION SERVICES
Jerry Johnson

DIRECTOR of MARKETING
and PUBLIC INFORMATION
Vacant

VICE PRESIDENT
ACADEMIC AFFAIRS
Kenneth Ender

TECH PREP
COORDINATOR
Linda Swinford

DEAN
STUDENT ASSESSMENT
and LEARNING
Madelyn Mihm (Interim)

DEAN
LEARNING RESOURCES
David Zindel

DEAN
LIFELONG
LEARNING DIVISION
Nancy Cooper

DEAN
TRANSFER
CAREER MAJORS
Lois Hamilton (Interim)

DEAN
OCCUPATIONAL and TECH.
CAREER MAJORS
Gary Morgan

ACADEMIC DIRECTOR
David Erlanson

ACADEMIC DIRECTOR
William Grieve (Interim)

ACADEMIC DIRECTOR
SCANS
Stuart Shepherd

VICE PRESIDENT
FINANCE and ADMINISTRATION
Patricia Williams

DIRECTOR
OPERATIONS / PURCHASING
David Holtfreter

SUPERVISOR
OPERATIONS / MAINTENANCE
Randy Kircher

CONTROLLER
Melinda Westwater

DIRECTOR
ADMINISTRATIVE
INFORMATION SYSTEMS
Sandra Harmison

VICE PRESIDENT
STUDENT DEVELOPMENT
and SERVICES
Jane Johnson

COORDINATOR
FINANCIAL AID
and VETERANS AFFAIRS
Deborah Comage

DEAN
ADMISSIONS
and RECORDS
D. Michael Beube

DIRECTOR
OPTIONS / OPPORTUNITIES
Janey Wilcockson

COORDINATOR
CAREER PLANNING
and PLACEMENT
Kathy Sorenson

DIRECTOR
CHILD CARE
LEARNING CENTER
Lezetta Farnham

DIRECTOR
MULTI-CULTURAL
STUDENT ENRICHMENT
Jim LeMaster

COUNSELOR
(STUDENT DEVELOPMENT)
Sheryl Mullis

RECRUITMENT and
MARKETING
SPECIALIST
Jody Hunt

COORDINATOR
TRANSFER CENTER
Marcus Brown

COUNSELOR
(ACADEMIC ADVISEMENT)
Gary O'Connor

DMH orglst97.ecw 6/17/97

Exhibit 3-10—Organizational Chart

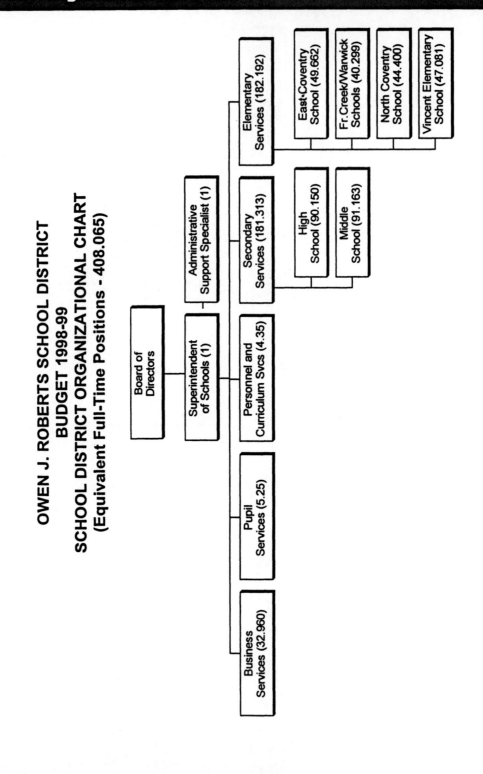

OWEN J. ROBERTS SCHOOL DISTRICT
BUDGET 1998-99
SCHOOL DISTRICT ORGANIZATIONAL CHART
(Equivalent Full-Time Positions - 408.065)

Board of Directors

Administrative Support Specialist (1)

Superintendent of Schools (1)

Business Services (32.960)

Pupil Services (5.25)

Personnel and Curriculum Svcs (4.35)

Secondary Services (181.313)

High School (90.150)

Middle School (91.163)

Elementary Services (182.192)

East-Coventry School (49.662)

Fr.Creek/Warwick Schools (40.299)

North Coventry School (44.400)

Vincent Elementary School (47.081)

Exhibit 3-10 (continued)

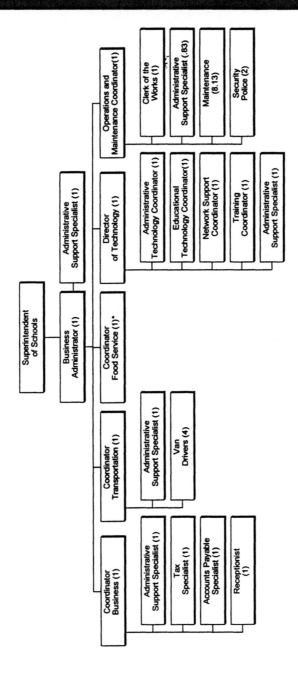

OWEN J. ROBERTS SCHOOL DISTRICT
BUDGET 1998-99
BUSINESS SERVICES
(Equivalent Full-Time Positions - 32.960)

Superintendent of Schools

Business Administrator (1)

Administrative Support Specialist (1)

Coordinator Business (1)
- Administrative Support Specialist (1)
- Tax Specialist (1)
- Accounts Payable Specialist (1)
- Receptionist (1)

Coordinator Transportation (1)
- Administrative Support Specialist (1)
- Van Drivers (4)

Coordinator Food Service (1)*

Director of Technology (1)
- Administrative Technology Coordinator (1)
- Educational Technology Coordinator (1)
- Network Support Coordinator (1)
- Training Coordinator (1)
- Administrative Support Specialist (1)

Operations and Maintenance Coordinator (1)
- Clerk of the Works (1)
- Administrative Support Specialist (.83)
- Maintenance (8.13)
- Security Police (2)

*This position is accounted for in the Food Service Fund.

Exhibit 3-10 (continued)

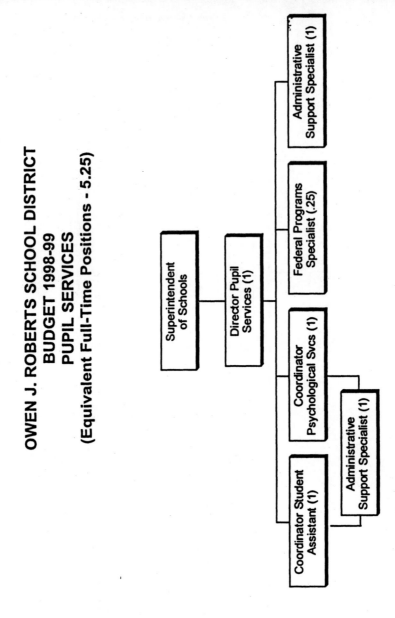

OWEN J. ROBERTS SCHOOL DISTRICT
BUDGET 1998-99
PUPIL SERVICES
(Equivalent Full-Time Positions - 5.25)

Superintendent of Schools

Director Pupil Services (1)

Coordinator Student Assistant (1)

Coordinator Psychological Svcs (1)

Federal Programs Specialist (.25)

Administrative Support Specialist (1)

Administrative Support Specialist (1)

Exhibit 3-10 (continued)

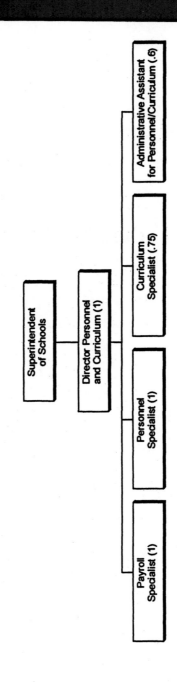

OWEN J. ROBERTS SCHOOL DISTRICT
BUDGET 1998-99
PERSONNEL AND CURRICULUM SERVICES
(Equivalent Full-Time Positions - 4.35)

Superintendent of Schools

Director Personnel and Curriculum (1)

Payroll Specialist (1)

Personnel Specialist (1)

Curriculum Specialist (.75)

Administrative Assistant for Personnel/Curriculum (.6)

Statement of the Mission

(Criterion C-4)

Exhibit 3-11

Exhibit 3-12

Exhibit 3-11—Statement of the Mission

VISION STATEMENT

In Prince William County Public Schools, all students will learn to their fullest potential. The education of each student will be individualized and developmentally appropriate. Student learning will be enhanced by national, global, and multicultural perspectives.

Students who graduate from Prince William County Public Schools will possess the basic knowledge and skills that will assure their proficiency in problem solving and the use of technology. Graduates will have a desire to learn and the skills to be life-long learners. They will be responsible citizens. All graduates will be competent to enter the work world and prepared to pursue advanced educational opportunities.

MISSION STATEMENT

Our Mission

is to provide a high quality, comprehensive and meaningful education for all students. In our schools, each student will experience success. Each student will be expected to succeed within the bounds of their abilities and chosen educational goals. Each student will be treated as an individual, given the tools to be a life-long learner, and taught to function effectively as a member of a group and as a productive member of society.

Exhibit 3-12: Statement of the Mission

SOUDERTON AREA SCHOOL DISTRICT

MISSION STATEMENT *

"The Mission of the Souderton Area School District is to prepare students to demonstrate competencies needed to contribute and to succeed in a changing world by building on a commitment to excellence and innovation; by working in partnership with family and community, and by assuring a quality education for all students in a safe and nurturing environment."

---

*   Mission Statement, as developed by the strategic planning process, was submitted to the School Board and approved with complete strategic plan on July 27, 1995.

June 12, 1997

Major Goals and Objectives

(Criterion C-5)

Exhibit 3-13

Exhibit 3-14

Exhibit 3-13—Majors Goals and Objectives

Prince William County Public Schools

Quality Management Plan
Fiscal Years 1997 thru 2000

Introduction

Purpose

The Quality Management Plan (QMP) has been developed in order to define a single purpose for all employees, to focus on that purpose, and to continuously improve the operation of Prince William County Public Schools. The major focus of the school division is the instruction of students. There are secondary functions and processes such as student services and transportation services that contribute to the instruction of students.

The Quality Management Plan is the school division's long-range plan. School level plans, central office department plans and the school division's budget reflect the QMP. Each plan will contain a section which will evaluate the degree to which conformance to customer requirements is met.

The Quality Management Plan provides basic guidance and direction to all budgetary units within the school division regarding the long-range vision of the division. Schools and central support departments will use a collaborative planning process to develop specific operational plans for implementing the division's long-range plan.

Background

School based management was initiated to improve the quality of education in Prince William County. Two questions guide the school division's efforts: Are the students learning and learning all they can learn? Are steps being taken to cause that learning to continue? School level and departmental plans are the mechanisms for implementing programs for improved student learning.

The long-range plan was developed and refined through meetings with groups of employees and citizens to determine the direction and focus for the school division. Teachers and administrators in concert with parents discussed school division needs and the desired direction for the school division. These discussions influenced the development of each component of the long-range plan.

Exhibit 3-13 (continued)

Framework

The Quality Management Plan contains six important elements. Each element has a specific design and purpose. These elements are vision statement, mission statement, standards of quality, goals, performance standards and implementation process.

1 . **Vision Statement:** The vision statement for the school division describes what the ideal is for the school division. It embodies the basic philosophy of the school division and sets a tone for individual units within the school division.

2. **Mission Statement:** The mission statement for the school division provides general information about how the school division expects to arrive at its vision. It describes the basic direction of the school division which will influence how the division uses its resources.

3. **Standards of quality:** The standards of quality describe desired goals for students upon graduation from Prince William County Public Schools. They identify what students will know and be able to do when they graduate. The standards of quality should serve to direct decision-making, i.e., how will these students be affected by the way resources are used, programs are developed, and the organization is structured?

4. **Goals:** A goal statement is a passive description of a desired result. A goal is essentially a vision for a single issue. Goals serve as guideposts to the school vision. Therefore, a goal must reflect an element of that vision. Goals refer to the "what" we are going to do.

5. **Performance Standards:** Criteria, indicators, and desired results are developed to assess and measure progress and successful implementation of the division's long-range plan. These provide the control system to measure, evaluate, and correct performance and progress towards the successful accomplishment of the long-range plan.

6. **Implementation Process:** Major strategies, implementation schedule of critical events, and elements of a control system provide for the plans implementation mechanisms.

Exhibit 3-13 (continued)

School and Department Plans

Each school and central department will develop long-range plans that include a statement of mission, goals, performance standards, objectives, and action plans. The plans will be developed through a collaborative partnership among school staff, parents, students, and the community. The division's Quality Management Plan will be used as the basis for developing these plans.

In addition to a statement of mission, goals, performance standards, objectives, and action plans, each school and departmental plan will also include the following components:

Process Narrative: The Process Narrative should provide an overview of the planning process, including needs assessment, issue identification, prioritization, problem analysis, definition of goals and objectives, and strategy identification. It is critical that the planning process include the opportunity for all stakeholders to review and react to both the plan and the budget in their development and finished forms.

Executive Summary: The Executive Summary should include an overview of the planned goals and objectives.

Composition of the Advisory Council: Membership of the council should be delineated along with notation of roles and responsibilities. Indicate if a facilitator was used and whether that facilitator was internal or external to the school.

Waivers and Deviations: Notation must be made if any strategy requires a waiver from regulation or deviation from current practice.

Critical Functions: In addition, department plans will include identification of the primary categories of continuing work, or critical functions, that must be performed to achieve the mission of the department and the mission of the school division.

Exhibit 3-13 (continued)

Standards of Quality

STANDARD 1: All students will become knowledgeable and proficient in the traditional basic academic skills.

Demonstrates proficiency in the traditional basic academic skills.

- English (including grammar, spelling, and composition)
- Reading (including phonics)
- Mathematics
- Science
- History (including U.S. and World History and Geography)
- Economics
- Foreign language
- The arts
- Physical education

Demonstrates positive work habits.

- Leadership skills
- Pride in quality
- Excellence
- Self-confidence
- Team work
- Dependability
- Regular attendance
- Self-respect
- Respect for others
- Interact well with others and work in groups

STANDARD 2: All students will become good thinkers, problem-solvers, and decision-makers.

Engages in individual and group problem-solving and decision-making processes using thinking skills and evaluates various solutions to a given problem.

- Acquires and integrates knowledge
- Extends and refines knowledge
- Uses knowledge meaningfully
- Thinks creatively, critically, analytically, and logically
- Identifies pros and cons to given problems

Exhibit 3-13 (continued)

Solves complex problems

- Uses various strategies to solve problems
- Demonstrates creative thinking skills through their original work (fluency, flexibility, originality, elaboration, etc.)

Recognizes problems and utilizes problem-solving and decision-making skills in daily life.

- Determines what products are the "best buy"
- Completes routine forms and documents
- Determines the total cost of items
- Evaluates information and develops own ideas on issues

STANDARD 3: All students will become effective communicators.

Uses appropriate oral, written, and nonverbal forms to represent ideas, images, and data.

- Demonstrates effective individual and group processing skills to create information
- Uses effective personal and practical communication skills which require quantitative and qualitative problem solving

Develops skills for life-long learning.

- Demonstrates use of standard spoken and written English
- Demonstrates use of standard math skills and concepts

STANDARD 4: All student will become users of technology.

Demonstrates technological literacy including communication and application.

- Demonstrates understanding of basic technological concepts and applies those skills to basic tasks
- Selects and applies appropriate technology to specific tasks
- Transfers technological concepts to practical applications

Investigates existing and emerging technologies.

- Analyzes current and emerging technologies to determine capabilities, potentials, and limitations for future use

Exhibit 3-13 (continued)

Demonstrates inter-personal and technical skills for continuing education and/or employability.

- Demonstrates basic technical skills for continuing education and/or job entry employment

STANDARD 5: All students will become knowledgeable of various racial and ethnic cultures, as well as differences based on gendger, age, and physical ability.

Is knowledgeable of various cultures.

- Understands and respects cultural similarities and differences
- Understands cultural diversity
- Understands the common humanity all people share through their differences and similarities

Utilizes skills for interacting with people of different cultures.

- Understands differences and makes judgements based on knowledge and fact
- Identifies the contribution of individuals who have made important contributions to various cultures and to society

STANDARD 6: All students will become good citizens.

Is a responsible, contributing member of the local, national, and world community.

- Understands the value of American citizenship
- Knows conflict resolution skills
- Understands and acts within the legal requirements of the school, community, state, and nation
- Voluntarily participates in school, community, state, or national service projects and/or activities

Analyzes national and world issues and possible results and consequences of these issues.

- Understands the effects of actions by the United States government on the state and local level
- Understands the effects of actions by the United States on other countries
- Understands the effects of actions by other countries on the United States

Exhibit 3-13 (continued)

Goals

Goal 1: *All students will acquire the skills and knowledge needed to meet their present and future needs within a global community.*

Performance Standards:

Knowledge and Skills

- Standards of Quality: All students will demonstrate proficiency on Prince William County tests administered to students in Grades 3, 5, 7, and 10.
- Literacy Passport: All students will pass all three Literacy Passport tests within three testing opportunities.
- Literacy Passport: Eighty percent (80%) of all 6th grade students will pass all three Literacy Passport Tests in the first testing opportunity.
- Reading Proficiency: All students in grades 5 and 8 enrolled in the Prince William County Public Schools for a minimum of 3 prior consecutive years will read at or above grade level.

External Comparisons

- Standardized Test Scores: The percent of students who take the Virginia Assessment Program standardized tests under standard conditions whose composite scores are above the national 25th percentile will exceed the state average.
- Standardized Test Scores: The percent of students who take the Virginia Assessment Program standardized tests under standard conditions whose composite scores are above the national 75th percentile will exceed the state average.
- Scholastic Aptitude Test Participation: The percent of eleventh and twelfth grade students who take the Scholastic Aptitude Test will exceed the state and national averages.
- Scholastic Aptitude Test Scores: The percent of eleventh and twelfth grade students taking the Scholastic Aptitude Test who score at or above 1,100 will exceed the state and national averages.
- Scholastic Aptitude Test Scores: The mean score of eleventh and twelfth grade students taking the Scholastic Aptitude Test will exceed the state and national averages.
- Advanced Placement Test Scores: The percent of eleventh and twelfth grade students taking advanced placement courses who score three or more on the advanced placement tests will exceed state averages.
- Advanced Studies Diploma: The percent of high school graduates who earn the advanced studies diploma will exceed the state average.

Exhibit 3-13 (continued)

Program Completion

- Drop-out rate: The percent of students in Grades 7-12 who dropped out of school will be less than the state average.
- Attendance: The percent of students in Grades K-12 who were absent ten days or fewer from school will be greater than the state average.
- Five-year Follow-up Survey: A follow-up survey and report of graduates will be conducted after five years to assess student success in post-secondary study and employment. The report will include the number and percent of graduates who have completed a bachelor's degree, who are employed in a field consistent with their secondary course of study, who are registered voters, and who are satisfied with the skills and knowledge acquired while attending Prince William County Public Schools.
- Prince William County Public Schools Proficiency Diploma: All tenth grade students will qualify for the Prince William County Proficiency Diploma.
- Research Project: All eleventh grade students will successfully complete the Prince William County Research Project requirement.

Goal 2: Parents, students, staff, and members of the community will have a high degree of satisfaction and support for all programs and schools.

Performance Standard:

- Surveys: At least 80% of parents, students, staff, and members of the community responding to the annual survey will rate their overall level of satisfaction with schools and the school division as good or excellent.

Goal 3: Central support departments will provide innovative and quality products and services that fully satisfy the requirements of their customers.

Performance Standard:

- Customer Satisfaction Surveys: At least 80% of the customers surveyed will rate the overall level of satisfaction with central services as good or excellent.

Exhibit 3-13 (continued)

Implementation Process
Major Strategies

The strategies listed below will provide guidance and direction to schools and departments during the next few years as plans are developed and implemented to meet the mission and goals stated in the Quality Management Plan.

1. The implementation of revised curriculum documents will continue to be essential in reflecting a rapidly changing knowledge base, demands for new technology, and innovative delivery models that facilitate critical thinking, collaboration, and hands-on experiences.

2. Educational programs will be designed to meet the present and future needs of all students.

3. A staff development plan which includes classroom support will be implemented to assist instructional employees to attain a high level of professionalism to meet the goals of the school division.

4. Appropriate facilities, technology, and equipment with equitable access will be provided for students and employees to accomplish the goals of the school division.

5. A site-based planning and budgeting process will be developed and implemented that ensures collaboration and shared decision-making within and across all levels of the school division.

6. Multicultural education will be provided, building upon the cultural diversity and similarities of our students and preparing them for successful interaction with other races, genders, cultures, and countries in the 21st century.

7. The principles of "Quality Management" will be implemented to provide a framework for effective planning and the successful implementation of school plans.

8. A school program review process will be implemented to ensure support for school and division efforts to improve continuously.

9. The school division will establish a program which recognizes individuals and groups for their contributions to the school division.

10. The school division will continue implementation of the Technology Plan with wide area networks, technical support, training, student and administrative systems.

11. A comprehensive communication plan will be developed for the school division.

Exhibit 3-13 (continued)

The Control System

The assessment component is the control system of the planning process. The control system must measure, evaluate, and correct performance and progress towards completion of the action plans and the continuing mission and goals of the school division. The control system for the school division's long-range plan will include the following:

- An annual report on the performance standards identified in the plan. This will include division-wide and individual school reports. Information will be presented for minority students and economically disadvantaged students.

- An annual report on the survey of staff, student, parent, and community satisfaction with each school and the school division.

- An annual report on the customer satisfaction survey for central services.

- All reports will include historic, trend, and <u>longitudinal</u> data.

- Superintendent's School Intervention Plan for schools that do not meet performance standards and school division goals and expectations.

- Program evaluation reports for innovative programs that require waivers.

- Site assessments conducted annually based on individual site goals and targets.

Implementation Schedule

The Quality Management Plan (QMP) was introduced and implemented beginning with the FY95 school year. Each school and department was responsible for a detailed budget plan which identified the major needs faced by the budget unit and specific plans and funding decisions to address those needs. This process continues for both schools and central office departments.

ANNUAL EVENTS:

- Budget development process.

- Continued training of principals and central department managers on the components and process for implementing the Quality Management Plan.

- Completion of school level and central department plans for FY98.

- QMP Performance Standard Report to the Prince William County School Board.

Exhibit 3-13 (continued)

NEW INITIATIVES:

September 1996	Continue review of the use of test item bank for quality control in classroom grading and instructional management system to align the documented curriculum with the taught curriculum and the assessed curriculum.
	Begin pilot Research Project
October 1996	Identify and plan implementation of test item bank and the instructional management technology.
Spring-Fall 1997	Pilot, training, and initial implementation of test item bank and the instructional management technology.
November 1996-February 1997	Continued test development Proficiency Test and Applications Assessments
April - May 1997	Complete implementation of Proficiency Tests in Grades 3, 5, 7, and 10 (language arts, mathematics, and information management) and Applications Assessments in Grades 3, 7, and 10 (language arts, mathematics, and science)
Summer 1997	Begin development of Technology Assessments
Fall 1998	Field test Technology Assessments Implement Research Project for Class of 2000
Spring 1999	Implement Technology Assessments
Summer 1999	Review and update Quality Management Plan

Exhibit 3-14—Major Goals and Objectives

OBJECTIVES *

1. All students will demonstrate the skills and discipline necessary to exercise and fulfill their rights and responsibilities as citizens.

2. All students will demonstrate analytical thinking and organizational skills by utilizing their knowledge and creativity to meet or exceed Souderton Area School District's standards of excellence.

3. Students at all levels will demonstrate achievement of district standards.

* As developed by the Strategic Plan Planning Committee September 1994. Complete plan approved by School Board on July 27, 1995.

Exhibit 3-14 (continued)

STRATEGIES *

CURRICULUM AND ASSESSMENT
We will design challenging curriculum and a framework for assessment that will measure each student's competency to meet the district's established standards.

STAFF DEVELOPMENT
We will create a structure and process to facilitate the competence of all staff in achieving the goals of the organization.

FACILITIES
We will develop and implement short and long range facilities' plans to accommodate educational program requirements, projected student enrollments, and building obsolescence.

STUDENT SUPPORT
We will establish guidelines, procedures, and definitions to direct student support programs, discipline, security, and extra-curricular activities.

COMMUNITY/PARENTS
We will develop and implement strategies to increase participation of students in their community, parents in their children's education, and community members and institutions in our schools.

TIME
We will reinvent the school system around learning, rather than time, so that the academic schedule is not limited by the traditional school schedule.

ORGANIZATIONAL STRUCTURE
We will put in place a process and structure for the organization that will facilitate communication, decision-making, and accountability throughout the organization.

FINANCIAL RESOURCES
We will develop and implement a financial plan to provide sufficient resources to fund all objectives of the Souderton Area School District Strategic Plan consistent with sound business practices.

INSTRUCTION
We will deliver the most effective instruction and interventions for all students.

TECHNOLOGY
We will develop an effective and efficient plan to acquire, continually update, and incorporate technology throughout every facet of the district.

---

*   As developed by the Strategic Plan Planning Committee September 1994. Complete plan approved by School Board on July 27, 1995.

Exhibit 3-14 (continued)

SOUDERTON AREA SCHOOL DISTRICT

FINANCIAL IMPLICATIONS - STRATEGIC PLAN

Attached is a copy of the document which outlines the financial implications to the strategic plan as developed through the 1995 strategic planning process.

The dollar amounts have been separated into two columns; column 1 being the regular budget and column 2 being non-regular budget. Amounts in the regular budget column indicate that the district currently budgets funds in its budget for similar items and the dollars in that column would either be an additional amount to an existing account or diverting use of the budgeted funds for strategic plan purposes. Items in the non-regular budget column indicate items that are in most cases over and above what would normally be provided in the budget and/or items that would require the establishment of a new code for budgeting purposes.

Behind some of the items under the facilities strategy there is a designation to refer to the BEC 90 study. The BEC90 is a study completed by Breslin, Ridyard, Fadero, the district architects, as a result of building projects that are ongoing. The BEC 90 study is a review of all district facilities with recommendations for upgrades, improvements, and compliance with current standards. Under the instruction strategy the miscellaneous notes that refer to technology mean that money to accomplish the instruction objective has been provided through the technology strategy for the same purpose.

Under the technology strategy the regular budget column, under item #2, indicates $600,000 which represents the approximate amount of one mil for each year of a six-year period. This is the amount that the Board has in the past designated towards technology upgrade.

As you can see from the total, the regular and non-regular budget amounts equal approximately 2.3 million dollars; however, when you factor out the amount provided for the technology strategy ($1,795,000), the approximate amount for the other parts of the strategic plan is about $531,000 (regular budget $129,000, non-regular budget $402,000).

June 12, 1997

Exhibit 3-14 (continued)

<u>STRATEGIC PLAN FINANCIAL IMPLICATIONS</u>
<u>STRATEGIES</u>

CURRICULUM & ASSESSMENT

We will design challenging curriculum and a framework for assessment that will measure each student's competency to meet the district's established standards.

	Reg Budget	Non - reg Budget
1. Review and assess the curriculum with reference to state requirements.	100	0
2. Provide flexible curriculum incorporating or exceeding state requirements to meet the needs of all students.	1,800	0
3. Create and implement a planned course format for all curricula that structures opportunities for active citizenship, analytical thinking, creative thinking, and organizational skills.	3,100	0
4. Foster, develop, and disseminate practices that encourage the integration of various curricula and resources for more relevant learning in academic and vocational education.	4,500	0
5. Develop performance standards and assessments to meet district and state outcomes at transitional school levels.	5,600	0
6. Create and implement a reporting system that reflects changes in assessments.	15,000	0
7. Implement and manage an assessment system, which includes portfolios, that will serve as a basis for ongoing evaluation.	4,000	0
8. Establish graduation requirements which include, but are not limited to, the state requirements.	26,500	0
9. Develop a comprehensive plan to enable students to meet academic standards at all levels.	0	60,000
10. Promote community awareness, involvement, and support for initiatives in curricula and assessment.	300	0
11. Develop, staff, and implement a management structure to coordinate curricula throughout the district.	5,000	0
12. Create a process that informs students and parents of career and educational opportunities.	25,000	0
TOTAL	90,900	60,000

Exhibit 3-14 (continued)

STAFF DEVELOPMENT

We will create a structure and process to facilitate the competence of all staff in achieving the goals of the organization.

	Reg Budget	Non-reg Budget
1. Provide time for purposeful, ongoing staff development.	0	0
2. Educate professionals to use a comprehensive range of strategies to ensure student achievement of learning standards.	0	0
3. Establish collaborative commitment to Staff Development utilizing community and staff resources.	500	0
4. Establish nurturing school cultures that support site-based staff development.	1,500	0
5. Assure that the Staff Development process maintains a balance by responding to individual, building, and district needs.	0	0
6. Establish a Staff Development Center for on-going learning that encourages a sense of community throughout the district.	0	50,000
7. Provide inservice opportunities for support staff (aides, custodians, cafeteria workers, secretaries, etc.).	0	1,000
8. Provide inservice opportunities for district administrators.	2,000	0
9. Create opportunities for school board members to participate in and benefit from inservice.	1,000	0
10. Afford to all staff the opportunities to become knowledgeable about alternative methods of student learning and assessment.	4,000	0
TOTAL	**9,000**	**51,000**

FACILITIES

We will develop and implement short and long range facilities' plans to accommodate educational program requirements, projected student enrollments, and building obsolescence.

	Reg. Budget	Non-reg Budget
1. Determine that all school facilities are designed and continually updated to meet curricular needs in accomplishing the educational mission. BEC 90	0	0
2. Ensure the safety of all elementary playgrounds.	0	45,200
3. Insure a safe environment in all school facilities--especially classrooms where subjects such as art, family and consumer science, physical education, science, and technology education are taught. BEC 90	0	0
4. Assure that adequate safety and security measures are met in all buildings.	0	70,800
5. Ascertain compliance with ADA (American Disabilities Act) in all schools. BEC 90	0	0
6. Periodically evaluate the demographic nature of the Souderton Area School District in determining its capability for accommodating projected enrollments.	0	0
7. Ensure safe and efficient traffic flow of students, staff, and guests (both pedestrian and vehicular).	0	0
8. Reduce and eventually eliminate all areas of obsolescence. BEC 90	0	0
TOTAL	**0**	**116,000**

Exhibit 3-14 (continued)

STUDENT SUPPORT

We will establish guidelines, procedures, and definitions to direct student support programs, discipline, security, and extra-curricular activities.

	Reg Budget	Non - reg Budget
1. Provide, develop, and maintain student support services.	0	0
2. Inform the school community about available support services available to students.	0	0
3. Foster positive attitudes and develop good citizenship skills through a citizenship campaign.	0	9,000
4. Inform students, parents, and community of expectations of behavior and enforce the established consequences.	2,000	0
5. Provide a safe school environment.	0	0
6. Develop preventive measures to insure security.	0	0
7. Foster participation of all students in extra-curricular activities.	0	0
TOTAL	**2,000**	**9,000**

TIME

We will reinvent the school system around learning, rather than time so that the academic schedule is not limited by the traditional school schedule.

	Reg Budget	Non - reg Budget
1. Assure that looping is an option available in all elementary schools.	0	0
2. Implement a team teaching program in the 6-7 building contingent upon the results of the pilot study.	0	65,000
TOTAL	**0**	**65,000**

ORGANIZATIONAL STRUCTURE

We will put in place a process and structure for the organization that will facilitate communication, decision-making and accountability throughout the organization.

	Reg Budget	Non reg Budget
1. Create an empowering organization structure which fosters and models the application of collaborative principles and practices.	0	2,000
2. Implement a comprehensive collaborative training program by qualified instructors for all SASD personnel to teach and/or refresh communication skills.	0	500
3. Establish open and effective communication channels for students, parents, district employees, and community members.	0	2,000
4. Ensure that the highest quality collaborative decisions are made within the school community.	0	500
5. Maximize the potential of all the stakeholders through shared accountability in providing a positive, productive learning and working environment.	0	0
TOTAL	**0**	**5,000**

Exhibit 3-14 (continued)

FINANCIAL RESOURCES

We will develop and implement a financial plan to provide sufficient resources to fund all objectives of the SASD Strategic Plan consistent with sound business practices.

	Reg Budget	Non - reg Budget
1. Compare privatization vs in-district options for appropriate services within the Souderton Area School District.		0	0
2. Implement Cost Savings team at all applicable sites for all appropriate services offered within the Souderton Area School District.	0	0
3. Determine alternative sources of revenue for the Souderton Area School District including both traditional and non-traditional sources.	0	0
4. Examine and eliminate, where possible, the duplication of services within the Souderton Area School District and other external agencies.	0	0
5. Bring about changes in the amount of state funding returned to the local school district.	0	0
TOTAL	0	0

INSTRUCTION

We will deliver the most effective instruction and interventions for all students.

	Reg Budget	Non - reg Budget
1. Use a variety of instructional strategies to maximize the opportunity for individual student learning.	2,000	0
2. Build an enriched learning environment through a resource support system. (Tech.)	10,000	0
3. Engage all students in authentic learning experiences that emphasize the meaningful application of knowledge beyond the school setting.	0	60,000
4. Incorporate flexible use of time and varied grouping formats in instruction at all levels.	0	0
5. Incorporate technology to enhance instruction. (Tech.)	0	0
6. Design a model for demonstration sites that would allow for the observation and implementation of effective instructional practices.	0	8,505
TOTAL	12,000	68,505

Exhibit 3-14 (continued)

TECHNOLOGY

We will develop an effective and efficient plan to acquire, continually update, and incorporate technology throughout every facet of the district.

	Reg Budget	Non - reg Budget
1. Provide a K-12 program that will help all students become literate in the use of technology.	0	47,200
2. Use technology to assist and enhance the educational program.	600,000	639,000
3. Develop and implement an integrated district-wide technology program for administrative/staff personnel.	25,000	76,900
4. Implement an effective and efficient communication system within the district and beyond.	5,000	60,000
5. Expand the availability, use, and integration of technology into the K-12 curriculum through the district's library media centers.	0	74,400
6. Establish a technology center/hub as a district and community information center.	6,000	250,035
7. Train all staff (in an ongoing and supportive manner) to enhance classroom instruction through the use of technology.	12,240	0
TOTAL	648,240	1,147,535

COMMUNITY/PARENTS

We will develop and implement strategies to increase participation of students in their community, parents in their children's education, and community members and institutions in our schools.

	Reg Budget	Non - reg Budget
1. Enhance the student's education through service learning extending beyond the classroom.	0	2,100
2. Ensure communication and extend the opportunities for all parents to become active partners in their child's education.	0	2,500
3. Provide resources and encourage involvement in parenting education programs.	0	3,500
4. Expand the Souderton Area School District's community outreach programs.	0	20,000
5. Broaden the scope of the Souderton Area School District's public relations program.	15,000	0
TOTAL	15,000	28,100
GRAND TOTAL	777,140	1,550,140
TOTAL REG AND NON-REG	2,327,280	

Operating and Capital Budget Development Process

(Criterion C-6)

Exhibit 3-15—Operating and Capital Budget Development Process

Mt. Lebanon School District
1997-98 Budget

BUDGET TIMELINE

Early-May	Strategic Planning Team meets to determine district goals.
July	Annual district performance report published in Mt. Lebanon Magazine.
Early-August	Management staff reviews and refines strategic plan and prepares individual annual goals.
Mid-August	Individual administrator goal and planning conferences begin.
Early-September	Superintendent reviews strategic plan with all staff and community.
Late-September	Determination of existing revenue trends and exploration of options among alternative revenue sources.
Mid-November	First draft of Five Year Forecast prepared by central office staff following input from all staff and administrators utilizing strategic plan priorities.
November	All management review of proposed Five Year Forecast.
December	School Board review and acceptance of Five Year Forecast assumptions and direction for the General Fund and Capital Projects Fund.
December	Management reviews revised Five Year Forecast conditions.
Mid-December	Central office plans for annual budget preparation based upon Five Year Forecast and strategic plan parameters.
Early-January	Management staff begins preparation of annual budgets.
January	Strategic Plan Planning Committee reviews implementation schedule of action plans.
Late January-March	Superintendent chairs Residents <u>Ad</u> <u>Hoc</u> Budget Committee.
February	School board reviews and approves the strategic plan implementation timeline. Strategic plan implementation costs are included in the budgets.
Mid-March	School board review of proposed General Fund and Capital Projects budgets.
Mid-April	Public begins study of proposed annual budget for public approval at May board meeting which includes televised budget shows and public forums.
Mid-May	Public approval of final budgets and implementations.

Exhibit 3-16—Operating and Capital Budget Development Process

TREDYFFRIN/EASTTOWN SCHOOL DISTRICT
BUDGET 1997-98

BUDGET DEVELOPMENT PROCESS

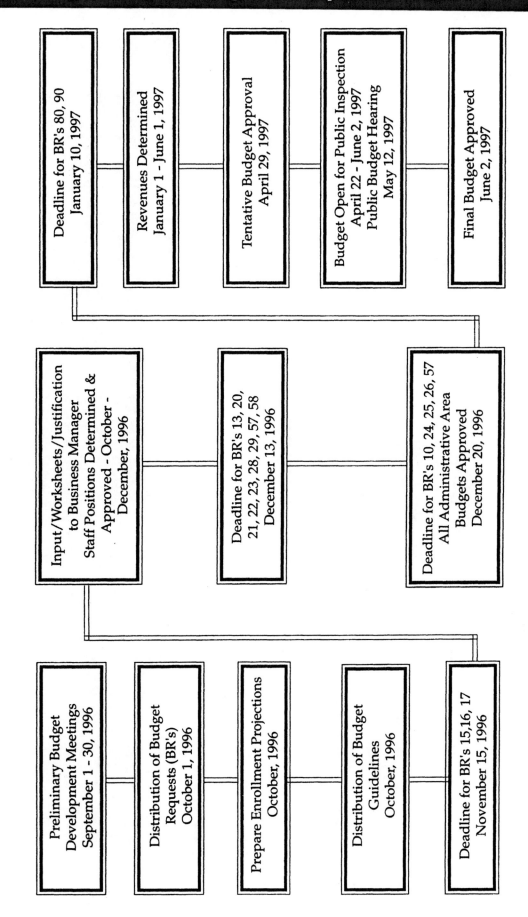

Preliminary Budget Development Meetings
September 1 - 30, 1996

Distribution of Budget Requests (BR's)
October 1, 1996

Prepare Enrollment Projections
October, 1996

Distribution of Budget Guidelines
October, 1996

Deadline for BR's 15,16, 17
November 15, 1996

Input/Worksheets/Justification to Business Manager
Staff Positions Determined & Approved - October - December, 1996

Deadline for BR's 13, 20, 21, 22, 23, 28, 29, 57, 58
December 13, 1996

Deadline for BR's 10, 24, 25, 26, 57
All Administrative Area Budgets Approved
December 20, 1996

Deadline for BR's 80, 90
January 10, 1997

Revenues Determined
January 1 - June 1, 1997

Tentative Budget Approval
April 29, 1997

Budget Open for Public Inspection
April 22 - June 2, 1997
Public Budget Hearing
May 12, 1997

Final Budget Approved
June 2, 1997

Exhibit 3-17—Operating and Capital Budget Development Process

VII.

BUDGET DEVELOPMENT TIMELINE

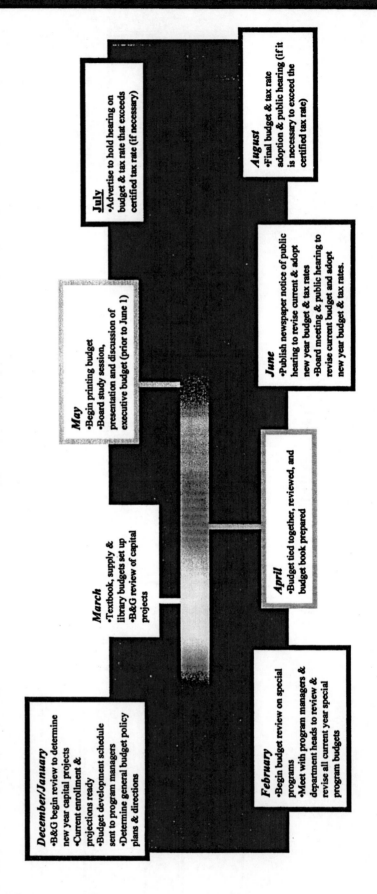

December/January
- B&G begin review to determine new year capital projects
- Current enrollment & projections ready
- Budget development schedule sent to program managers
- Determine general budget policy plans & directions

February
- Begin budget review on special programs
- Meet with program managers & department heads to review & revise all current year special program budgets

March
- Textbook, supply & library budgets set up
- B&G review of capital projects

April
- Budget tied together, reviewed, and budget book prepared

May
- Begin printing budget
- Board study session, presentation and discussion of executive budget (prior to June 1)

June
- Publish newspaper notice of public hearing to revise current & adopt new year budget & tax rates
- Board meeting & public hearing to revise current budget and adopt new year budget & tax rates.

July
- Advertise to hold hearing on budget & tax rate that exceeds certified tax rate (if necessary)

August
- Final budget & tax rate adoption & public hearing (if it is necessary to exceed the certified tax rate)

Exhibit 3-18—Operating and Capital Budget Development Process

BUDGET DEVELOPMENT PROCESS

The budget process can be disaggregated conceptually into a five step process that includes: planning, preparation, adoption, implementation, and evaluation. The process is driven by two objectives - to provide every child in the District with the best possible educational opportunities and to maximize the use of available resources. Within this framework, the Board attempts to balance the educational needs of students and the resources available to the District from local, state, and federal sources. The product, the School District's budget that details the revenues and expenditures to support educational programs and services, is a delicate balance of policy choices.

Budget Planning

For the fiscal year that begins July 1, the planning process for budgeting starts the prior September when the Board adopts a budget calendar. The calendar includes all of the important activities in the budgeting process; the dates on which important decisions are scheduled to be made; and the person responsible for the activity. Once adopted the calendar represents the guidelines for the preparation and adoption of the financial plan of the School District.

Preparation of the Operating Budget

The preparation of the budget is the process of defining service levels such as the course offerings in the educational program; projecting student enrollment; developing staffing allocations; estimating expenditure needs to support programs and services; and projecting available revenues. The process begins when the Director of Pupil Services provides a five-year forecast of elementary enrollment and a ten-year forecast of secondary enrollment to the Board. The Board agrees to a forecast of enrollments in October which establishes an important assumption on which per pupil expenditure appropriations, instructional staffing allocations, and service levels such as the number of course sections and the number of transportation vehicles are based.

At the pupil meeting in December, the Board approves building budgets that are primarily based on per pupil allocations for the projected student enrollment. The per pupil appropriations are established early in the budget cycle to permit staff involvement in the determination of resource allocations within the buildings. This also permits the acquisition of supplies, materials and equipment at the lowest price through the public bidding process and timely delivery of purchases prior to the opening of the school term. The budget process is continued at the January meeting at which the Board approves the course offerings that will form the educational programs for the next year.

Since salaries and fringe benefits constitute approximately three-quarters of budget expenditures, the Board gives careful consideration to staffing allocations for both instructional and noninstructional positions to provide for defined service levels. The professional staffing needed to support the educational program is a function of both the projected student enrollment approved by the Board in October and the course offerings approved by the Board in January. The staffing needs of the District are constructed on a zero base approach at all levels. The Board considers staffing allocations during the months of February and March at public workshops. Staffing allocations are formally approved in March.

Preparation of the Capital and Other Budgets

The budget development process for the Special Revenue Funds that include the Athletic Fund and the Capital Reserve Fund (the capital budget), the Debt Service Fund Budget and the Enterprise Fund (the food service budget) proceeds concurrently with the foregoing process for the development of the operating budget.

Each year the District updates its five year Capital Reserve Fund plan that provides for the maintenance of facilities. Projects are prioritized based on resolution of safety matters, compliance with

Exhibit 3-18 (continued)

state and federal statutes, maintenance of existing facilities, and improvements to District buildings. In the update of the plan, the Directors consider recommendations from the District's architect-of-record, the representatives of the property and casualty insurance providers, members of the District's safety committee, the Director of Operations and Maintenance, the Board's Building and Grounds Committee, and building principals. Funds in the amount equal to one (1) mill of real estate taxes are transferred from the operating budget to help fund expenditures in the five-year building maintenance plan.

In accord with the requirements of the Pennsylvania Department of Education for the establishment of a capital project for new construction or major renovation, the Directors periodically convene a task force comprised of Board members, staff members, and citizens of the community to assess the facility needs of the District. The recommendations from the task force are based on the needs of the educational program, capacity needs derived from enrollment forecasts, and the physical condition of the buildings. Funds for new construction or major renovations are provided for through the issuance of debt. The impact of capital projects are considered in the development of the proposed and projected operating budgets.

The critical elements in the development of the athletic budget are the estimation of program needs and gate receipts for ticketed events. The difference is the contribution required from the operating budget to support the extra-curricular and athletic programs.

The Debt Service Fund Budget is determined based on the principal and interest payments required to meet debt obligations that are set forth in bond amortization schedules. The debt reflects funds borrowed to construct, renovate and maintain school facilities.

The food service budget also has an impact on the operating budget. The food service budget is formulated from an estimation of the participation levels in each school based on projected enrollments. Expenses for labor are predicated on the projected levels of participation in the breakfast and lunch programs converted into meals prepared per day to determine staff. Costs for food are estimated based on the number of meals to be provided. Revenue is based on projected sales to students and staff as well as estimated state and federal support for the school breakfast and lunch programs. The difference between revenues and expenses is the amount of contribution required from the operating budget to provide the food service program.

Budget Adoption, Implementation, and Evaluation

The budgets of the District for the next year are proposed at a Board meeting in May. In May and June, the Board considers the budgets and provides for public input and comment on the financial plan to fund the District's educational programs and services. Final passage of the budgets occurs in June. The implementation of the approved financial plan is discussed in the following section referred to as the budget administration and management process. The final step in the budget process is the evaluation of the financial plan. The results of operations for the fiscal year are set forth annually in the District's Comprehensive Annual Financial Report (CAFR).

Exhibit 3-18 (continued)

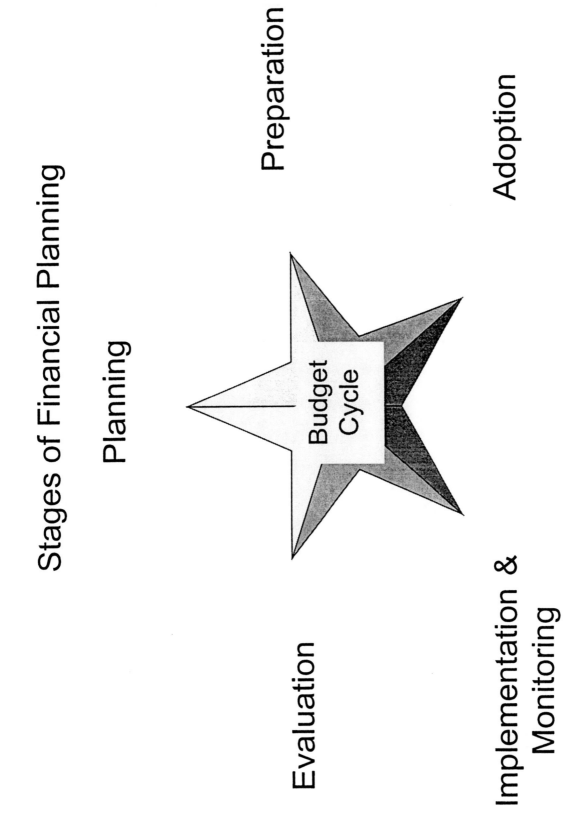

Stages of Financial Planning

Preparation

Adoption

Planning

Budget Cycle

Evaluation

Implementation & Monitoring

Exhibit 3-18 (continued)

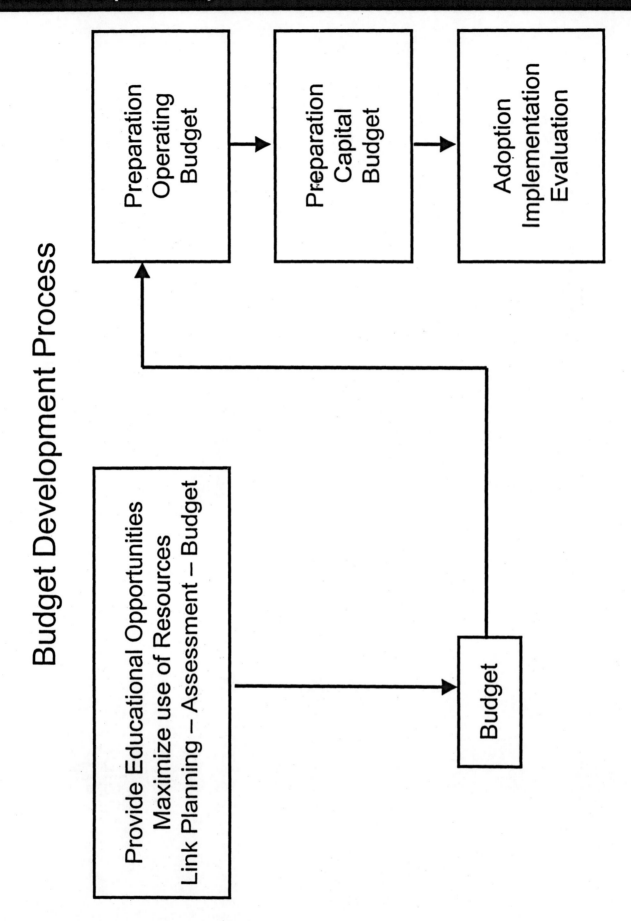

Budget Development Process

Exhibit 3-18 (continued)

BUDGET DEVELOPMENT CALENDAR

July 1997						
S	M	T	W	T	F	S
		1	2	3	4	5
6	7	8	9	10	11	12
13	14	15	16	17	18	19
20	21	22	23	24	25	26
27	28	29	30	31		

August 1997						
S	M	T	W	T	F	S
					1	2
3	4	5	6	7	8	9
10	11	12	13	14	15	16
17	18	19	20	21	22	23
24/31	25	26	27	28	29	30

September 1997						
S	M	T	W	T	F	S
	1	2	3	4	5	6
7	8	9	10	11	12	13
14	15	16	17	18	19	20
21	22	23	24	25	26	27
28	29	30				

October 1997						
S	M	T	W	T	F	S
			1	2	3	4
5	6	7	8	9	10	11
12	13	14	15	16	17	18
19	20	21	22	23	24	25
26	27	28	29	30	31	

November 1997						
S	M	T	W	T	F	S
						1
2	3	4	5	6	7	8
9	10	11	12	13	14	15
16	17	18	19	20	21	22
23/30	24	25	26	27	28	29

December 1997						
S	M	T	W	T	F	S
	1	2	3	4	5	6
7	8	9	10	11	12	13
14	15	16	17	18	19	20
21	22	23	24	25	26	27
28	29	30	31			

DATE	ACTIVITY
10/27/97	Presentation of: • Enrollment Forecasts (Board Action) • School Calendar Approval of Contract for Transportation Vehicles (Board Action)
11/25/97	Management Review of Building Budget Allocations
12/1/97	Approval of: • Enrollment Forecasts (Board Action) • Building Budget Allocations (Board Action) • Contract for Audit Services (Board Action) • Budget Development Calendar (Board Action)
1/6/98	Management Review of Annual Goals
1/26/98	Approval of: • School Calendar (Board Action) • Contract for Boiler Replacement-MS (Board Action) • Contract for North Coventry Project (Board Action)
2/3/98	Management Review of Staffing Allocations – Elementary
2/4/98	Management Review of Staffing Allocations – Middle School
2/5/98	Management Review of Staffing Allocations – High School
2/5/98	Management Review of Staffing Allocations – District
2/23/98	Presentation of Staffing Allocations (Board Action)
2/23/98	Approval of: • PlanCon G for North Coventry Project (Board Action) • Contract for High School Project (Board Action) • Annual Census (Board Action) • Annual Goals (Board Action) • Contract for Building Infrastructures: EC, Vin, FC, War (Board Action)
2/23/98	Management Review of: • Transportation Services Budget • Plant Services Budget • Negotiations Agreement with RFSA (Board Action) • Capital Reserve Fund Budget • Capital Projects Budget • Debt Service Fund Budget • Athletic Fund Budget
3/2/98	Committee Review of: • Transportation Services Budget • Plant Services Budget • Capital Reserve Fund Budget • Capital Projects Budget
3/6/98	Management Review of: • Technical Services Budget • Community Swim Program Budget • Business Services Budget
3/9/98	Board Review of Staffing Allocations
3/16/98	Committee Review of: • Athletic Fund Budget • Educational Program • Proposed Curriculum Proposals
3/23/98	Management Review of Public Information Services Budget
3/24/98	Approval of PlanCon G for High School Project (Board Action)

Exhibit 3-18 (continued)

BUDGET DEVELOPMENT CALENDAR (continued)

January 1998

S	M	T	W	T	F	S
				1	2	3
4	5	6	7	8	9	10
11	12	13	14	15	16	17
18	19	20	21	22	23	24
25	26	27	28	29	30	31

February 1998

S	M	T	W	T	F	S
1	2	3	4	5	6	7
8	9	10	11	12	13	14
15	16	17	18	19	20	21
22	23	24	25	26	27	28

March 1998

S	M	T	W	T	F	S
1	2	3	4	5	6	7
8	9	10	11	12	13	14
15	16	17	18	19	20	21
22	23	24	25	26	27	28
29	30	31				

April 1998

S	M	T	W	T	F	S
			1	2	3	4
5	6	7	8	9	10	11
12	13	14	15	16	17	18
19	20	21	22	23	24	25
26	27	28	29	30		

May 1998

S	M	T	W	T	F	S
					1	2
3	4	5	6	7	8	9
10	11	12	13	14	15	16
17	18	19	20	21	22	23
24/31	25	26	27	28	29	30

June 1998

S	M	T	W	T	F	S
	1	2	3	4	5	6
7	8	9	10	11	12	13
14	15	16	17	18	19	20
21	22	23	24	25	26	27
28	29	30				

DATE	ACTIVITY
3/30/98	• Approval of Contract for Unit Ventilators/DDC Controls: EC, Vin (Board Action)
3/30/98	• Award of Contract for Mowing Services (Board Action)
3/30/98	• Approval of:
	• Staffing Allocations (Board Action)
	• Educational Program (Board Action)
	• IU 24 Core Services Budget (Board Action)
	• Occupational Educational Services Budget (Board Action)
	• IU 24 Special Education Contracted Services Budget (Board Action)
	• IU 24 Marketplace Contracted Services (Board Action)
	• Management Review of:
3/30/98	• Staff Services Budget
	• Pupil Services Budget
	• Pupil Health Services Budget
	• Staff Development Services Budget
	• Federal Programs Budget
	• Curriculum Development Services Budget
	• Summer School Budget
	• Adult Education Budget
	• Executive Services Budget
	• Renewal of:
3/30/98	• Contract for Housekeeping Services (Board Action)
	• Contract for Transportation Services (Board Action)
	• Refrigeration Services (Board Action)
	• Contract for Yearbook Printing-HS (Board Action)
	• Plumbing Services (Board Action)
4/1/98	• Management Review of Staff Alignment
4/2/98	• Management Review of Staff Alignment
4/3/98	• Management Review of Staff Alignment
4/6/98	• Management Review of:
	• Professionals Services Budget
	• Proprietary Fund (Food Service) Budget
	• Revenue Forecast
4/27/98	• Approval of Contracts for:
	• Replacement Vehicles (Board Action)
	• Heating Services (Board Action)
	• Electrical Services (Board Action)
	• Snow Removal Services (Board Action)
	• Instructional & Non-Instructional Supplies (Board Action)
	• Athletic/Medical Supplies (Board Action)
4/27/98	• Approval of PlanCon H for North Coventry Project (Board Action)
4/27/98	• Approval of PlanCon H for High School Project (Board Action)
4/27/98	• Approval of Curriculum Proposals (Board Action)
5/18/98	• Presentation of Budgets (Board Action)
6/22/98	• Adoption of Budget (Board Action)
6/22/98	• Approval of:
	• Tax Resolution (Board Action)
	• Contract-Fluid Products-Food SVCS(Board Action)
	• Property & Casualty Ins. Program (Board Action)
7/5/98	• Submission of Budget
	• For Review in ASBO Budget Awards Program
	• To Pennsylvania Dept. Of Education
	• To Chester County Intermediate Unit

Budget Administration and Management Process

(Criterion C-7)

Exhibit 3-19—Budget Administration and Management Process

DeSoto Parish School Board
Organization Section
Fiscal Year 1997-98

Budget Administration and Management Process

After the budget has been approved, controls on spending are the most significant emphasis in the administration and management of the budget because the Board demands that we follow the established spending policies set in the budget. Below is a synopsis of other significant financial policies.

Fixing Responsibility

The superintendent shall assign various budgetary line items to members of the administrative staff. Each staff member is held responsible for seeing that expenditures stay within budget boundaries. Should any staff member encounter problems in any budget area, the Business Office should be notified immediately in order that adjustments might be made according to Board policies.

Quarterly Financial Statements

The Business Office shall print a quarterly financial statement comparing actual expenditures against detailed budgets. This report is sent to each staff member who is responsible for seeing that expenditures are within budget boundaries.

Purchasing

All purchases of $1.00 or more made with School Board funds shall be made by the central purchasing office on official purchase orders. All purchase orders shall be numbered, thus providing a permanent record of every transaction executed by the purchasing department. The purchase order system (1) keeps staff members from overspending, and (2) enables staff members to know how much money is available for new commitments.

Sales Tax Reports

The Business Office shall present a monthly report to the Finance Committee detailing the collections from sales and use taxes. Budget adjustments are presented to the Board if actual collections vary significantly.

Minimum Foundation Program Receipts

The Business Office shall monitor and compare the monthly receipts to the formula approved by the Louisiana Legislature. The Superintendent shall be notified of any change to the budgeted amount or delays in the receipt of funds. Budget adjustments are presented to the Finance Committee and the Board if actual collections vary significantly.

Exhibit 3-19 (continued)

DeSoto Parish School Board
Organization Section
Fiscal Year 1997-98

Property Tax Receipts

The Business Office shall monitor and compare the property tax receipts during the months of January, February, and March. The Superintendent shall be notified of any change to the budgeted amount or delays in the receipt of funds. Budget adjustments are presented to the Finance Committee and the Board if actual collections vary significantly.

Cash Management

All cash receipts shall be deposited on a daily basis and secured by the bank against loss. This security shall at all times be equal to 100% of the balance on deposit. All monies not immediately needed shall be invested at the greatest possible rate. The goal is to be 100% invested 100% of the time, be 100% liquid and 100% secured.

Fixed Assets

The Business Office has been directed to oversee the physical control and accountability, as well as, to provide tools for enhanced management of all lands, buildings, and equipment. Building level administrators conduct semi-annual physical inventories of all fixed assets and an annual audit is conducted by the Business Office using random sampling techniques.

Financial Records

The Business Office shall exercise diligence and care in preserving records for the periods of time specified in formal record retention schedules developed and approved by the Louisiana Secretary of State, Archives and Records Division. This schedule shall be reviewed and updated annually in the event that a particular record is not identified on the record retention schedule.

Financial and Compliance Audit

The financial statements of the DeSoto Parish School Board shall be audited annually by a licensed certified public accountant (CPA) and presented to the Board and the Legislative Auditor of Louisiana.

Staffing

Personnel Rosters, that are presented in the budget, list the number of employees that will be hired. Staffing according to the these rosters is the responsibility of the Director of Personnel and Administrative Services. The Business Office shall monitor the number of employees hired during the month of October and shall notify the Superintendent of any changes to the number of employees hired. Budget adjustments are presented to the Finance Committee and the Board if actual expenditures and the number employed exceed budget projects.

Exhibit 3-20—Budget Administration and Management Process

SAN CARLOS UNIFIED SCHOOL DISTRICT NO. 20
1997-98 BUDGET

VII.   BUDGET IMPLEMENTATION

In order to determine if budgeted expenditures are in keeping with the adopted budget, a monthly report of expenditures shall be presented to the Board. Variances within budget categories shall be a part of this report.

Any required overexpenditures in a major subsection of the maintenance and operation budget shall require Board approval.

LEGAL REFERENCE: A.R.S. §15-905

VIII.   AUDIT REQUIREMENTS

The district is required to have its records and financial statements audited by a certified public accountant or independent consultant, subject to the requirements of the Single Audit Act of 1984 and the State Auditor General for internal control procedures.

A certified public accountant or independent consultant shall be appointed by the Board pursuant to the Arizona Administrative Code requirement for the procurement of services. Audit fees shall be charged to the appropriate funds as required by law.

The completed audit report shall be presented to the Board for examination and discussion. The audit report shall be a public record, and copies shall be filed with the state and other appropriate authorities.

Financial And Compliance Audits

A.   The governing board of a school district which is required to comply with the single audit act of 1984 (P.L. 98-502) shall contract for at least biennial financial and compliance audits of financial transactions and the accounts subject to the single audit act of 1984 (P.L. 98-502) kept by or for the school district.

B.   Contracts for financial and compliance audits and completed audits shall be approved by the auditor general as provided in §41-1279.21.

Exhibit 3-20 (continued)

SAN CARLOS UNIFIED SCHOOL DISTRICT NO. 20
1997-98 BUDGET

C.   If the school district will incur costs of financial and compliance audits for the budget year, the governing board of a school district may increase its base support level for the budget year by an amount equal to the amount expended for the district's financial and compliance audits in the year before the current year, increased by the growth rate as prescribed by §15-901, subsection B, paragraph 2, subdivision (f). In determining the amount expended for the district's financial and compliance audits, the school district shall include only the portion of the audit which must be paid from monies other than federal monies. The department of education and the auditor general shall prescribe a method for determining the increase in the base support level and shall include in the maintenance and operation section of the budget format, as provided in §15-903, a separate line for financial and compliance audits expenditures.

LEGAL REFERENCE: A.R.S. §15-914

IX.   POLICIES AND PRACTICES

SCHOOL-BASED BUDGETING

San Carlos Unified School District has implemented school-based budgeting. In school-based budgeting, the principals in collaboration with their staff have been delegated the responsibility to prepare budgets at the individual building level. The school-based budgeting process helps this school district in the sense that the staff and the administrators feel a sense of ownership and commitment for improvement in the activities and programs within their school.

Budget development, allocation, capital improvements, major maintenance and construction are best planned and directed from the district level as are other major district-wide activities, such as energy management, food services and transportation.

BUDGET MANAGEMENT

The budget is managed through a decentralized financial management system. All the principals, administrators and supervisors have been allocated a certain amount of funds based on their program's goals and objectives. The district office controls all accounts. The principals, administrators and supervisors receive printouts from the business office at least monthly to update the financial position at the building level. Budget modification, transfer of funds, journal entries and adjustments are made at the district office. The business office at the district level maintains effective control over the district's funds and general fixed assets.

Exhibit 3-21—Budget Administration and Management Process

BUDGET ADMINISTRATION AND MANAGEMENT PROCESS

Budget administration and management is the process of regulating expenditures during the fiscal year to ensure that they do not exceed authorized amounts and that they are used for intended, proper, and legal purposes. The management of the budget is accomplished in a variety of ways: monitoring program implementation; controlling expenditures; tracking revenue receipts; making corrections in expenditure allocations to reflect changes in costs, service levels or plans; and reporting to the Board and public on fiscal operations.

During the preparation of the budget, the document itself serves as the vehicle for planning and resource allocation decisions in the District. After the budget is adopted by the Board in June and the appropriations made to the various accounts, it then becomes the major fiscal management tool for administering and controlling expenditures. There are, however, other budget administration and management issues important to the budget process that are discussed below.

Organization for Budget Management

The decision making philosophy and organizational structure of the District for budgeting combines elements of the management team and school site management concepts. It is an approach between centralization and decentralization in philosophy and structure. Many of the decisions in the District are formulated by management teams with the responsibility for budget control at the building or department level (such as: transportation or pupil services).

For example, the Administrative Council, which is comprised of central office administrators and building principals, reviews and approves curriculum recommendations of the Curriculum Advisory Council prior to presentation to the Board for final consideration. The Curriculum Advisory Council is comprised of building principals and members of the professional staff. Teams of administrators and teachers at the central office and building level are thus an important part of the decision-making process for educational programs and curriculum in the District. Funds to support curriculum revisions are then controlled by the Director of Personnel and Curriculum.

The overall spending and revenue plans are coordinated by the central office to keep the District's total expenditures within available revenues. District level coordination is also exercised in such areas as personnel policies which are established and monitored centrally to maintain general uniformity and compliance with negotiated collective bargaining agreements as well as state and federal statutes. However, budgetary allocations to responsibility cost centers, particularly the building budget appropriations, are provided in an unrestricted, lump-sum amount and decisions on how to allocate these monies are made at the site or department level. For example, principals, who are responsibility cost center managers, are required by Board policy to provide participation for the professional staff in the decision making process on the use of building resources through Building Instructional Improvement Committees.

Expenditure Control and Approvals

For management control purposes, the operating budget (General Fund) of the District is disaggregated into twenty-four (24) responsibility cost centers. A budget manager (an administrator or coordinator such as a Building Principal or Transportation Coordinator) is accountable for the management of the financial resources approved by the Board for each of the twenty-five responsibility cost centers in the operating budget. In addition, the Athletic Coordinator and the Food Service Coordinator are assigned as the budget manager for the Athletic Fund and the Enterprise Fund, respectively. The Business Administrator is the budget manager for the Debt Service Fund and Capital Reserve Fund. Thus, every expenditure appropriation in the District's budgets is assigned to a responsibility cost center manager who is accountable for the proper expenditure of funds.

Exhibit 3-21 (continued)

Each of the budget managers is authorized to approve the expenditure of funds within their respective responsibility cost center appropriations, provided that funds are expended in accord with District purchasing procedures and legal requirements. Administrative regulations require that all purchase orders be forwarded to the business office to verify availability of funds, proper account coding, and compliance with legal purchasing procedures. All bid awards and contracts must be approved by the Board of Directors. The Business Administrator also carefully monitors comparisons between budget and actual expenditures to maintain cost control and to insure against overspending.

Encumbrance Control

Another important component in the District's financial control and reporting system is the encumbrance of funds. Encumbrances are obligations in the form of purchase orders, contracts, or salary commitments chargeable to an appropriation and for which part of the appropriation is reserved. The purpose for the encumbrance of funds is to insure that obligations are recognized as soon as financial commitments are made. Otherwise, the accounting system would only record actual amounts entered into the expenditure accounts, not those that are planned or anticipated. In short, the encumbrance of funds is an important control measure to prevent the inadvertent overexpenditure of budget appropriations due to the lack of information about future commitments. For budgetary purposes, appropriations lapse at fiscal year-end and outstanding encumbrances at year-end are canceled.

Transfers between Budget Accounts

The budget is a spending plan based on a series of assumptions and estimates. Rarely, if ever, will all of the actual expenditures be equal to the detailed budget estimates. As actual expenditures are incurred, adjustments are required in the budget between accounts to cover higher than expected costs or to provide for an unanticipated expense. However, District controls on the transfer of funds insure that expenditures do not exceed available financial resources.

Responsibility cost center managers have the authority to transfer funds between accounts that increase or decrease appropriated amounts with certain constraints. Such constraints include that transfers between responsibility cost centers, whether between funds or within a fund, or revisions that alter the total revenues and expenditures of any fund, must be approved by the School Board in advance. In addition, transfers between functions within a responsibility cost center must also have the prior approval of the Board of School Directors. For example, appropriations for instruction cannot be transferred to support services or vice versa without prior Board approval.

Management Information and Reporting for Control

The District maintains an interactive, on-line budgetary accounting and control system that provides reports to assist Board Members, the Business Administrator, and responsibility cost center managers in administering, monitoring and controlling the implementation of the budget. The information from the automated accounting information system is important and relevant in evaluating the financial condition of the District and the fiscal performance of responsibility cost center managers.

The reports produced from the information system are designed for specific District needs and to meet state and federal reporting requirements. Among the most important of the documents for management control purposes are expenditure reports which are prepared by function and by responsibility cost center. Revenue reports are also prepared that track receipts against budget.

While revenue and expenditure reports are primarily for internal use for management control, the District also prepares a Comprehensive Annual Financial Report (CAFR) to report the results of operations. The CAFR includes such reports as a combined balance sheet for all fund types and a combined statement of revenue, expenditures and changes in fund balances for all governmental funds.

CHAPTER 4

Financial Section

Budgets are financial planning and decision-making documents. They contain information to assist school entity legislative bodies and administrative officials with revenue raising and spending decisions. Because budgets are financial planing documents, they place heavy emphasis on the presentation of financial information. The Financial Section is the heart of the school budget document. The budget financial schedules present the proposed and adopted budgets for a school entity compared with the results of past budget plans and with future projections. The MBA criteria set minimum requirements for the manner and methods by which these budgets are presented.

CONTENTS

The MBA criteria set minimum requirements for this section of the budget document, including:

1. Scope and format of budget presentations(i.e., schedules)
2. Use of the pyramid approach in the Presentation of budgets
3. Complete information presented including fund balances, revenues, expenditures and other financing sources/uses
4. Inclusion of capital budgets and a list of major capital projects
5. Description of capital spending impact on the operating budget
6. Current debt, legal debt limits and effects on current/future budgets

Although the criteria allow for latitude in how these items are presented, they are very specific about the minimum scope and the order of data presented and the use of the pyramid approach for the summarization of data.

Scope and Format of Budget Presentations (Criterion D-1)

The core of a budget document consists of a series of individual budgets — separate presentations or schedules of budgeted resources and resource allocations, usually for each of the entity's individual funds and programs, groups of funds or programs and in some cases for each school and department of the school entity. The Financial Section contains both summary and detailed budget schedules. State and/or local law may stipulate the level of detail contained in these schedules, or the local governing board and administration may determine the level of detail required. The MBA criteria address the design and makeup of these budget schedules. These criteria set some minimum requirements as well as offer some alternatives.

INCLUDE ALL GOVERNMENTAL AND PROPRIETARY FUNDS

The budget should include presentations for all governmental and proprietary funds at required levels of detail. Some entities may include budget presentations for fiduciary funds although there is little practical reason to budget for these funds and such budgets are not required by the award criteria.

At a minimum, the criteria require presentations to include revenues by source and expenditures by function and object. If there is a difference between the legal level of presentation and the minimum level of presentation set by the entity's governing board and administration, budget presentations (schedules) should be shown at the lower level (most detailed level) of presentation.

In addition to the minimum level of presentation required above, as an option, budgets may also be presented by program, location and/or administrative unit.

Cross-classification — displaying the expenditures in more than one way (e.g., function, object, program, groups of programs, location, and administrative unit) — can provide decision-makers with different perspectives on spending. This methodology will allow the requirement for minimum level of detail to be met while still providing ways of presenting the budget information, which is of most interest to citizens and other parties who have an interest in the budget and/or the budget process.

Use a Pyramid Approach (Criterion D-2)

The criteria establish a sequence for the presentations or schedules contained in the financial section. The pyramid approach in school budgeting refers to the presentation of summary schedules first, followed by the more detailed schedules. This approach allows for totals to be aggregated from the more detailed schedules to the highly aggregated schedules at the top of the pyramid through the use of combining schedules. This approach makes it easy for the reader to see exactly what budgets are aggregated from the lower levels (most detailed) to the highly aggregated or summarized schedules at the top of the pyramid. Specifically, the criteria require that a summary of all funds precede budget presentations of individual funds. Optional program, location and administrative unit budget presentations should follow the individual fund presentations. Whenever a summary budget schedule groups individual budgets, the school entity should follow this pyramid approach.

Complete information presented including fund balances, revenues, expenditures and other financing sources/uses (Criterion D-3)

Budget presentations should include complete information on all available resources and planned spending; specifically, budget schedules should display information on fund balances, revenues, expenditures and other financing sources/uses. This data should be shown for at least two years: the current year budget or the estimated current year expenditures, and the proposed budget year. The criteria prefer that the financial section also include actual data for three prior years at the same level of detail as presented for the current year and the proposed budget year. The school entity may choose instead to show this latter information in the document's informational section.

Exhibit 4-1 through 4-7 illustrates how four different school entities presented their summary of all funds, all governmental fund type budgets, or all governmental and proprietary fund budgets. They are all very good illustrations of the pyramid approach and good illustrations of presenting the "complete picture" i.e. Revenues by source, expenditures by function/object, including other financial sources and uses and beginning and ending fund balances. Exhibit 4-3 illustrates how this school district presented the individual fund (Maintenance and operation Fund Budget)

that folds into the summary shown in Exhibit 4-2. Again, this is a very good example of the preferred presentation of three prior years actual data and the current year in a format that is comparable to the budget being presented. Exhibit 4-4 is a chart showing how the funds of this school entity are organized, it is a map showing how the individual fund line item budgets are summarized and incorporated into the "Summary All Budgets" shown in Exhibit 4-5. Such a chart is not a requirement of the MBA criteria but is a nice touch to show visually at a glance the number of individual funds included in this budget and how they are incorporated into the summary. Exhibit 4-6 is an illustration of a school district that started the presentation with a summary of just total revenue and expenditures of each fund and then to moved a presentation of revenue by sources and expenditures by function in the next schedule which is shown in Exhibit 4-7. The permutations of different presentations are almost endless but these exhibits are good examples of presentations that meet the MBA criteria. Not shown here, but included in these budget documents, are summary and detailed schedules for other individual governmental and proprietary funds.

Those school entities from which Exhibits 4-1 through 4-5 are taken do not have any proprietary funds; therefore, the summary is less complicated than that shown in exhibits 4-6 and 4-7. The reader is reminded that the MBA criteria encourage the use of charts and graphs throughout the budget document. Budget presentations that have won the award contain numerous examples of the creative use of charts and graphs to communicate information that is required in the financial section and other sections of the budget. Exhibits 4-6 and 4-8 are examples of the chart and graph presentations, pie charts are used in these examples but many other forms of charts and graphs are used. Not shown in this exhibit are the summary and detailed schedules for the other governmental and proprietary funds.

The MBA criteria allow school entities to also present budgets by program, location, and/or administrative unit. Exhibits 4-9 through 4-11 illustrate how this is done by three different school entities that have won the award. Exhibit 4-9 is an example of a program budget for an individual program. Exhibit 4-10 is an example of an individual school or location budget. And, Exhibit 4-11 is an example of an individual department or administrative unit budget. Keep in mind that these individual school, department and program budgets should be summarized using combining schedules and the pyramid approach, as are other schedules in the budget presentation. Exhibit 4-12 is an example of this type of combining schedule used to summarize the department budgets of this school district. Similar schedules should be used to summarize school or location and program budgets.

The number of variations on program, department and individual school or location budget presentations is nearly limitless. The MBA criteria do not require these presentations as a part of the minimum requirements but these presentations are often desirable to satisfy the information needs of the users of the budget document. The MBA criteria requires only a presentation for all Governmental and Proprietary Funds, a presentation of revenues by source, and expenditures by function and object at the level of detail required by law or formally approved by a school entity's governing body. The criteria encourage presentations tailored to the individual needs of each entity so long as these minimum requirements are satisfied.

Inclusion of capital budgets and a list of major capital projects (Criterion D-4)

Some entities budget for capital spending in a separate budget document. Whether appropriations for capital projects are included in the annual budget document or authorized in a separate capital budget, MBA criteria require schools to include capital expenditures for the budget year in the budget presentation. In addition, the criteria require a listing of major capital projects within the document.

Exhibit 4-13 is one example of a capital project listing with the corresponding expenditures by year; major capital projects often require expenditures in more than one year. This schedule reports the total expenditure for the project by year as well as the amount for the budget year. Exhibit 4-14 is another example of a capital spending summary listing major capital projects for the year. This summary includes a more detailed description of each project, including a breakdown of project costs and the operating budget impact. Many school entities will have a long-range capital plan, which is included in their budget document providing information on planned capital projects for five or more years into the future. The inclusions of such long range capital plans in the budget document is encouraged because it provides information of great interest to the community, however, such information is not required by the MBA criteria.

Description of capital spending impact on the operating budget (Criterion D-5)

Capital improvements and other types of capital spending can have a major impact on the operating budgets. The construction of new schools can have the most dramatic effect on operating budgets. Smaller capital projects, such as new lighting in a school or a new heating ventilation and air-conditioning system, can also affect the operating budget. The MBA criteria require some assessment, preferably quantitative, of direct and indirect costs and savings or other service impacts that result from capital spending.

Exhibit 4-14 provides one example of such an assessment. Incorporated in the listing of major capital projects for the year is a brief description of the operating budget impact. This assessment could be improved with an estimate of actual dollar savings or costs.

Current debt, legal debt limits and effect on current/future budgets (Criterion D-6)

Like capital spending, debt can also affect future operating budgets. In addition, state laws and regulations most often place strict limitations on the use and amount of debt incurred by public agencies. Because of the far-reaching implications of indebtedness, the MBA criteria require information on current debt obligations, the relationship between current and legal debt limits, and the effects of existing debt levels on current and future budgets.

Exhibit 4-15 gives the history of the district's current debt load, and explains the district's legal debt limit. Exhibit 4-16 shows what the total outstanding debt for the district will be as a result of past transactions and the bonds planed to be issued during the budget year. Exhibit 4-16 also shows what the future debt service expenditures will be and therefore the impact on future budgets of the current and planed budget year debt. This district successfully used a combination of narrative and data to satisfy this award criterion. A number of different formats could succeed as well.

CHECKLIST

○ Budget presentations for all governmental and proprietary funds at either legal level required by state law or at the level adopted by the governing body are included.

○ These budget presentations include revenues by source and expenditures by function and object.

○ A summary of all budgeted funds is presented first in this section, followed by presentations for individual funds.

○ Budget presentations include fund balances, revenues, expenditures and other financing sources/uses for at least the current year and budget year and preferably for three prior years.

○ Capital expenditures and major capital projects for the budget year are listed in this section.

○ A description of the impact of capital spending on current and future operating budgets is provided.

○ This section includes financial data on current debt obligations and information on current debt margins and the impact of existing debt levels on current and future budgets.

Scope and Format of Budget Presentations

(Criterion D-1)

Use of the Pyramid Approach

(Criterion D-2)

Complete Information Presented Including Fund Balances, Revenues, Expenditures and Other Financing Sources/Uses

(Criterion D-3)

Exhibits 4-1 through 4-8

Optional Presentation: Budgets by Program, Location, and/or Administrative Unit

Exhibits 4-9 through 4-12

Exhibit 4-1—Budget Summary of All Funds

DeSoto Parish School Board
Budget Summary of All Funds
Fiscal Year 1997-98

	Total Budget				
		Special	Debt	Capital	
	General	Revenue	Service	Projects	
Revenues	Fund	Fund	Fund	Fund	Total
Local Revenues	$8,682,716	$1,388,223	$3,242,961	$262,596	$13,576,496
State Revenues	15,172,687	423,571	29,754	0	15,626,012
Federal Revenues	538	3,441,496	0	0	3,442,034
Total Revenues	$23,855,941	$5,253,290	$3,272,715	$262,596	$32,644,542
Expenditures					
Regular Programs	$11,085,531	$0	$0	$0	$11,085,531
Special Education Programs	2,936,177	155,602	0	0	3,091,779
Vocational Programs	801,968	53,705	0	0	855,673
Other Instructional Programs	416,373	0	0	0	416,373
Special Programs	77,475	1,078,502	0	0	1,155,977
Adult Education Programs	74,860	66,115	0	0	140,975
Pupil Support Services	896,337	100,956	0	0	997,293
Instructional Staff Services	930,369	458,775	0	0	1,389,144
General Administration	695,284	36,815	95,577	2,950	830,626
School Administration	1,564,511	0	0	0	1,564,511
Business Services	384,316	50	0	270	384,636
Maintenance of Plant	1,887,246	1,026,907	0	0	2,914,153
Student Transportation Services	2,474,925	2,800	0	0	2,477,725
Central Services	86,085	0	0	0	86,085
Food Service	0	2,285,004	0	0	2,285,004
Facility Acquisition & Constructio	0	0	0	172,900	172,900
Debt Service	0	0	3,209,903	0	3,209,903
Total Expenditures	$24,311,457	$5,265,231	$3,305,480	$176,120	$33,058,288
Other Sources of Funds	$96,245	$0	$0	$0	$96,245
Other Uses of Funds	0	(47,665)	0	0	(47,665)
Total Other Sources & Uses	$96,245	($47,665)	$0	$0	$48,580
EXCESS (DEFICIENCY)	($359,271)	($59,606)	($32,765)	$86,476	($365,166)
Beginning Fund Balance	$4,379,797	$571,660	$2,787,124	$654,389	$8,392,970
Ending Fund Balance	$4,020,526	$512,054	$2,754,359	$740,865	$8,027,804

Exhibit 4-2—Summary of Budgets

SAN CARLOS UNIFIED SCHOOL DISTRICT NO. 20
Summary of Budgets - All Governmental Fund Types
For Fiscal Year 1997-98

	Maintenance & Operation (General) Fund	Special Revenue Funds	Capital Projects Fund	Total All Governmental Funds
Revenues:				
Interest on investments	$ -	$ -	$ 500,000	$ 500,000
Intergovernmental grants and aid				
County	231,053	-	122,401	353,454
State	3,658,733	132,519	1,938,228	5,729,480
Federal	3,684,570	1,430,729	-	5,115,299
Food services sales	-	35,000	-	35,000
Auxiliary operations sales	-	70,000	-	70,000
Other	-	283,800	-	283,800
Total revenues	7,574,356	1,952,048	2,560,629	12,087,033
Expenditures:				
Current:				
Administration	911,430	42,205	-	953,635
Instruction	4,245,995	740,838	-	4,986,833
Instruction support	1,150,372	118,974	-	1,269,346
Operation	1,437,356	272,300	12,000	1,721,656
Pupil transportation	447,465	-	-	447,465
Food services	-	650,000	-	650,000
Auxiliary operations	-	70,000	-	70,000
Capital outlay	-	68,231	2,680,151	2,748,382
Total expenditures	8,192,618	1,962,548	2,692,151	12,847,317
Excess (deficiency) of revenues over expenditures	(618,262)	(10,500)	(131,522)	(760,284)
Other financing sources (uses)				
Operating transfers in	-	-	3,000,000	3,000,000
Operating transfers out	(3,000,000)	-	-	(3,000,000)
Total other financing sources (uses)	(3,000,000)	-	3,000,000	-
Excess (deficiency) of revenues over expenditures and other sources (uses)	(3,618,262)	(10,500)	2,868,478	(760,284)
Fund balances at beginning of year	4,650,335	721,625	7,548,465	12,920,425
Fund balances at end of year	$ 1,032,073	$ 711,125	$ 10,416,943	12,160,141

Exhibit 4-3—Maintenance and Operational Fund Budget

SAN CARLOS UNIFIED SCHOOL DISTRICT NO. 20

Maintenance and Operation Fund Budget

For Fiscal Year 1997-98 With Comparative Information for Years 1993-94 Through 1996-97

Fund Expenditures by Function

	1993-94 Actual	1994-95 Actual	1995-96 Actual	1996-97 Budget	1997-98 Budget
Revenues:					
Interest on investments	$ 2,264	$ -	$ 3,023	$ -	$ -
Intergovernmental grants and aid					
County	528,976	349,924	353,353	303,439	231,053
State	4,210,756	4,547,615	4,879,655	5,029,416	3,658,733
Federal	2,091,406	2,698,497	4,334,789	3,684,570	3,684,570
Other	1,435	1,608	3,707	-	-
Total revenues	6,834,837	7,597,644	9,574,527	9,017,425	7,574,356
Expenditures:					
Current:					
Administration	367,860	472,570	627,121	1,360,960	911,430
Instruction	3,717,933	3,511,792	3,979,602	4,019,378	4,245,995
Instruction support	777,669	826,680	1,042,709	952,702	1,150,372
Operation	1,020,984	1,044,435	1,231,844	1,260,261	1,437,356
Pupil transportation	376,892	373,942	445,058	418,913	447,465
Total expenditures	6,261,338	6,229,419	7,326,334	8,012,214	8,192,618
Excess (deficiency) of revenues over expenditures	573,499	1,368,225	2,248,193	1,005,211	(618,262)
Other financing sources (uses)					
Operating transfers out	-	(1,346,997)	(1,271,407)	(3,000,000)	(3,000,000)
Reversions	(81,632)	-	-	-	-
Total other financing sources (uses)	(81,632)	(1,346,997)	(1,271,407)	(3,000,000)	(3,000,000)
Excess (deficiency) of revenues over expenditures and other sources (uses)	491,867	21,228	976,786	(1,994,789)	(3,618,262)
Fund balances at beginning of year	1,356,296	1,940,654	1,951,989	2,297,953	4,650,335
Increase (decrease) in reserve for inventories	92,491	(9,893)	(16,315)	-	-
Fund balances at end of year	$ 1,940,654	$ 1,951,989	$ 2,912,460	$ 303,164	$ 1,032,073

Exhibit 4-4—Summary of All Budgets

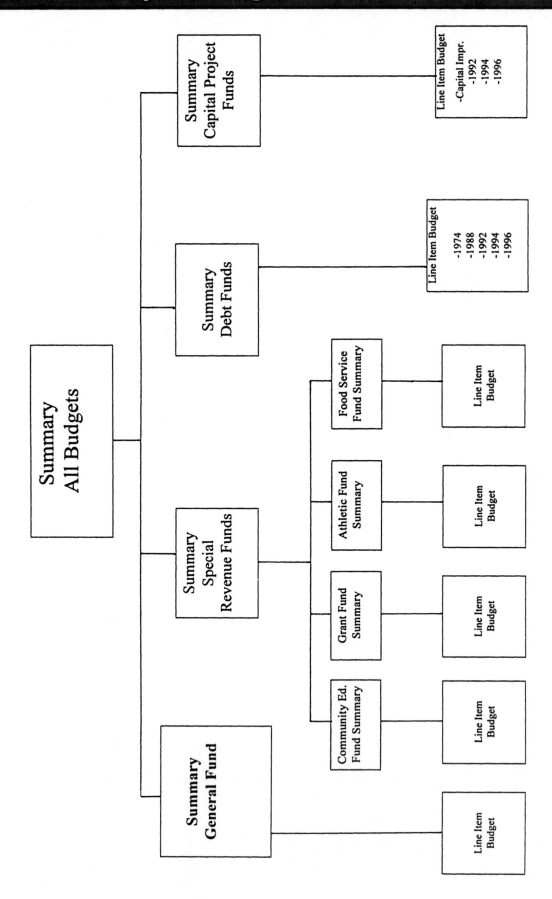

Exhibit 4-5—Summary Budget of All Funds

1997-98 Summary Budget
All Funds

	General Fund	Special Revenue Funds	Debt Funds	Capital Project Funds	Total
Revenues:					
Property taxes	$ 4,670,000	$ 0	$ 4,799,378	$	$ 9,469,378
Other local revenue	314,812	1,554,016	82,000	0	1,950,828
State of Michigan	26,426,498	113,664	0	0	26,540,162
Federal government	0	624,745	0	0	624,745
Other	385,888	59,211	0	0	445,099
Proceeds from long-term debt	0	0	0	0	0
Transfers from other funds	26,009	339,699	0	474,821	840,529
Total Revenues	$ 31,823,207	$ 2,691,335	$ 4,881,378	$ 474,821	$ 39,870,741
Expenditures:					
Salaries	$ 18,898,002	$ 1,480,100	$ 0	$ 0	$ 20,378,102
Employee benefits	6,952,438	444,837	0	0	7,397,275
Purchased services	1,592,830	157,965	0	0	1,750,795
Supplies, materials, other	2,280,747	521,168	0	0	2,801,915
Debt Service	385,053	0	5,014,246	0	5,399,299
Capital Outlay	646,369	14,492	0	1,974,821	2,635,682
Other expenditures	113,409	7,880	0	0	121,289
Transfer to other funds	774,253	47,725	0	0	821,978
Total Expenditures	$ 31,643,101	$ 2,674,167	$ 5,014,246	$ 1,974,821	$ 41,306,335
Excess of revenues and other sources (uses) over expenditures:	$ 180,106	$ 17,168	$ (132,868)	$ (1,500,000)	$ (1,435,594)
Fund Balance July 1	$ 1,752,038	$ 6,526	$ 483,865	$ 2,167,300	$ 4,409,729
Fund Balance - June 30	$ 1,932,144	$ 23,694	$ 350,997	$ 667,300	$ 2,974,135

Exhibit 4-6—Summary All Government and Proprietary Funds

MSD of Washington Township, Indianapolis, Indiana
Summary All Governmental and Proprietary Funds
1998 Annual Budget

	Total All Funds	Governmental Funds[1]					Proprietary Funds			
		General Fund	Debt Service Fund	Capital Projects Fund	Transportation Fund	Special Education Preschool Fund	School Lunch Fund	Textbook Rental Fund	J. Everett Light Vocational Fund	Educational Fees Fund
Total Revenue	$ 81,957,688	$ 52,802,239	$ 2,839,909	$ 15,811,320	$ 5,409,798	$ 287,422	$ 2,350,000	$ 610,000	$ 1,666,000	$ 175,000
Total Expenditures	81,426,647	53,629,948	2,860,157	13,911,320	5,737,293	285,179	2,404,000	650,000	1,766,500	176,250
Excess (deficiency) of revenues over expenditures	531,041	(827,709)	(20,248)	1,900,000	(327,495)	2,243	(54,000)	(40,000)	(100,500)	(1,250)
Budgetary Reconciliation[2]	934,434	934,434	-	-	-	-	-	-	-	-
Net Interfund Transfers In(out)	23,000	-	-	-	-	-	-	30,000	-	(7,000)
Fund Balance, January 1, 1998	5,460,657	3,113,963	21,009	339,300	680,569	(1,316)	350,375	(216,640)	1,069,137	104,260
Fund Balance, December 31, 1998	$ 6,949,132	$ 3,220,688	$ 761	$ 2,239,300	$ 353,074	$ 927	$ 296,375	$ (226,640)	$ 968,637	$ 96,010

[1] Source: State Board of Accounts, School Budget Forms 1, 1-S, 2 & 3.

[2] Refer to page 29 in the Financial Section for a detailed explanation.

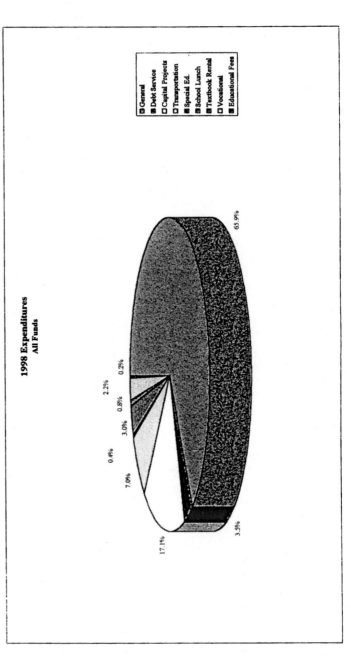

1998 Expenditures
All Funds

Legend:
- General
- Debt Service
- Capital Projects
- Transportation
- Special Ed.
- School Lunch
- Textbook Rental
- Vocational
- Educational Fees

65.9% 3.5% 0.2% 2.2% 0.8% 3.0% 0.4% 7.0% 17.1%

Exhibit 4-7—Sumary of Governmental Fund Budgets

MSD of Washington Township, Indianapolis, Indiana
Summary of Governmental Fund Budgets[1]
1998 Annual Budget

	Total all Governmental Funds	General Fund	Debt Service Fund	Capital Projects Fund[2]	Transportation Fund	Special Education Pre-School Fund
Revenues						
Property Taxes	$ 45,560,947	$ 26,205,969	$ 2,492,909	$ 12,105,791	$ 4,596,134	$ 160,144
Other Local Taxes	6,507,578	3,685,407	347,000	1,811,529	648,000	15,642
State and Federal	21,225,663	20,948,363			165,664	111,636
Interest on Investments	850,000	850,000				
Tuition and Fees	730,000	730,000				
Other	2,282,500	382,500		1,900,000		
Total Revenue	77,156,688	52,802,239	2,839,909	15,817,320	5,409,798	287,422
Expenditures						
Instruction	$ 32,096,035	$ 31,820,856				$ 275,179
Support Services						
Pupils	1,566,845	1,566,845				
Instruction Staff	1,452,844	1,452,844				
General Administration	622,311	622,311				
School Administration	3,110,274	3,110,274				
Business	24,254,496	5,294,949		13,659,820	5,299,727	
Central	9,286,435	8,581,369		257,500	437,566	
Total Support Services	40,293,205	20,628,592		13,917,320	5,737,293	
Community Services	142,000	142,000				
Nonprogrammed Charges	1,038,500	1,038,500				
Debt Service	2,860,157		2,860,157			
Total Expenditures	$ 76,429,897	$ 53,629,948	$ 2,860,157	$ 13,917,320	$ 5,737,293	$ 285,179
Excess (deficiency) of revenues over expenditures	$ 726,791	$ (827,709)	$ (20,248)	$ 1,900,000	$ (327,495)	$ 2,243
Budgetary Reconciliation[2]	934,434	934,434	-	-	-	-
Fund Balance, January 1, 1998	4,153,525	3,113,963	21,009	339,300	680,569	(1,316)
Fund Balance, December 31, 1998	$ 5,814,750	$ 3,220,688	$ 761	$ 2,239,300	$ 353,074	$ 927

[1] Source: State Board of Accounts School Budget Forms 1, 1-S, 2 & 3.
[2] Refer to page 29 in the Financial Section for a detailed explanation.

Exhibit 4-8—The General Budget

MSD of Washington Township, Indianapolis, Indiana
The General Fund
1998 Annual Budget

"1998 Expenditures include the school district's operating balance."

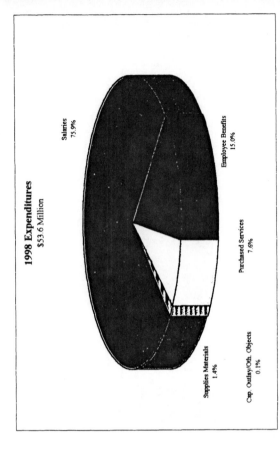

1998 Expenditures
$53.6 Million

Salaries
75.9%

Employee Benefits
15.0%

Purchased Services
7.6%

Supplies Materials
1.4%

Cap. Outlay/Oth. Objects
0.1%

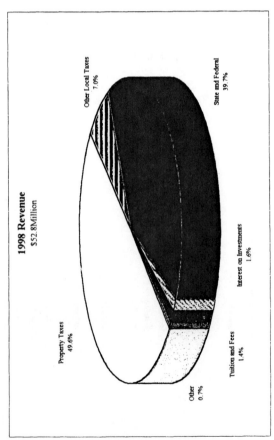

1998 Revenue
$52.8Million

Other Local Taxes
7.0%

State and Federal
39.7%

Interest on Investments
1.6%

Tuition and Fees
1.4%

Other
0.7%

Property Taxes
49.6%

Exhibit 4-9—Budgets by Program, Location, and/or Administrative Unit

ALPINE SCHOOL DISTRICT
TRADES AND INDUSTRY
PROGRAM 6600-6800
DIRECTOR: Clay Christensen

	1994-95 Final	1995-96 Final	1996-97 Original Budget	1996-97 Estimated Final	1997-98 Budget
REVENUES					
Local Revenue	980,240	1,181,707	937,334	903,934	1,056,070
Miscellenous Revenue	0	0	0	0	0
Vocational & Tech Ed.	785,592	571,932	1,012,995	1,267,594	1,145,935
Retirement and Social Security	237,684	265,396	306,381	319,444	339,845
Federal Revenue	0	13,691	0	0	0
Total Revenues	2,003,516	2,032,726	2,256,710	2,490,972	2,541,850
EXPENDITURES					
Certified Teacher Salary	1,074,155	1,203,763	1,312,334	1,368,786	1,457,091
Substitute teacher	0	0	0	0	0
Hourly Certified Salary	8,576	4,413	11,700	11,700	11,700
State Retirement	155,707	174,414	205,092	213,837	230,013
Social Security	81,976	90,982	101,289	105,607	112,362
Industrial Insurance	4,224	4,711	5,164	5,384	4,408
Health & Accident Insurance	118,086	120,077	133,348	146,798	162,246
Disability Insurance	4,070	4,671	5,001	5,436	5,601
Inservice Training	13,691	0	0	0	0
Community College Registration	129,350	103,099	99,300	110,000	110,000
Mileage - Travel	203	578	550	550	550
Materials and Supplies	62,172	60,461	58,405	72,469	72,469
Special Supply Account	0	376	2,148	500	500
Equipment	274,231	185,061	212,459	328,623	296,623
Built Portable/Home	0	11,250	9,000	9,000	9,000
Indirect Charges	77,075	68,873	100,920	112,282	69,287
Total Expenditures	2,003,516	2,032,729	2,256,710	2,490,972	2,541,850
ALLOCATED FTE					
Certified Teacher Salary	24.66	28.24	30.24	32.47	33.47

PROGRAM DESCRIPTION AND GOALS

A clustering of courses which prepare students for a variety of careers in the Trades and Industrial areas. Students may prepare to enter careers in such areas as manufacturing, construction, transportation, power and energy, or or in such trades as computer programming, personal services, building trades, sheet metal, cabinetry, commercial art/photography, etc. They may also prepare for post high school training in such areas as technicians in areas such as Automotive/Diesel, Electronics, Heating/Refrigeration, Industrial Maintenance, Collision Repair, Drafting/CAD, Machine, Tool/CNC, Metal Fabrication, Composites, etc. Courses may include, but are are not limited to: Construction, Manufacturing/Materials Processing, Drafting Tech and CAD, Graphic Arts, Communications, Woodworking Tech, Cabinet/Millwork, Automotive Technician, Principles of Technology, Occupational Computer Programming, Cosmetology/Barbering, Carpentry, Electronics Technician, Heating/Air Conditioning/Refrigeration, Heavy Duty Mechanics/Diesel, Automotive Body/Painting Technician, Television Equipment Operations, Graphics/Printing Communications, Commercial Art, Commercial Photography, Machine Tool/CNC, Welding Processes, and Industrial Plastics.

Exhibit 4-10—Budgets by Program, Location, and/or Administrative Unit

BROWARD COUNTY PUBLIC SCHOOLS
ANNUAL BUDGET 1997-98

SCHOOL: W. C. YOUNG COMMUNITY   **AREA: SOUTH**   **LOCATION: 3001**

STAFF

POSITIONS	1996-97	1997-98	INCR/(DECR)	POSITIONS	1996-97	1997-98	INCR/(DECR)
INSTRUCTIONAL PERSONNEL:				INSTRUCTIONAL SUPPORT PERSONNEL:			
Basic K-12				Basic K-12			
At Risk				At Risk			
Exceptional				Exceptional			
Voc Ed - 7-12				Adult		1.40	1.40
Adult	5.80	4.30	(1.50)	Other			
Other				TOTAL		1.40	1.40
TOTAL	5.80	4.30	(1.50)				
				SCHOOL SUPPORT PERSONNEL:			
ADMINISTRATIVE PERSONNEL:				Clerical (Incl. Confidential)	2.00	2.60	0.60
Principal				Media Clerk			
Asst Principal	1.10	1.10		Head/Asst Fac Service			
TOTAL	1.10	1.10		Facilities Service/Fac Aide	1.30	2.40	1.10
				Yardperson			
INSTRUCTIONAL SPECIALISTS:				Security Specialist/Monitor		0.50	0.50
Media Spec/Libr.				Other			
Couns/Director				TOTAL	3.30	5.50	2.20
ESE Specialist							
Other							
TOTAL				GRAND TOTAL STAFF	10.20	12.30	2.10

REVENUE

INSTRUCTIONAL ALLOCATION	UNWTD FTE	WTD FTE	REVENUE	* CATEGORICAL ALLOCATION BREAKDOWN	REVENUE
Basic K-12				Accountability	
At Risk				Advanced Academic	
Exceptional				Custodial Allocation	31,352
Voc Ed - 7-12				DOP Local Adjustment	
Adult	341.89	271.52	304,373	ESE Matrix Adjustment	
TOTAL	341.89	271.52	304,373	ESE Specialist Allocation	
				Instructional Allocation Adjustment	
				Instructional Materials	
SUPPORT ALLOCATION			182,388	Instructional Staff Training	543
				Magnet	
CATEGORICAL ALLOCATION *			57,620	Rotating 7th Period	
				Other	25,725
TOTAL REVENUE			544,381	TOTAL CATEGORICAL ALLOCATION	57,620

APPROPRIATIONS

ACCOUNT TITLE	FUNCTION	1996-97	1997-98	INCR/(DECR)	APPROPRIATION PER FTE
INSTRUCTIONAL					
Basic Education (K-12)	5100				
Exceptional Education	5200				
Vocational Education	5300	38,794	44,029	5,235	162.16
Adult General Education	5400	236,707	208,173	(28,534)	766.69
Other Instructional	5000	58,750	28,437	(30,313)	104.73
TOTAL INSTRUCTIONAL		334,251	280,639	(53,612)	1,033.58
Pupil Personnel	6100	31,128	29,330	(1,798)	108.02
Media Services	6200				
Curriculum Development	6300				
Instructional Staff Training	6400	6,860	543	(6,317)	2.00
School Administration	7300	196,226	130,652	(65,574)	481.19
Facilities Acquisition & Construction	7400	2,824		(2,824)	
Central Services	7700				
Pupil Transportation	7800				
Operations of Plant	7900	55,868	91,187	35,319	335.84
Maintenance of Plant	8100				
Community Services	9100	17,697	12,030	(5,667)	44.31
Transfers	9700				
TOTAL APPROPRIATIONS		644,854	544,381	(100,473)	2,004.94

Exhibit 4-11—Budgets by Program, Location, and/or Administrative Unit

BROWARD COUNTY PUBLIC SCHOOLS
ANNUAL BUDGET 1997-1998

DEPARTMENT: SUPERINTENDENT OF SCHOOLS **LOCATION: 9511**

POSITIONS AND SALARY

Job Class	Days	Position Title	Function	1996-97 Positions	1997-98 Positions	Salary	Fringe Benefits
100229	244	Clerk Specialist A (Conf)	7200	2.0	2.0	$57,185	$20,612
100864	244	Executive Secretary - Supt	7200	3.0	3.0	132,043	43,872
100866	244	Department Secretary (Conf)	7200	1.0	1.0	33,846	11,777
840602	244	Executive Asst - Board Liaison	7200	1.0	1.0	106,174	32,029
841071	244	Superintendent	7200	1.0	1.0	167,948	49,325
		SUB - TOTAL		8.0	8.0	$497,196	$157,615
		OTHER SALARIES	7200			36,200	10,136
		OVERTIME	7200			75,000	21,000
		PARTTIME	7200			0	0
		SUBSTITUTES	7200			0	0
		TOTAL		8.0	8.0	$608,396	$188,751

DEPARTMENT SUMMARY

Object Number	Object Title	Function	1995-96 Actual	1996-97 Budget	1997-98 Budget	Increase/ (Decrease)
100	Salaries		$686,440	$608,396	$608,396	$0
200	Employee Benefits		215,181	188,751	188,751	0
	Total Salaries and Benefits		901,621	797,147	797,147	0
311	Attorney Fees	7200	0	10,000	10,000	0
312	Consultant & Professional/Technical	7200	4,450	6,468	6,468	0
314	Other Personal Services	7200	0	1,500	1,500	0
332	Travel In-County	7200	268	900	900	0
333	Travel Out-of-County	7200	3,373	15,196	15,196	0
351	Repairs & Maintenance	7200	611	1,000	1,000	0
362	Equipment Rental	7200	15,751	24,500	24,500	0
364	Facility Rental - Noninstructional	7200	0	8,028	8,028	0
371	Postage & Freight	7200	193	550	550	0
372	Communications (Telephone)	7200	4,144	3,500	3,500	0
382	Water & Sewer	7200	228	500	500	0
391	Advertising	7200	500	0	0	0
395	Printing	7200	9,356	29,240	29,240	0
399	Other Purchased Services	7200	45,230	14,000	14,000	0
511	Supplies	7200	19,155	8,300	8,300	0
514	Professional Books	7200	230	50	50	0
531	Periodicals	7200	1,060	2,000	2,000	0
641	Furn, Fixtures & Equip more than $500	7200	0	6,000	6,000	0
642	Furn, Fixtures & Equip less than $500	7200	469	1,500	1,500	0
692	Computer Software less than $500	7200	478	1,000	1,000	0
733	Professional Dues & Registration Fees	7200	24,781	44,130	44,130	0
794	Miscellaneous Broward Ctr	7200/62007	4,427	5,000	5,000	0
	Total Non-salary		134,704	183,362	183,362	0
	Department Total		$1,036,325	$980,509	$980,509	$0

L~11

Exhibit 4-12—Budgets by Program, Location, and/or Administrative Unit

BROWARD COUNTY PUBLIC SCHOOLS
ANNUAL BUDGET 1997-1998
Overview of Department Budgets

Division Summary	1996-1997 Current Budget			1997-1998 Tentative Budget			Increase/ (Decrease)
	Salary & Fringe	Non-salary Items	Total Budget	Salary & Fringe	Non-salary Items	Total Budget	
BOARD	$1,179,236	$617,544	$1,796,780	$1,179,236	$617,544	$1,796,780	$0
SUPERINTENDENT	2,826,850	422,539	3,249,389	2,735,409	422,539	3,157,948	(91,441)
SCHOOL OPERATIONS	17,341,343	4,342,629	21,683,972	17,285,218	4,342,629	21,627,847	(56,125)
EDUCATIONAL PROG	19,099,162	4,204,268	23,303,430	18,946,392	4,234,685	23,181,077	(122,353)
ACCOUNTABILITY	10,195,042	4,677,930	14,872,972	10,191,298	4,228,453	14,419,751	(453,221)
FINANCIAL MGMT	74,807,631	18,338,753	93,146,384	54,579,265	38,969,549	93,548,814	402,430
DISTRICT ADMIN	11,276,447	11,282,612	22,559,059	11,400,884	11,230,082	22,630,966	71,907
FACILITIES AND CNSTR	2,471,867	4,300,801	6,772,668	2,477,203	4,300,801	6,778,004	5,336
	$139,197,578	$48,187,076	$187,384,654	$118,794,905	$68,346,282	$187,141,187	($243,467)

Inclusion of Capital Budgets and a List of Major Capital Projects

(Criterion D-4)

Description of Capital Spending Impact on the Operation Budget

(Criterion D-5)

Exhibit 4-13

Exhibit 4-14

Exhibit 4-13—Capital Budget

SALT LAKE CITY SCHOOL DISTRICT
Capital Bond Fund
For Fiscal Year 1998-99 With Comparative Information for Years 1994-95 Through 1997-98
Capital Bond Fund Projects

	Total Project	Prior Expenditures	1994-95 Actual	1995-96 Actual	1996-97 Actual	1997-98 Revised Budget	1998-99 Budget
Bond Sale Expenditures	$ 126,759	$ 40,061	$ 42,116	$ 44,582	$ 0	$ 0	$ 0
East High Track & Stadium	4,186,274	2,169,983	1,780,247	236,044	0	0	0
East High School	35,281,836	3,423,199	14,700,299	11,085,540	4,829,044	1,243,754	0
Highland High School	17,125,437	191,749	2,363,779	8,433,704	5,723,031	413,174	0
Horizonte	10,513,243	1,738,299	6,879,992	1,809,973	84,979	0	0
Horace Mann Demolition	531,600	0	0	0	0	531,600	0
Portables	678,015	450,900	0	227,115	0	0	0
West High School	23,273,719	240,847	2,536,564	7,706,739	9,926,648	2,862,921	0
Total	$ 91,716,883	$ 8,255,038	$ 28,302,997	$ 29,543,697	$ 20,563,702	$ 5,051,449	$ 0

Contributions from the community were collected for the following projects which are included in the above totals.

East High Track & Stadium	$ 214,858
West Field House Statues	2,200

Exhibit 4-14—Capital Budget

Capital Projects Summary

Project: Reroofing

Description:

The planned upgrading of roofs at rotating sites helps the district maintain its school buildings at a level cost. This eliminates many would-be emergency repairs which would arise if the buildings were not on a routine roofing replacement schedule.

Operating Budget Impact: Roofing emergency repair costs will be maintained at a lower level.

Project Costs	Actual 1992-93	Budget 1993-94	Budget 1994-95
Sites			132,000
Buildings	192,000		3,654,000
Equipment			
Bond Issuance			47,668
Total	$192,000		$3,833,668

Project: Handicapped/Life Safety

Description:

This includes the upgrading for alarm systems, replacing and expanding cushioning under playground equipment, and making classroom and building space increasingly accessible to handicapped individuals.

Operating Budget Impact: Increased safety lessons the district's liablity in case of accidents. Improving handicapped facilities ensures that the district will continue to benefit from state and federal funds which require handicapped facilities be in place for students and faculty who have a need.

Project Costs	Actual 1992-93	Budget 1993-94	Budget 1994-95
Sites	26,695	20,000	
Buildings		180,000	1,509,000
Equipment	5,547		
Bond Issuance			18,999
Total	$32,242	$200,000	$1,527,999

Project: Manitou Elementary School

Description:

In the 1983 facilities inventory, Manitou Elementary School was described as "unsafe and unhealthy", and located on too small of a site. The district purchased a new site and replaced the entire school with an expanded building to accomodate growing enrollment.

Operating Budget Impact: The new school is energy efficient which will reduce utility costs. All fixtures and furnishings are new which will keep repair and maintence costs at a minimum for the next few years.

Project Costs	Actual 1992-93	Budget 1993-94	Budget 1994-95
Sites	356,443		
Buildings	1,199,816	4,900,000	1,000,000
Equipment			250,000
Bond Issuance			9,443
Total	$1,556,259	$4,900,000	$1,259,443

Current Debt, Legal Debt Limits and Effect on Current/Future Budgets

(Criterion D-6)

Exhibit 4-15

Exhibit 4-16

Exhibit 4-15—Current Debt, Legal Debt Limits and Effect

The District's Current Debt Obligations

On May 15, 1990, the district entered into an agreement with Salt Lake City Corporation for the payment of a share of the City's debt financing of the Steiner Aquatic Center. In consideration of this agreement, the district's swimming teams have priority use of the aquatic center and the rate paid by the district for the use of the center is discounted 50%. The agreement requires the district to pay the City an annual installment equal to 60/157 of the City's debt service on lease revenue bonds issued by the City's Building Authority. The Steiner Aquatic Center is owned and operated by the City, and the district has no obligation other than as described herein.

The debt service requirements of this contract with the City to maturity, including interest are as follows:

Year Ending June 30	Principal	Interest	Total
1999	78,339	6,234	84,573
2000	76,908	3,089	79,997
	$ 155,247	$ 9,323	$ 164,570

The annual contract payments will be funded by the recreation program as a part of the Special Programs Fund Budget.

At an election held on November 2, 1993, the citizens of Salt Lake City approved a proposition authorizing the district to issue and sell General Obligation Bonds in the amount of not more than $70 million dollars. The proposition was approved by 80.43% of those voting in the election (an approval ratio of 4.1 to 1). Pursuant to that authorization, the district has sold $10 million in General Obligation Bonds dated February 1, 1994, $15 million dated January 15, 1995, and an additional $15 million dated January 15, 1996, for a total of $40 million. On December 1, 1997, $8,550,000 of the 1995 bonds were refunded by issuing $9,305,000 series 1997 bonds. The district plans to issue another $10 million in bonds in fiscal year 1998-99.

The district's current unused legal debt capacity is $517,244,375. The general obligation bonded debt of the district is limited by Utah law to 4% of the fair market value of the total taxable property in the district. For tax purposes primary residential property is assessed at 55% of its fair market value. All other taxable property is assessed at 100% of its fair market value. The following is the amortization schedule for these bond issues showing the debt service to be paid in the 1998-99 budget and future years on bonds currently outstanding and those planned to be issued during fiscal year 1998-99.

Exhibit 4-16—Current Debt, Legal Debt Limits and Effect

SALT LAKE CITY SCHOOL DISTRICT
Bonded Debt Amortization Schedule
General Obligation School Building Bonds

Year Ending June 30	Series 1994 $10,000,000 Principal	Interest	Series 1995A $15,000,000 Principal	Interest	Series 1996A $15,000,000 Principal	Interest	Series 1997 $9,305,000 Principal	Interest	Proposed Series 1998 (3) $10,000,000 Principal	Interest	Grand Totals Total Principal	Total Interest	Total Debt Service
1999	$ 410,000	$ 394,805	$ 595,000	$ 263,873	$ 975,000	$ 545,870	$ 55,000	$ 432,672	$ 885,000	$ 359,199	$ 2,920,000	$ 1,996,419	$ 4,916,419
2000	425,000	379,430	625,000	231,743	1,025,000	502,970	60,000	430,527	675,000	425,833	2,810,000	1,970,503	4,780,503
2001	445,000	362,430	660,000	199,243	1,070,000	457,870	60,000	428,127	365,000	392,082	2,600,000	1,839,752	4,439,752
2002	460,000	344,185	695,000	164,593	1,115,000	410,790	65,000	425,667	385,000	373,833	2,720,000	1,719,068	4,439,068
2003	485,000	324,865	730,000	127,410	1,160,000	360,615	65,000	422,938	405,000	354,582	2,845,000	1,590,410	4,435,410
2004	505,000	304,010	770,000	87,990	1,215,000	308,415	70,000	420,175	420,000	337,977	2,980,000	1,458,567	4,438,567
2005	530,000	281,790	815,000	45,640	1,270,000	253,740	70,000	417,165	440,000	320,548	3,125,000	1,318,883	4,443,883
2006	555,000	257,940	0 (1)		1,330,000	196,590	935,000	414,120	460,000	301,847	3,280,000	1,170,497	4,450,497
2007	580,000	232,410	0 (1)		1,390,000	135,410	985,000	372,980	475,000	282,068	3,430,000	1,022,868	4,452,868
2008	605,000	205,150	0 (1)		1,460,000	70,080	1,025,000	329,148	500,000	261,167	3,590,000	865,545	4,455,545
2009	640,000	176,110	0 (1)				1,075,000	282,510	920,000	238,918	2,635,000	697,538	3,332,538
2010	670,000	144,750	0 (1)				1,125,000	232,523	955,000	197,057	2,750,000	574,330	3,324,330
2011	705,000	111,250	0 (1)				1,180,000	179,648	1,000,000	152,172	2,885,000	443,070	3,328,070
2012	740,000	76,000	0 (1)				1,235,000	123,598	1,040,000	104,172	3,015,000	303,770	3,318,770
2013	780,000	39,000	0 (1)				1,300,000	63,700	1,075,000	53,212	3,155,000	155,912	3,310,912
Totals	$ 8,535,000	$ 3,634,125	$ 4,890,000	$ 1,120,492	$ 12,010,000	$ 3,242,350	$ 9,305,000	$ 4,975,498	$ 10,000,000	$ 4,154,667	$ 44,740,000	$ 17,127,132	$ 61,867,132

(1) The principal and interest due in fiscal 2006 through 2013 on the series 1995A bonds were refunded resulting in the defeasance of the old debt and substitution of the "Refunding Bonds" series of 1997.

(2) There is an annual Paying Agent fee of $250.00 that must be added to the debt service listed for the Series 1997 and another $250.00 for the 1998 Bonds.

(3) The district plans to issue another $10,000,000 in Bonds early in the 1998-99 fiscal year.

CHAPTER 5
Informational Section

The last section of a school budget contains information on past and future budgets as well as factors that influence the proposed budget. The Informational Section of the document puts the proposed budget into context and it explains past budget decisions. The data in the Informational Section also helps reveal the impact of past and current decisions on future budgets and budget results should current trends continue beyond the budget year. It is therefore designed to give both an historical as well as a future perspective to the proposed budget. This section helps users of the budget document to better understand the past and future directions of the school entity.

CONTENTS

At a minimum, the MBA criteria require the following information in this section of the budget:

1. Revenue Sources, Assumptions and Trends (Criterion E-1)
2. Values of Taxable Properties (Criterion E-2)
3. Property Tax Rates and Collections (Criterion E-3)
4. Analysis of Tax Burden (Criterion E-4)
5. Comparison of Revenues and Expenditures (Criterion E-5)
6. Budget Forecasts (Criterion E-6)
7. Student Enrollment History and Forecasts (Criterion E-7)
8. Personnel Resource Allocations (Criterion E-8)
9. Bond Amortization Schedules (Criterion E-9)
10. Performance Measurements (Criterion E-10)
11. Other Useful Information (Criterion E-11)
12. A Glossary of Terms (Criterion E-12)

The criteria in the Informational Section specify the years to be covered by this data but do not prescribe a particular format for presenting this information.

Revenue Sources, Assumptions and Trends (Criterion E-1)

There are two critical procedures to the understanding of changes and trends in budget revenue estimates. The first procedure is to make comparisons to explain the causes of the changes from one year to the next or a future year to the next future year. This kind of analysis is known as baseline budget analysis. This technique uses the current year budget or estimated current year actual (or any other base year) as a benchmark or baseline against which to measure, explain, and evaluate changes in the budget proposed for the next year (or a future year). Conceptually, all changes between the baseline budget and the proposed budget can be categorized by changes due to workload, price, and program standards. The general approach with this kind of analysis is to explain the change due to one factor with the other two factors held constant. This analysis helps to deductively reveal underlying assumptions.

While baseline budget analysis is one way to help deduce the critical presumptions about future trends on which revenue estimates are based, it is equally important to explicitly disclose revenue estimate assumptions. Disclosure of the assumptions is essential to evaluating the credibility of the budget forecasts. In order to present understandable information on revenue sources, underlying assumptions, and significant revenue trends, it might be necessary to briefly explain the structure or system of local, state or federal funding.

Exhibit 5-1 provides a separate narrative presentation of the revenue and expenditure assumptions on which projections and forecasts are based. While not explicitly identified, many of the factors and assumptions can be classified into workload (student enrollment), price (employee compensation), or program standard (class size) changes whose impact is reflected in the budget forecasts. The narrative also explains future changes in the projected sources and uses of funds based on assumptions about the capital budget for technology and for the strategic plan. Exhibits 5-2 and 5-3 are examples that present the assumptions on the same page as the revenue and expenditure projections. Exhibit 5-2 is interesting in that it presents the projected growth rate (a critical assumption) next to the revenue and expenditure data. These two examples both provide some brief explanation of state sources of revenue to help explain the revenue forecast.

REAL ESTATE PROPERTY TAX INFORMATION

The single largest local source of revenue for most school districts is the property tax. It is therefore not surprising that the MBA criteria require considerable information on the property tax in school budget documents. If a school entity does not levy property taxes, these particular criteria do not apply and the entity should indicate such in a cover letter accompanying its application (See Chapter 1, Background and General Requirements). Criteria 2, 3 and 4 of the Informational Section deal with the property tax base, rates and collections as well as its impact on taxpayers. Specifically, a minimum of three years of actual, current year budget and/or estimated current year actual, and the proposed budget year are required for the following data:

■ Values (assessed and market) of taxable property (Criterion E-2)
■ Property tax rates and collections (Criterion E-3)
■ Analysis of tax burden (Criterion E-4)

The above data can be shown separately or consolidated into one or more tables. For purposes of illustration, most of the examples present information discretely.

Values of Taxable Property (Criterion E-2)

Since real estate taxes are, in most cases, the largest source of local funding in most school entities, data about the tax base is very significant. It is therefore important to understand the stability of the revenue source for the school entity. The stability of a revenue source is the degree to which the yield will change with regard to economic cycles as well as with regard to local economic factors. One approach to evaluate the stability of the revenue source is to examine information about the past history of the tax base. Historical experience is useful in the projection of revenue sources provided there are no anticipated changes in the trend factors.

Another way to evaluate the stability of the revenue source is to assess the natural growth in the tax base. The

relationship between the assessed value on which taxes are levied and the market value is important to this understanding. This criterion therefore requires both the presentation of assessed value as well as market value for a minimum of three years actual, the current year budget and/or estimated current year actual and the proposed budget year.

Exhibits 5-4 and 5-5 both exceed the requirements of the criterion with the presentation of ten or more years of information on both the assessed and market values. Both exhibits provide a useful calculation of the percentage change in the assessed value from year to year as well as a calculation of the ratio between the assessed and market values for each year. Exhibit 5-5 also provides a further breakdown of the assessed valuation by the two municipal governments that are within the boundaries of the school entity along with a chart that graphs the gross value of a mill of real estate taxes over the years of the presentation.

Property Tax Rates and Collections (Criterion (E-3)

Another measure of a revenue source is productive yield. This is a measure of the amount of revenues that a tax will yield. Gross yield is equal to the tax rate times the tax base. Net yield of a tax source, or the amount of revenue that the tax source actually will generate, reflects additions and reductions to the gross yield. For the real estate property tax, the net yield is a function of the gross yield less discounts and uncollected (liened) taxes plus penalties.

To evaluate the productive yield of the real estate tax, the Informational Section requires the presentation of information about property tax rates and collections for a minimum of three years actual, the current year budget and/or estimated current year actual and the proposed budget year. The presentation must also indicate if the tax rate is a rate per $100 of taxable value or on some other basis.

Both Exhibits 5-6 and 5-7 exceed the requirements for the presentation of tax rates and collections for the required number of years. Both presentations state the basis of the tax rate and provide very useful information to help evaluate the productive yield of the tax source. Such useful information includes the gross yield (total tax levy or taxes assessed) as well as the net yield (productive yield), which is stated in terms of actual tax collections. In addition, the presentations set forth a calculation of the percentage of taxes collected which is in effect the productive yield percentage. Exhibit 5-7 provides a more detailed presentation of the tax rates along with charts that help with the understanding of the information.

Analysis of Tax Burden (Criterion E-4)

The final element of real estate property information is the impact of the tax source on citizens in the community. This information translates the economic impact of this tax source of the budget on the residents of the school atity. It is frequently referred to as the "tax burden on citizens." The presentation must include a minimum of three years actual, the current year budget and/or estimated current year actual and the proposed budget year.

There are many ways to present the tax burden, none of which may actually calculate the tax impact on a specific taxpayer in the community. The school entity must therefore develop a meaningful presentation that fairly presents the tax consequences to the typical, median or average taxpayer.

Exhibit 5-8 presents the tax burden in terms of the actual numbers for a 2400 square foot home with three bedrooms in a specific subdivision, which is presumably typical of the dwellings in the community. The information is presented with such information as the market value, assessment ratio, assessed value, the tax rate with the basis denoted, and the actual tax levy. Exhibit 5-9 and 5-10 present much the same information based on the average market value of a home in the community that has escalated over time while Exhibit 5-11 presents the tax burden based on a fixed market value for a property. All of the exhibits communicate the tax burden information with the effective use of charts or graphs.

Comparison of Revenues and Expenditures (Criterion E-5)

At a minimum, the budget must include a five-year comparative history for all governmental funds. A schedule or schedule(s) of revenues and expenditures for three prior years actual, the current year budget and/or estimated current year actual and proposed budget year should be included. This comparison may be made either in the Informational Section or in the Financial Section of the document. If the three years actual data is presented in the Financial Section, it does not need to be repeated in the Information Section. However, if the three prior years actual data is presented in the Information Section, it must be in a format that is comparable to the data presented for the current year and the proposed budget year in the Financial Section. Presentation of similar data for other funds is optional.

There are a number of ways of satisfying this criterion. The school entity in Exhibit 5-12 chose to present separate schedules for revenues and expenditures in addition to separate schedules for each governmental fund. Shown in this example is the five-year history of revenues and expenditures by function and object for the General Fund on separate schedules. Splitting this data into separate schedules allows the entity to present budget history information in greater detail.

Exhibit 5-13 presents the revenue and expenditure summary data in a single schedule for the Maintenance and Operation fund. The presentation also includes the average annual percentage growth in specified sources and uses of funds. Exhibit 5-14 presents the required information

for the five years along with the percentage changes from year to year as well as the average percentage change. Finally, Exhibit 5-15 provides the historical information with annual and average annual percentage changes in revenue and expenditure classifications along with a graph of data that displays total revenues and expenditures. The graph adds to the understanding of the data with the labeling of annual percentage change information for both total revenues and total expenditures. All of the exhibits include beginning and ending fund balance information.

Budget Forecasts (Criterion E-6)

Budget forecasts can help decision-makers assess the fiscal consequences of budget proposals. Sometimes the full effect of current budgetary decisions is not realized until future years. For example, a proposal to create a new program after the start of the fiscal year will not include an entire year of costs in the proposed budget. A forecast of subsequent budget years would show the full impact of such budgetary actions. Budget forecasts can also measure the impact of countervailing factors. For example, if a major revenue base is shrinking while a major spending item is growing, a budget forecast may help identify when future budget gaps will occur. The budget forecast will also reveal the financial consequences on future year budgets of the use of non-recurring revenues to fund recurring expenditures.

The MBA criteria require a presentation of three years of budget forecasts beyond the proposed budget year. These forecasts should include beginning and ending fund balances, and revenue and expenditures for all governmental funds. Exhibit 5-16 offers an example of one way to present these budget forecasts. Data is presented for major revenue sources and major objects of expenditures in the district's general fund for three subsequent budget years. Separate schedules are provided for the other governmental funds.

In another example, the school entity presented the projections that met the criterion supplemented with a schedule of incremental revenue and expenditure changes. This augmentation, set forth in Exhibit 5-17, is of interest since the projections reflect the impact of new resource requirements for such things as state mandates and the strategic plan of the school entity. The example is also of interest in that it provides the percentage of total resources available that would be consumed by new recurring resource demands.

Exhibit 5-18 is an example that also exceeds the forecast criterion with the calculation of projected annual percentage change for each of the revenue and expenditure classifications. Finally Exhibit 5-19 illustrates a presentation that includes historical, budget, and projected revenue and expenditure data on a single schedule. The schedule is followed in the budget document with a table that graphs total revenues, total expenditures, revenues over expenditures, and cumulative fund balance for each year. The chart provides major assumptions on which the estimates are based. Exhibit 5-19 from the same school entity also includes an example of the presentation of revenue and expenditure estimates for a capital projects fund that is supported with a schedule of planned projects for each school building.

Student Enrollment History and Forecasts (Criterion E-7)

The single greatest determinant of resource needs for any school is the size of its student enrollment. Spending on personal services, materials and supplies, and capital infrastructure is often derived directly or indirectly from student populations. In many cases, student enrollment levels are also used to calculate intergovernmental aid to school districts.

Because of its importance to budget development and budget forecasts, the MBA criteria require a narrative discussion of the forecasting methodology and techniques used to project student enrollments in addition to the presentation of enrollment data. The required data includes a minimum of three years of actual student enrollment history, the current budget and/or estimated current year enrollment, the proposed budget year enrollment and a minimum of three years of enrollment projections.

Exhibit 5-20 offers a thorough discussion of enrollment forecasting technology and techniques as well as a tabular display of enrollment histories and projections. The display sets forth the enrollment projections for the required number of years by grade level. Exhibits 5-21 and 5-22 exceed the criterion with not only a complete discussion of methodology as well as the required years of data but also with excellent charts and graphs that enhance the presentation. Although not required, the tables in Exhibit 5-21 display enrollment data by school level for the current and proposed budget years. Finally, Exhibit 5-22 provides additional enrollment statistics and demographic data that give more insight into the enrollment characteristics of the school entity.

Personnel Resource Allocations (Criterion E-8)

A significant portion of school budgets is allocated to personnel costs. A good indicator of these costs is personnel resource allocations or staffing levels. Staffing levels can also be an indicator of a school entity's commitment to specific programs (e.g., number of special education teachers). There are a number of different ways to display staffing levels. Whichever format is used, position or personnel counts should be expressed in full-time equivalent (FTE) units. To meet the criterion, the display must include personnel resources allocations for a minimum of three prior years actual, the current year budget and/or estimated current year actual, and the proposed budget year.

Exhibit 5-23 meets the requirements of the criterion with a display of personnel resource allocations by positions within the school entity for the required number of years. Exhibit 5-24 presents much the same information but organized by instruction and support services. Exhibit 5-25 demonstrates the use of charts to enhance the presentation of information about personnel resource allocations. Exhibit 5-26 displays personnel resource allocations by function and budget account code as a crosswalk to budget expenditures. Exhibit 5-27 is interesting in the presentation of two different formats by purpose and by classification to help better understand staffing patterns. The exhibit also provides a calculation of the changes in staffing for the proposed budget as well as information about the historical changes in program standards for class size. Finally, Exhibit 5-28 displays personnel resource allocations by position classification by function with differences calculated between the estimated actual budget and the proposed budget.

Bond Amortization Schedules (Criterion E-9)

Because of the significance of debt service payments on current and future budgets, a bond amortization schedule should be included in the budget. Exhibits 5-29 and 5-30 present typical formats used for these schedules. The schedules should include principal, interest and total annual payment for each debt issue over the term of the bond(s). Exhibit 5-30 provides a total of the financial impact of the debt service for each budget year until outstanding debt is retired.

Performance Measurements (Criterion E-10)

The last piece of historical information required for this section is three prior years of performance data. The concept and promise of reporting performance in measurable terms has been an ongoing issue for school entities. Performance measurement systems provide accountability to the citizenry by identifying results and evaluating past resources allocation decisions. Furthermore, performance measurement facilitates future decision-making regarding resource allocation and service-delivery options.

Today, many school entities use and report at least some concrete measures of performance. However, the measures commonly in use need significant development and refinement. Moreover, few school entities fully integrate performance measurement data in their core resource allocation process. However, performance measurement systems can provide the tools to identify problems and effect program and service improvements.

Essentially, performance measurement is a process for determining how well a school entity is accomplishing its mission through the delivery of programs, services, or processes. Performance measurement systems attempt to measure performance through ongoing data collection efforts, as opposed to program evaluations, operational audits, and other special studies that generally are more extensive and less frequently performed. In other words, performance measurement is a periodic rather than an episodic form of evaluation. The process of measuring and reporting performance is similar to financial reporting systems, which routinely collect financial data and report financial performance. Performance measurement reporting adds another dimension of accountability to taxpayers.

The four key steps of performance measurement are:

- Identification and definition of indicators;
- Collection of the appropriate data;
- Analysis or comparison of performance to previous results or relevant norms;
- Reporting the results.

Performance measurement encompasses indicators that measure performance along several dimensions. Although there are many different terms and combinations of indicators, most attempt to measure performance along one of three dimensions: quantity (measures of efforts), effectiveness (measures of outputs and outcomes), or efficiency (measures that relate efforts to accomplishments).

- Measures of efforts are input indicators that define the amount or volume of monetary and nonmonetary resources used in carrying out a program or service. Measures of efforts can therefore take the form of financial or nonfinancial information. The amount spent per pupil per year would be an example of a financial measure of effort. Nonfinancial measures of effort could include the number of staff members allocated to a specific program or service like special education for example.
- Measures of accomplishments can be divided into "output" and "outcome" measures. "Output" measures tend to focus on the quantity or volume of services provided by a program. Output indicators are commonly referred to as workload indicators. The number of students served by a music program is an example of an output measure. "Outcome" measures provide information on program results, accomplishments, or quality of the service provided. It is a measure of the effectiveness of a program or service. The dropout rates or the percentages of students that graduate from a school entity are examples of outcome measures.
- Measures of efficiency quantify the relationship between inputs (service efforts) to outputs (service accomplishments). Efficiency indicators can be expressed as productivity ratios (i.e., output divided by input) or as unit-cost ratios (i.e., input divided by output). They measure how much output or outcome can be produced or provided by a given resource level. They also measure how much input

it takes to produce a given level of output or outcome. An example would be the cost of a program or service in terms of dollars or work hours for each student in the program.

Performance data can be a powerful tool in measuring the effectiveness and efficiency of school programs and services. If linked to specific budget goals and objectives, performance data can help managers and elected officials to assess a program's success or failure rate. If resources are allocated on the basis of performance, the focus of budgeting can be shifted from inputs to results. As indicated, performance measures can be quantitative or qualitative.

Outcome measures and efficiency indicators can be the best barometers of program success, but often they are the ones that administrators and faculty have the least influence over. Because input indicators are already an integral part of budgets, schools should strive to present a mix of output, outcome and efficiency measures within their budgets. The most effective presentations of performance data are those which provide comparative data over a number of budget years and attempt to link indicators with long-standing, critical goals.

Two other terms often expressed in relationship to performance measurement are benchmarks and service efforts and accomplishments. "Benchmarks" often is used synonymously with performance measures, but for many it connotes additional meaning that goes beyond performance measurement. The term benchmarking first emerged in the private sector, which uses it to refer to the process of seeking best practices and attempting to emulate them. Benchmarking is used in school entities when referencing comparisons of performance to a goal, past performance, or another program's measurement data.

"Service efforts and accomplishments" is a term that was coined by the Governmental Accounting Standards Board (GASB) in its research into the status of performance measurement practice and research. GASB recommends use of the "classic" performance measurement indicators – inputs, outputs, outcome, and efficiency – but labels inputs as service efforts, outputs and outcomes as service accomplishments, and efficiency measures as indicators that relate service efforts to service accomplishments.

GASB also uses the term "explanatory information" to refer to descriptive text that accompanies presentations of performance measurement data. Relevant information to include would be factors or events that influence program operations that affect performance. GASB and others group this information into two types: 1) demographic data or events that are outside the control of program personnel and 2) elements that the entity does control. An example of the former information would be an explanation that test scores for secondary students could be affected by the percentage of students who do not speak English as their first language. An example of the latter information would be the staffing patterns of the school entity.

Exhibits 5-31 through 5-35 illustrate several different formats for presenting performance data. Exhibit 5-31 provides performance information in a report in a state mandated format for specified measures. They include such measures as graduation rate, standardized reading test scores, attendance rate, dropout rate, and retention rate. The indicators are presented for the school entity compared to state averages or standards. Exhibit 5-32 displays academic performance data based on the entity's own competency tests as well as national standardized tests. The standardized test scores are then used to compare the performance of the students of the school entity to other students within the same state.

Some school entities use a combination of both qualitative as well as quantitative data to evaluate the results of the programs and services. Exhibit 5-33 is such an example that uses narrative descriptive information supported with standardized test scores over a several year period. Exhibit 5-34 effectively uses graphs and charts to present performance data in more detail by subject matter. Finally, Exhibit 5-35 provides comparative performance data for school entities within the same geographical area along with charts to improve the presentation.

Other Useful Information (Criterion E-11)

A wide array of other information can help readers to understand a school entity's budget. MBA criteria encourage schools to include supplemental information, particularly information that helps to explain the connections between past and current budget decisions. The types of information, which might be included, are such items as:

- Demographic and economic profile of the school or district
- Histories and projections of intergovernmental aid
- Comparative information on teacher and administrator salaries
- History of teacher-student ratios
- Major changes in teaching technologies and curricula

Exhibits 5-36 through 5-38 provide vastly different kinds of information to help readers better understand the district and its budgets. Everything from a map of school locations to a history of per pupil costs can provide some insight into the makeup of school budgets. None of this information is required by the MBA criteria. School entities must decide on their own whether this or other supplemental information is needed to shed additional light on budgetary decisions.

A Glossary of Terms (Criterion E-12)

Every budget document should include a glossary of terms. The glossary should not be a substitute for a well-written budget but should define those terms and acronyms that a budget novice might not know. Rather than simply include a list of standard terms provided in finance or accounting texts, budget makers should develop their own list of terms which are particularly relevant to their budget and school entity. The glossary should be updated every year to remain current.

Exhibit 5-39 is an excerpt from a glossary that provides a mix of standard terms and those unique to the district. Note also that even standard definitions are tailored to fit the district's special circumstances.

CHECKLIST

1. The document should:
   a) Describe major revenue sources
   b) Explain underlying assumptions for each major revenue estimates
   c) Discuss significant trends for each major revenue
   d) Explain state/local funding structure, if necessary
2. Present the assessed value of taxable property and the market value of taxable property for:
   a) A minimum of three years actual
   b) The current year budget and/or estimated current year actual
   c) The proposed budget year
3. Include property tax rates and collections for:
   a) A minimum of three years actual
   b) The current year budget and/or estimated current year actual
   c) The proposed budget year
   d) Describe whether the tax rate is per $100 of taxable value or on some other form of rate
4. Include an analysis of the budget's effect on taxpayers for:
   a) A minimum of three years actual
   b) The current year budget and/or estimated current year actual
   c) The proposed budget year
5. The document should provide a:
   a) Five-year summary comparison of revenues and expenditures (three prior years actual, current year budget and/or estimated actual, and the proposed budget year. If the three years actual data is presented in the Financial Section, this presentation is not required). All years must be presented in a comparable form and format, whether presented in the Financial or Information Section
   b) Five-year summary should be presented for all governmental funds. (Presentation of similar data for other funds is optional.)
6. Present a minimum of three years of budget forecasts beyond the proposed budget year.
   a) Include beginning and ending fund balance

b) Revenue

c) Expenditures

d) The three years of budget forecasts is for each governmental fund. Forecasts for other funds are optional.

7. The document should present:

a) A minimum of three years of actual student enrollment history

b) Current budget and/or estimated current year enrollment

c) Proposed budget year enrollment

d) A minimum of three years of enrollment projections

e) Forecasting methodology and techniques

8. Present personnel resource allocations for:

a) A minimum of three years actual

b) The current year budget and/or estimated current year actual

c) The proposed budget year

9. Include the bond amortization schedule(s) of the school entity.

10. Provide performance measures for three prior years.

a) Standardized test scores

b) Dropout rates

c) Accomplishment of goals and objectives

d) Parent/student satisfaction surveys

e) Other performance measures

11. Include other information to help the reader understand the past and future directions of the school entity.

12. Include a glossary of terms.

Revenue Sources, Assumptions and Trends

(Criterion E-1)

Exhibit 5-1

Exhibit 5-2

Exhibit 5-3

Exhibit 5-1—Revenue Sources, Assumptions and Trends

Colorado Springs School District No. 11
GENERAL FUND
3 Year Projection Summary of Incremental Revenue & Expenditure Change
FY1997-98

A five year budget forecast is prepared each year and provided for public information. This projection includes FY1998-99 through FY2000-01 of the forecast and helps provide an important frame of reference for budget and policy decision making. The budget forecast is but one of many tools used in budget development and is prepared using an incremental approach which projects increases in revenues and other resources as well as new expenditure demands for each year. All figures are subject to change and are for preliminary planning purposes only.

Revenue Assumptions

1. The number of funded pupils will increase by 902 during the 3 year period.

2. Charter school pupil counts will to increase as the Edison Charter continues to phase in through FY2000-01.

3. The total program funding per pupil revenue amount will increase by total factor of 3.25% each year. In addition, growth is expected to be fully funded each year.

4. Charter schools will continue to buy services from the district. The revenue amount will increase with the continued phase in of the Edison Charter.

5. The district may become eligible for Medicaid reimbursements as a result of legislative action. Potential revenue amounts will be projected when the state's plan is completed.

6. Other potential resources are expected to increase at relatively minor amounts.

Expenditure Assumptions

1. Mandatory/Statutory Requirements
   - Maintain the required 3% emergency reserve (Amendment I).
   - Maintain the required per pupil funding for Capital & Insurance needs.
   - Maintain the required per pupil funding for instructional needs.
   - Provide funding for new mandates.

2. Strategic Plan - Student Achievement Priorities
   - The Edison Charter phase in will continue to consume new year resources until fully implemented.
   - ESL (English as a Second Language) will require additional resources in order to reach full implementation plus resources to maintain pupil teacher ratios.
   - The need for instructional staff increases will be partially offset until the Edison Charter school is fully implemented.
   - The special education population will continue to increase requiring additional resources.
   - Some funding will be allocated to various instructional programs with a major focus on low achieving schools and at risk student groups.
   - The average rate of reduction for middle school class size will accomplish full implementation by FY2001-02.
   - Additional new resources will continue to be made available for instructional initiatives as well as standards development and assessment.

3. Strategic Plan - Community Partnerships
   - Additional new resources will be needed to continue strategic plans for community involvement in schools as well as maintaining a safe learning environment.

Exhibit 5-1 (continued)

Colorado Springs School District No. 11
GENERAL FUND
3 Year Projection Summary of Incremental Revenue & Expenditure Change
FY1997-98

Expenditure Assumptions (continued)

4. Strategic Plan - Technology Plan
   - Passage of the bond election and mill levy override has provided substantial resources which will be used for implementation of the Technology Plan. However, additional resources will be needed for full plan implementation.

5. Strategic Plan - Capital Needs
   - Passage of the bond election has provided substantial resources which will be used to significantly address the capital needs of the district. However, additional resources will be needed for continued upkeep of district facilities.

6. Other Budget Needs
   - The most significant future budget need is funding for operating costs as construction of new schools is completed in FY1998-1999, FY1999-2000 and FY2000-2001.
   - Recurring funding for a two tier bus scheduling system will be necessary in FY1998-1999.
   - Restoration of the contingency reserve to 1% of revenues is planned over the next five years.
   - Reversing the recurring sources/uses mismatch is planned over the next five years.
   - Other non-strategic plan budget needs are expected to occur over the next five years.

7. Employee Compensation
   - Funding for employee pay increases and benefits will be provided from new resources each year. An amount similar to the actual amount provided in FY1997-98 has been used to illustrate employee compensation needs each year. The cost of a 5% health insurance premium increase has been shown for information purposes only and would likely be part of the total employee compensation package.
   - Post employment benefits will require additional funding in order to maintain existing programs at close to current levels.
   - Savings created by retirements will be rolled back into salary schedules.

8. Reallocation of Existing Budget
   - Use of existing resources will be challenged and justified for continuation. Even with targeted levels of reallocation, expected new demands exceed projected levels of new resources, which will require additional prioritization in order to balance the budget.

Exhibit 5-2—Revenue Sources, Assumptions and Trends

SALT LAKE CITY SCHOOL DISTRICT
Maintenance and Operation Fund Budget Projected
For Fiscal Year 1997-98 Through 2000-2001
Fund Expenditures by Object

	1997-98 Budget	1998-99 Projected	1999-2000 Projected	2000-2001 Projected	Projected Growth Rate
Revenues:					
Property taxes	$ 42,843,695	$ 43,700,569	$ 44,574,580	$ 45,466,072	2.00%
Interest on investments	988,941	1,018,609	1,049,168	1,080,643	3.00%
Other local revenue	405,395	417,557	430,084	442,986	3.00%
State of Utah	59,600,208	63,176,220	66,966,794	70,984,801	6.00%
Federal government	5,945,847	6,064,764	6,186,059	6,309,780	2.00%
Total Revenues	109,784,086	114,377,719	119,206,684	124,284,282	4.40%
Expenditures & Encumbrances:					
Salaries	72,452,861	75,350,975	78,365,014	81,499,615	4.00%
Employee benefits	23,598,727	24,542,676	25,524,383	26,545,358	4.00%
Contract services - professional & educational	1,426,689	1,469,490	1,513,574	1,558,982	3.00%
Maintenance & repairs	4,117,915	4,282,632	4,453,937	4,632,094	4.00%
Field trips, insurance, phone & travel	1,625,817	1,674,592	1,724,829	1,776,574	3.00%
Supplies, textbooks & utilities	7,685,999	7,916,579	8,154,076	8,398,699	3.00%
Equipment	2,901,374	2,901,374	2,901,374	2,901,374	0.00%
Total Expenditures & Encumbrances	113,809,382	118,138,317	122,637,188	127,312,696	3.95%
Excess (deficiency) of revenues and other sources (uses) over expenditures	(4,025,296)	(3,760,598)	(3,430,504)	(3,028,414)	
Fund Balances Unreserved & Undesignated - July 1	4,025,296	0	(3,760,598)	(7,191,102)	
Fund Balances Unreserved & Undesignated-June 30	$ 0	$ (3,760,598)	$ (7,191,102)	$ (10,219,516)	

The column under the heading "Projected Growth Rate" is the rate of growth used in making the projection. The following explains reasoning supporting the projected growth rate. For property tax, only an educated judgment is used. Interest on investments and other local revenue is set according to current information. For State revenue, past experience is adjusted for projected average daily membership (ADM) and Federal revenue is based on judgment only. Employee benefits and salary are projected using most recent experience adjusted by some judgment. Contracted service is assumed to grow in relation to expected inflation. Maintenance and repairs are projected based on inflation plus one percent growth. Student transportation, insurance, etc. is set at expected inflation. Supplies, textbooks, and utilities are projected at expected inflation. The most encouraging news regarding this projection is the relationship of the revenue growth to the growth of expenditures. Revenue growth is slightly higher than expenditure growth. This continues our most recent experience in actual revenue and expenditures as shown on page 122.

Exhibit 5-3—Revenue Sources, Assumptions and Trends

GENERAL FUND	1996-97 Approved Budget	1997-98 Adopted Budget	1998-99 Projected Budget	1999-2000 Projected Budget	2001-01 Projected Budget
Revenues:					
Local Revenue	$ 58,643,509	$ 63,055,565	$ 64,647,878	$ 64,836,853	$ 64,501,440
State Revenue	51,373,339	55,330,430	62,661,712	70,964,389	80,367,170
Total Revenues	$ 110,016,848	$ 118,385,995	$ 127,309,590	$ 135,801,242	$ 144,868,610
Expenditures:					
Instruction	$ 74,347,031	$ 79,986,277	$ 83,185,735	87,444,845	$ 91,922,021
Supporting Services	42,828,032	46,186,502	50,089,261	54,321,804	58,911,996
Community Services	57,926	-	-	-	-
Total Expenditures	$ 117,232,989	$ 126,172,779	$ 133,274,996	$ 141,766,649	$ 150,834,017
Excess of Revenues Over (Under) Expenditures)	$ (7,216,141)	$ (7,786,784)	$ (5,965,406)	$ (5,965,407)	$ (5,965,407)
Other Financing Sources (Uses):					
Transfers from Other Funds	$ 5,956,407	$ 5,818,484	$ 5,965,406	$ 5,965,407	$ 5,965,407
Transfer to Other Funds	$ (96,000)	$ (179,481)	$ -	$ -	$ -
Payments to Other Governmental Units	(26,000)	(26,000)	-	-	-
Total Other Financing Sources (Uses)	$ 5,834,407	$ 5,613,003	$ 5,965,406	$ 5,965,407	$ 5,965,407
Excess of Revenues Over (Under) Expenditures and Other Sources (Uses)	$ (1,381,734)	$ (2,173,781)	$ -	$ -	$ -
Fund Balance, July 1	15,625,616	14,243,882	12,070,101	12,070,101	12,070,101
Fund Balance, June 30	$ 14,243,882	$ 12,070,101	$ 12,070,101	$ 12,070,101	$ 12,070,101

Revenue Assumptions:

Local

(1) Ad valorem taxes are projected at a rate that will maintain funds for the solvent operation of the General Fund Budget.

(2) Other local revenue is projected to increase by 3% for each of the three ensuing years based on historical trends.

State

(3) Education Finance Act revenue is based on a historical five-year trend indexed for the three ensuing years.

(4) Fringe Benefit Contributions revenue is based on a historical five-year trend indexed for the three ensuing years.

(5) Other state revenue is projected based on a historical five-year trend indexed for the three ensuring years.

Other Financing Sources

(6) Transfers from Other Funds are projected for 1998-99 based on a historical five-year trend with the expectation for 1999-2000 and 2000-01 to remain at a constant level.

(Assumptions continued on page 179)

Horry County Schools

Exhibit 5-3 (continued)

Expenditure and Other Financing Uses Assumptions:

(1) All salary projections for the three ensuring years are based on a 2% longevity step increase for eligible employees applied to the 1996-97 indexed salary. An additional 2.5% cost-of-living adjustment (COLA) based upon a historical five-year average was applied to the step and accordingly indexed for each ensuing year.

(2) Fringe benefits for the last three years experienced no significant changes. These rates were used to project the three ensuing years: Group Life - .15%; Retirement – 9.597%; FICA – 7.65%; and Group Health and Dental based on actual coverage or an average of $2,500.

(3) For all non-salary accounts the forecasting for the three ensuing years is based on 1996-97 budgeted expenditures increased upon a historical five-year average consumer price index of 3.12%.

(4) For 1997-98 through 2000-01 project no payments to Other Governmental Units.

Fund Balance Assumptions:

(1) Assumes no growth in Fund Balance for the next three years. Forecasted to appropriate excess accumulation in Fund Balance.

Horry County Schools

Values of Taxable Properties

(Criterion E-2)

Exhibit 5-4

Exhibit 5-5

Exhibit 5-4—Values of Taxable Properties

SOUDERTON AREA SCHOOL DISTRICT
ASSESSED VALUE/MARKET VALUE HISTORY

Year	Assessed Value**		% Incr/ (Decr)	Market Value	Ratio
1983-84	71,662,520		***	437,137,700	16.40%
1984-85	73,925,370		3.16%	494,304,600	15.00%
1985-86	77,400,020		4.70%	520,914,300	14.90%
1986-87	80,027,960		3.40%	607,325,600	13.20%
1987-88	82,276,180		2.81%	632,893,692	13.00%
1988-89	84,053,850		2.16%	761,389,700	11.00%
1989-90	85,431,910		1.64%	780,097,500	11.00%
1990-91	88,125,790		3.15%	964,702,300	9.13%
1991-92	90,774,900		3.01%	1,000,825,799	9.07%
1992-93	91,611,630		0.92%	1,172,141,900	7.81%
1993-94	93,534,080		2.10%	1,204,355,300	7.76%
1994-95	97,272,080		4.00%	1,383,980,400	7.03%
1995-96	101,165,720		4.00%	1,447,796,600	6.99%
1996-97	105,247,466	**	4.03%	1,505,686,209	6.99%
1997-98*	107,701,904	*	2.33%	1,540,799,771	6.99%

* Estimated
** Based on July 1 School Tax Duplicate
Note: All information through 1995-96 was obtained from documentation from the St Equalization Board reports for each applicable year.

June 12, 1997

Exhibit 5-5—Values of Taxable Properties

TREDYFFRIN/EASTTOWN SCHOOL DISTRICT
Assessed and Market Value of Taxable Property
Last Ten Fiscal Years
(Unaudited)

Year	Market Value (1)	Total Assessment (2)	Percentage
1996-97	$ 3,333,158,800	$ 261,653,960	7.9
1995-96	3,112,562,900	257,979,610	8.3
1994-95	3,054,537,200	253,537,550	8.3
1993-94	2,924,917,400	255,539,800	8.7
1992-93	2,960,758,500	257,818,830	8.7
1991-92	2,619,211,800	256,783,730	9.8
1990-91	2,577,909,700	253,491,900	9.8
1989-90	2,134,201,900	245,029,250	11.5
1988-89	1,980,727,100	232,889,190	11.8
1987-88	1,530,747,500	223,053,390	14.6

Source: (1) Determined by the Pennsylvania State Tax Equalization Board (Latest Data Available)

(2) Chester County Board of Assessment Appeals, West Chester, Pennsylvania

Exhibit 5-5 (continued)

Tredyffrin/Easttown School District
Revenue Raising Options
Property Tax
Assessed Valuation Millage

Year	Easttown Township	Mills	Tredyffrin Township	Mills	Total	Assessment Increase Amount	Percent
1987-1988	49,261,660	111.33	173,791,730	111.33	223,053,390	11,484,420	5.4
1988-1989	51,346,530	111.33	181,542,660	111.33	232,889,190	9,835,800	4.4
1989-1990	54,664,660	111.33	190,364,590	111.33	245,029,250	12,140,060	5.2
1990-1991	56,695,590	130.02	196,796,310	130.02	253,491,900	8,462,650	3.5
1991-1992	58,166,190	133.41	198,617,540	133.41	256,783,730	3,291,830	1.3
1992-1993	59,197,850	139.26	198,620,980	139.26	257,818,830	1,035,100	0.4
1993-1994	59,067,530	150.56	196,472,270	150.56	255,539,800	(2,279,030)	(0.9)
1994-1995	60,145,420	157.78	193,392,130	157.78	253,537,550	(2,002,250)	(0.8)
1995-1996	60,487,290	160.87	197,492,320	160.87	257,979,610	4,442,060	1.8
1996-1997	61,353,300	163.22	200,300,660	163.22	261,653,960	3,674,350	1.4
1997-1998	62,127,500	167.72	200,370,160	167.72	262,497,660	843,700	0.3

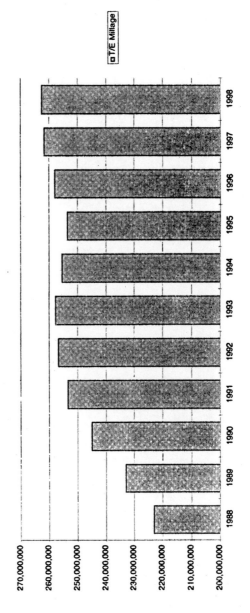

Gross Value Of A Mill

□ T/E Millage

Property Tax Rates and Collections

(Criterion E-3)

Exhibit 5-6

Exhibit 5-7

Exhibit 5-6—Property Tax Rates and Collections

Tredyffrin/Easttown School District
Property Tax Levies and Collections
Last Ten Fiscal Years
(Unaudited)

Year	Established Millage	Total Tax Levy	Current Tax Collections	% of Levy Collected	Current Taxes Liened	% of Total Levy
1997-98	167.72	$44,026,108	$42,101,980	95.63%	$632,387	1.44%
1996-97	163.22	$42,013,303	$40,618,660	96.03%	$594,847	1.42%
1995-96	160.87	$41,066,252	$39,572,650	95.70%	$606,808	1.48%
1994-95	157.78	$39,450,912	$37,906,536	96.09%	$694,475	1.76%
1993-94	150.56	$37,819,836	$36,203,386	95.73%	$855,685	2.26%
1992-93	139.26	$35,592,396	$34,256,361	96.25%	$813,038	2.28%
1991-92	133.41	$34,027,032	$32,729,717	96.19%	$660,812	1.94%
1990-91	130.02	$32,749,025	$31,686,391	96.76%	$599,209	1.83%
1989-90	111.33	$27,277,105	$26,479,548	97.08%	$419,092	1.54%
1988-89	111.33	$25,702,538	$25,199,664	98.04%	$344,283	1.34%

1. One mill of tax is equal to $1.00 for every $1,000 of assessed valuation of real estate property
2. Does not include delinquent or interim taxes
3. Budgeted

Exhibit 5-7—Propterty Tax Rates and Collections

SOUTH LYON COMMUNITY SCHOOLS

Schedule of Property Tax Rates
1992-93 through 1997-98

	1992-93	1993-94	1994-95	1995-96	1996-97	1997-98
Homesteads:						
Operating	34.28	34.58	6.00	6.00	6.00	6.00
Debt	6.25	5.88	5.88	5.88	6.25	6.25
Total	40.53	40.46	11.88	11.88	12.25	12.25
Non-Homesteads:						
Operating	34.28	34.58	24.00	24.00	24.00	24.00
Debt	6.25	5.88	5.88	5.88	6.25	6.25
Total	40.53	40.46	29.88	29.88	30.25	30.25

NOTE: Tax rate is 1 mill per $1,000 taxable value.

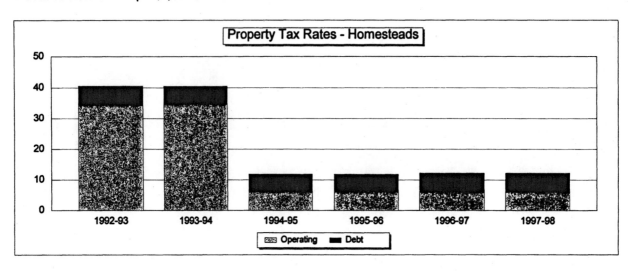

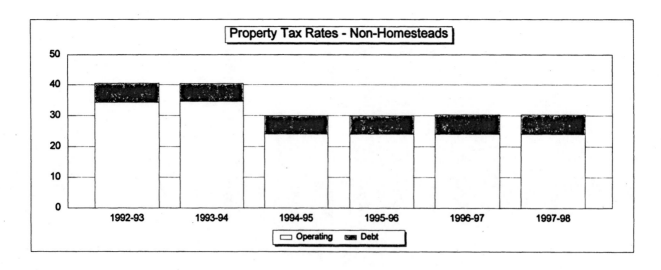

Exhibit 5-7 (continued)

SOUTH LYON COMMUNITY SCHOOLS

Schedule of Operating Property Taxes Assessed and Collected
1992-93 through 1996-97 Actual and 1997-98 Estimated

Fiscal Year	Taxes Assessed	Collections to March 1, each year	Current Percentage of Taxes Collected	Delinquent Collections	Collections to June 30, each year	Total Percentage of Taxes Collected
1992-93	18,376,249	16,846,459	91.68%	1,488,789	18,335,248	99.78%
1993-94	20,943,606	19,495,004	93.08%	1,320,913	20,815,917	99.39%
1994-95	3,701,028	3,480,514	94.04%	136,102	3,616,616	97.72%
1995-96	4,267,645	3,883,835	91.01%	288,711	4,172,546	97.77%
1996-97	4,375,446	4,047,136	92.50%	228,631	4,275,767	97.72%
1997-98 est.	4,972,528	4,599,588	92.50%	259,566	4,859,154	97.72%

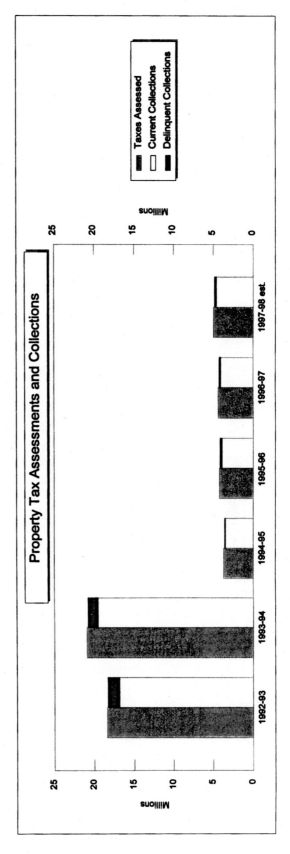

Property Tax Assessments and Collections

Taxes Assessed
Current Collections
Delinquent Collections

Analysis of Tax Burden

(Criterion E-4)

Exhibit 5-8

Exhibit 5-9

Exhibit 5-10

Exhibit 5-11

Exhibit 5-8—Analysis of Tax Burden

Colorado Springs School District No. 11
Annual Property Tax Informational Summary
Tax Burden On Home Owner (1)

District 11:

*estimated

Assessment Year	1990	1991	1992	1993	1994	1995	1996	1997*
Actual Value	89,180	89,180	89,180	92,587	92,587	127,052	127,052	127,052
Assessment Rate	14.34%	14.34%	14.34%	12.86%	12.86%	10.36%	10.36%	10.36%
Assessed Value	12,790	12,790	12,790	11,910	11,910	13,160	13,160	13,160
Levy Rate (per 1,000)	38.779	41.033	41.033	40.93	40.93	38.865	45.975	38.618
Tax Levy	496	525	525	487	487	511	605	508

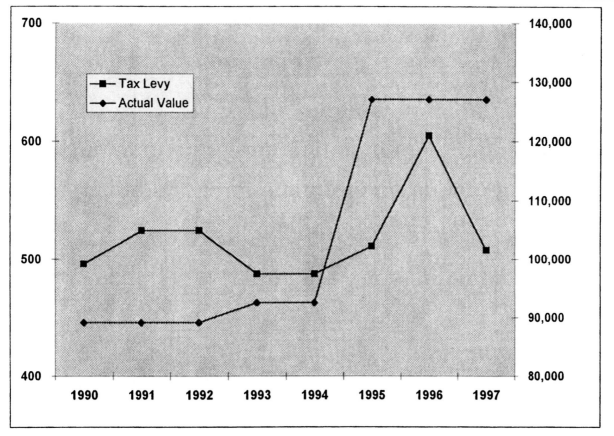

(1) Figures are actual numbers for a 3-bedroom, 2,400 sq. ft. home in the Village Seven subdivision.

Exhibit 5-9—Analysis of Tax Burden

MSD of Washington Township, Indianapolis, Indiana
Analysis of Budget Effect on Taxpayers
Five Calendar Years

	Actual 1994	Actual 1995	Actual 1996	Revised 1997	Budget 1998[4]
Market Value of a Home	$ 122,859	$ 124,304	$ 138,652	$ 141,674	$ 143,577
Certified Assessed Valuation	40,953	41,435	46,217	47,225	47,859
Percent Increase in Assessed Valuation	0.38%	1.18%	12.85%	2.18%	1.34%
Property Tax Rate[1,2,3]	4.1245	4.3014	3.7443	3.818	4.2676
Property Tax Due	1,689	1,782	1,731	1,803	2,042
Property Tax Increase (Decrease) from Prior Year	$ (18)	$ 93	$ (52)	$ 73	$ 239

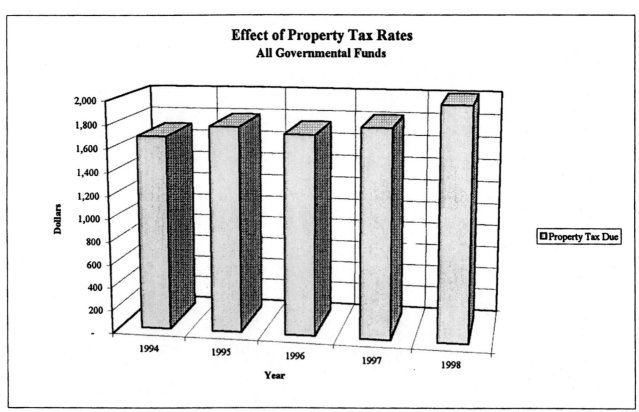

Effect of Property Tax Rates
All Governmental Funds

[1] Source: State Board of Tax Commissioners Final Budget Order 1994-1997.
[2] Source: Calculated using School Budget Form No. 3 - Estimated Funds to be Raised 1997.
[3] Property Tax Rate for 1998 is advertised tax rate.
[4] The 1998 tax rate is an estimated rate. Differences between the advertised and final tax rate may be material.

Exhibit 5-10—Analysis of Tax Burden

SOUTH LYON COMMUNITY SCHOOLS

Schedule of Tax Burden on Citizens
1992-93 through 1997-98

HOMESTEADS	1992-93 Actual	1993-94 Actual	1994-95 Actual	1995-96 Actual	1996-97 Actual	1997-98 Actual
Estimated Market Value	75,000	81,075	84,723	88,112	91,636	95,301
Average Taxable Value Increase	N/A	8.1%	2.5%	1.1%	1.4%	2.8%
Taxable Value	37,500	40,538	41,551	42,008	42,596	43,789
Total Property Tax Rate Assessed (per $1,000)	40.53	40.46	11.88	11.88	12.25	12.25
Property Taxes Due	1,520	1,640	494	499	522	536
Property Tax Increase - Tax Rate	N/A	(3)	(1,159)	0	16	0
Property Tax Increase - Assessment Increase	N/A	123	12	5	7	15

NON-HOMESTEADS	1992-93 Actual	1993-94 Actual	1994-95 Actual	1995-96 Actual	1996-97 Actual	1997-98 Actual
Market Value of Non-Homestead	75,000	81,075	84,723	88,112	91,636	95,301
Average Taxable Value Increase	N/A	8.1%	2.5%	1.1%	1.4%	2.8%
Taxable Value	37,500	40,538	41,551	42,008	42,596	43,789
Total Property Tax Rate Assessed (per $1,000)	40.53	40.46	29.88	29.88	30.25	30.25
Property Taxes Due	1,520	1,640	1,242	1,255	1,289	1,325
Property Tax Increase - Tax Rate	N/A	(3)	(429)	0	16	0
Property Tax Increase - Assessment Increase	N/A	123	30	14	18	36

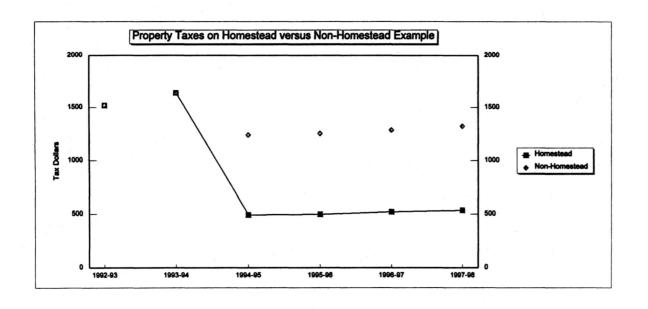

Exhibit 5-11—Analysis of Tax Burden

SALT LAKE CITY SCHOOL DISTRICT

Impact of Budget on Taxpayers
For Fiscal Year 1997-98 With Comparative Information for Years 1993-94 Through 1996-97

	1993-94 Actual	1994-95 Actual	1995-96 Actual	1996-97 Actual	1997-98 Budget
Market value of a home	$75,000	$75,000	$75,000	$75,000	$75,000
Appraised % of market value	66.98%	68.00%	55.00%	55.00%	55.00%
Taxable value	$50,231	$51,000	$41,250	$41,250	$41,250
Total property tax rate assessed	.008732	.008677	.007029	.006268	.006207
Property tax due	$438.62	$442.53	$289.95	$258.56	$256.04
Property Tax increase (decrease) from prior year	$9.34	$3.91	($152.58)	($31.39)	($2.52)

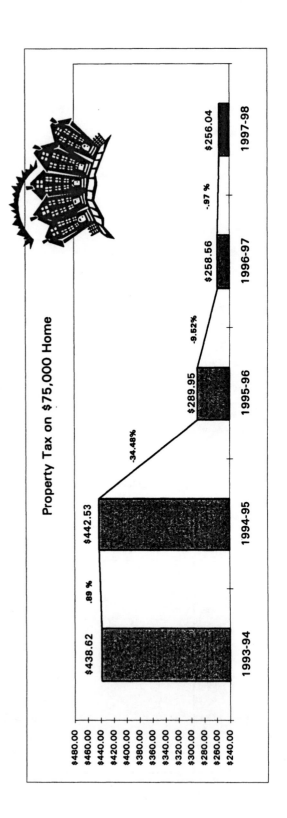

Property Tax on $75,000 Home

Comparison of
Revenues and Expenditures

(Criterion E-5)

Exhibit 5-12

Exhibit 5-13

Exhibit 5-14

Exhibit 5-15

Exhibit 5-12—Comparison of Revenues and Expenditures

Tredyffrin/Easttown School District
General Fund Budget 1997-98
Five Year Historical Comparison of Revenues - by Function

	1993-94 Actual	1994-95 Actual	1995-96 Actual	1996-97 Budget	1997-98 Budget
6000 Local Sources					
6111 Current Real Estate	$36,203,386	$37,906,536	$39,572,650	$40,359,949	$42,101,980
6112 Interim Taxes	1,143,977	1,437,326	908,791	650,000	655,000
6113 Public Utility Tax	511,334	505,830	523,170	525,000	525,000
6153 Transfer Tax	1,191,571	1,331,577	1,515,839	1,100,000	1,100,000
6154 Amusement Tax	368,222	304,062	356,233	145,000	6,680
6410 Delinquency Tax	637,237	1,104,600	905,310	800,000	728,881
6510 Earning on Investments	703,461	1,254,416	1,496,822	1,300,000	1,400,000
6800 Revenue from Intermediate Sources	13,232	63,238	18,327	0	0
6910 Rentals	77,932	135,552	148,241	125,000	145,000
6940 Tuition	108,978	84,221	92,765	75,000	75,000
6990 Miscellaneous Revenue	41,169	2,288	16,393	1,000	1,000
Total Revenue from Local Sources	$41,000,499	$44,129,646	$45,554,541	$45,080,949	$46,738,541
7000 State Sources					
7110 Basic Instructional Subsidy	$1,802,667	$1,823,105	$1,905,148	$1,899,606	$1,971,070
7150 School Performance Incentive	0	0	0	0	0
7160 State Sec. 1305 & 1306	65,829	59,034	37,291	55,000	35,000
7220 Vocational Education	0	0	0	0	0
7170 Instructional Support Teams	29,000	0	29,000	0	0
7210 Homebound Instruction	168	87	127	100	100
7240 Driver Education	6,885	0	0	0	0
7271 Special Education for School Aged Pupils	1,163,939	1,028,112	1,247,256	1,259,440	1,440,600
7310 Transportation	737,318	806,578	755,564	825,000	700,000
7320 Rentals and Sinking Fund Payments	82,020	81,883	220,198	85,000	134,000
7330 Health Services	103,025	99,985	108,600	100,000	100,000
7810 State Share of Social Security & Medicare	986,062	1,056,763	1,038,599	1,172,000	1,230,000
7820 State Share of Retirement Contributions Taxes	0	36,065	1,725,400	1,713,000	1,410,000
Total Revenue from State Sources	$4,976,913	$4,991,612	$7,067,183	$7,109,146	$7,020,770
Total Revenue	$45,977,412	$49,121,258	$52,621,724	$52,190,095	$53,759,311
9000 Other Financing Sources					
9300 Interfund Transfers	$0	$0	$0	$0	$0
9400 Sale of Fixed Assets	0	301	16,370	0	0
9500 Refund of Prior Years' Expenditures	0	475,128	257,799	0	0
Total Other Financing Sources	$0	$475,429	$274,169	$0	$0
Total Revenue and Other Financing Sources	$45,977,412	$49,596,687	$52,895,893	$52,190,095	$53,759,311

Exhibit 5-12 (continued)

Tredyffrin/Easttown School District
General Fund Budget 1997-98
Five Year Historical Comparison of Expenditures - by Function

	1993-94 Actual	1994-95 Actual	1995-96 Actual	1996-97 Budget	1997-98 Budget
1100 **Regular Programs**					
100 Personal Services - Salaries	$16,633,491	$18,627,774	$18,352,991	$19,988,465	$20,554,753
200 Personal Services - Benefits	4,668,281	4,355,264	4,851,678	3,651,663	3,563,660
300 Purchased Professional	11,736	20,568	21,791	40,609	42,101
400 Purchased Property	57,385	53,579	47,818	55,788	57,798
500 Other Purchased Services	49,141	57,238	72,196	86,532	94,679
600 Supplies	634,969	897,477	812,453	994,944	1,053,232
700 Equipment	246,708	466,898	509,096	483,271	546,586
800 Other Objects	3,505	3,722	8,786	12,195	12,451
Total Regular Programs	$22,305,216	$24,482,520	$24,676,810	$25,313,467	$25,925,259
1200 **Special Programs**					
100 Personal Services - Salaries	$983,024	$1,227,807	$1,315,346	$1,327,793	$1,467,991
200 Personal Services - Benefits	283,788	287,452	350,848	218,335	213,891
300 Purchased Professional	623,800	690,129	707,339	751,137	857,098
400 Purchased Property	0	0	0	0	0
500 Other Purchased Services	169,447	126,770	260,073	295,000	295,010
600 Supplies	8,069	11,243	8,937	10,100	10,127
700 Equipment	7,483	7,452	8,255	7,500	9,214
800 Other Objects	0	0	127	100	100
Total Special Programs	$2,075,611	$2,350,854	$2,650,925	$2,609,965	$2,853,432
1300 **Vocational Programs**					
100 Personal Services - Salaries	$0	$0	$0	$0	$0
200 Personal Services - Benefits	0	0	0	0	0
300 Purchased Professional	0	0	0	0	0
400 Purchased Property	0	0	0	0	0
500 Other Purchased Services	349,546	382,996	367,438	319,732	299,395
600 Supplies	0	0	0	0	0
700 Equipment	0	0	0	0	0
800 Other Objects	0	0	0	0	0
Total Vocational Programs	$349,546	$382,996	$367,438	$319,732	$299,395
1400 **Other Instructional Programs**					
100 Personal Services - Salaries	$12,448	$14,976	$8,082	$26,622	$20,020
200 Personal Services - Benefits	3,593	3,219	1,908	2,676	1,714
300 Purchased Professional	0	0	0	0	0
400 Purchased Property	0	0	0	0	0
500 Other Purchased Services	0	0	0	0	0
600 Supplies	1,011	0	0	0	2,000
700 Equipment	0	0	0	0	0
800 Other Objects	0	0	0	0	0
Total Other Instructional Programs	$17,052	$18,195	$9,990	$29,298	$23,734

Exhibit 5-13—Comparison of Revenues and Expenditures

JORDAN SCHOOL DISTRICT

FUND 10 - MAINTENANCE AND OPERATION

REVENUES, EXPENDITURES AND FUND BALANCES - FIVE YEAR SUMMARY

	Actual 1993-94	Actual 1994-95	Actual 1995-96	Final Amended 1996-97	Proposed 1997-98	Four Year Average Percent Growth
REVENUES						
Property Taxes	$ 41,148,825	$ 43,486,604	$ 39,540,362	$ 38,960,719	$ 40,913,454	-0.14%
Interest from Investments	1,374,639	2,382,209	2,213,767	2,827,000	3,027,000	30.05%
Other Local Sources	4,574,255	5,457,043	5,300,105	5,383,679	5,717,920	6.25%
State Sources	142,822,699	153,123,764	165,453,767	197,797,229	196,153,147	9.34%
Federal Sources	5,702,933	6,671,685	6,851,741	7,947,154	7,893,457	9.60%
Total Revenues	195,623,351	211,121,305	219,359,742	252,915,781	253,704,978	7.42%
EXPENDITURES						
Salaries	125,026,089	134,117,125	143,045,039	157,902,503	164,095,474	7.81%
Employees Benefits	45,300,589	50,070,200	53,264,564	59,279,599	62,314,431	9.39%
Purchased Services	5,422,283	5,322,046	6,022,405	8,394,496	7,789,756	10.92%
Supplies and Materials	14,323,102	14,278,480	16,573,364	21,640,274	18,606,498	7.48%
Equipment	2,184,506	3,710,015	3,982,574	6,789,102	4,328,394	24.54%
Other	482,565	486,760	400,218	456,006	533,668	2.65%
Total Expenditures	192,739,134	207,984,626	223,288,164	254,461,980	257,668,221	8.42%
Excess (Deficiency) of Revenues Over Expenditures	2,884,217	3,136,679	(3,928,422)	(1,546,199)	(3,963,243)	59.35%
Fund Balance, Beginning of Year	9,582,311	12,466,528	15,603,207	11,674,785	10,128,586	1.43%
Ending Fund Balance	$ 12,466,528	$ 15,603,207	$ 11,674,785	$ 10,128,586	$ 6,165,343	12.64%

Exhibit 5-14—Comparison of Revenues and Expenditures

SAN CARLOS UNIFIED SCHOOL DISTRICT NO. 20
Maintenance and Operation Fund Budget
For Fiscal Year 1997-98 With Comparative Information for the Years 1993-94 Through 1996-97
Fund Expenditures by Object
With Percent Growth from Previous Year and Average Percent Growth for Period

	1993-94 Actual	% Growth	1994-95 Actual	% Growth	1995-96 Actual	% Growth	1996-97 Budget	% Growth	1997-98 Budget	Average % Growth
Revenues:										
Interest on investments	$ 2,264	-100.00%	$ -	0.00%	3,023	-100.00%	$ -	0.00%	$ -	-50.00%
Intergovernmental grants and aid										
County	528,976	-33.85%	349,924	0.98%	353,353	-14.13%	303,439	-23.86%	231,053	-17.71%
State	4,210,756	8.00%	4,547,615	7.30%	4,879,655	3.07%	5,029,416	-27.25%	3,658,733	-2.22%
Federal	2,091,406	29.03%	2,698,497	60.64%	4,334,789	-15.00%	3,684,570	0.00%	3,684,570	18.67%
Other	1,435	12.06%	1,608	130.53%	3,707	-100.00%	-	0.00%	-	10.65%
Total revenues	6,834,837	11.16%	7,597,644	26.02%	9,574,527	-5.82%	9,017,425	-16.00%	7,574,356	3.84%
Expenditures:										
Salaries - certified	3,168,239	3.73%	3,286,536	6.90%	3,513,325	1.88%	3,579,506	6.65%	3,817,485	4.79%
Salaries - classified	1,167,942	10.82%	1,294,317	2.02%	1,320,513	10.44%	1,458,358	12.44%	1,639,763	8.93%
Employee benefits	976,132	-35.19%	632,603	65.03%	1,044,016	5.66%	1,103,106	8.50%	1,196,924	11.00%
Supplies and materials	409,675	0.53%	411,844	2.85%	423,581	-3.32%	409,524	3.98%	425,835	1.01%
Utilities and communications	219,844	7.87%	237,153	13.09%	268,208	0.76%	270,250	4.81%	283,250	6.63%
Tuition	16,787	-38.72%	10,287	-76.63%	2,404	44.88%	3,483	474.22%	20,000	100.94%
Other	302,719	17.83%	356,679	111.48%	754,287	57.50%	1,187,987	-31.87%	809,361	38.73%
Total expenditures	6,261,338	-0.51%	6,229,419	17.61%	7,326,334	9.36%	8,012,214	2.25%	8,192,618	7.18%
Excess (deficiency) of revenues over expenditures	573,499	138.57%	1,368,225	64.31%	2,248,193	-55.29%	1,005,211	-161.51%	(618,262)	-3.48%
Other financing sources (uses)										
Operating transfers out	(81,632)	0.00%	(1,346,997)	-5.61%	(1,271,407)	135.96%	(3,000,000)	0.00%	(3,000,000)	#REF!
Reversions	-	0.00%	-	0.00%	-	0.00%	-	0.00%	-	0.00%
Total other financing sources (uses)	(81,632)	1550.08%	(1,346,997)	-5.61%	(1,271,407)	135.96%	(3,000,000)	0.00%	(3,000,000)	420.11%
Excess (deficiency) of revenues over expenditures and other sources (uses)	491,867	-95.68%	21,228	4501.40%	976,786	-304.22%	(1,994,789)	81.39%	(3,618,262)	1045.72%
Fund balances at beginning of year	1,356,296	43.08%	1,940,654	0.58%	1,951,989	17.72%	2,297,953	102.37%	4,650,335	40.94%
Increase in reserves for inventories	92,491	-110.70%	(9,893)	64.91%	(16,315)	-100.00%	-	0.00%	-	-36.45%
Fund balances at end of year	$ 1,940,654	0.58%	$ 1,951,989	49.20%	2,912,460	-89.59%	303,164	240.43%	1,032,073	50.16%

Exhibit 5-15—Comparison of Revenues and Expenditures

SALT LAKE CITY SCHOOL DISTRICT

Maintenance and Operation Fund Budget
Comparative Information for Years 1991-92 Through 1995-96
**Fund Revenue & Expenditures
With Percent Growth from Previous Year**

	1991-92 Actual	1992-93 Actual	% Growth	1993-94 Actual	% Growth	1994-95 Actual	% Growth	1995-96 Actual	% Growth
Revenue	$ 80,193,824	$ 83,121,137	3.65%	$ 87,782,707	5.61%	$ 92,110,950	4.93%	$ 100,337,227	8.93%
Expenditures	80,533,353	83,185,426	3.29%	87,694,201	5.42%	91,198,856	4.00%	98,268,786	7.75%

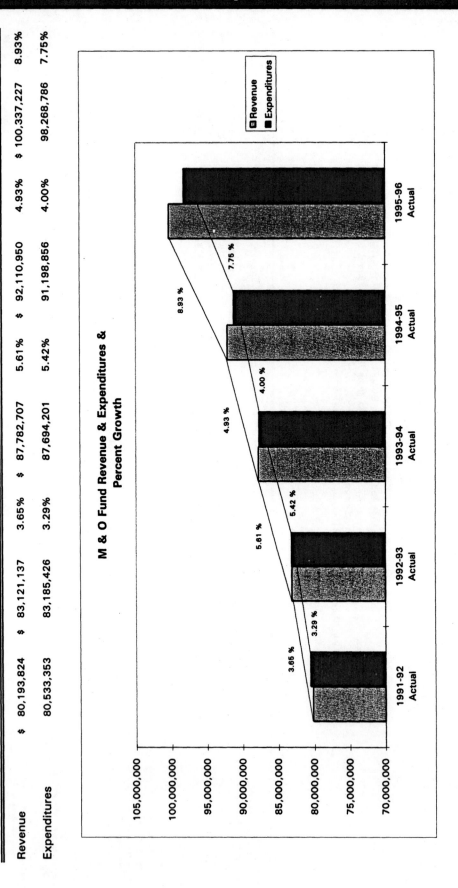

M & O Fund Revenue & Expenditures & Percent Growth

Exhibit 5-15 (continued)

SALT LAKE CITY SCHOOL DISTRICT
Maintenance and Operation Fund Budget
Comparative Information for Years 1991-92 Through 1995-96
Revenue and Expenditure Growth History
With Percent Growth from Previous Year and Average Percent Growth for Period

	1991-92 Actual	1992-93 Actual	% Growth	1993-94 Actual	% Growth	1994-95 Actual	% Growth	1995-96 Actual	% Growth	Average % Growth
Revenues:										
Property taxes	$ 41,171,574	$ 42,191,643	2.5%	$ 43,293,994	2.6%	$ 45,667,867	5.5%	$ 40,828,916	-10.6%	-0.2%
Interest on investments	1,658,462	1,455,602	-12.2%	1,417,033	-2.6%	1,731,925	22.2%	2,453,044	41.6%	12.0%
Other local revenue	893,901	962,929	7.7%	1,424,336	47.9%	1,433,186	0.6%	1,426,139	-0.5%	14.9%
State of Utah	32,010,920	33,582,203	4.9%	35,814,797	6.6%	37,552,199	4.9%	49,707,137	32.4%	13.8%
Federal government	4,458,967	4,928,760	10.5%	5,832,547	18.3%	5,725,773	-1.8%	5,921,991	3.4%	8.2%
Total Revenues	80,193,824	83,121,137	3.7%	87,782,707	5.6%	92,110,950	4.9%	100,337,227	8.9%	6.3%
Expenditures & Encumbrances:										
Salaries	52,378,643	54,765,149	4.6%	57,483,978	5.0%	59,927,877	4.3%	63,862,708	6.6%	5.5%
Employee benefits	17,108,183	17,225,109	0.7%	17,835,612	3.5%	18,951,259	6.3%	19,678,145	3.8%	3.8%
Contract services - professional & educational	732,907	746,735	1.9%	1,125,293	50.7%	1,217,609	8.2%	1,285,700	5.6%	18.9%
Maintenance & repairs	2,631,993	2,595,810	-1.4%	3,192,985	23.0%	3,332,206	4.4%	3,737,551	12.2%	10.5%
Field trips, ins., phone & travel	1,303,931	1,271,584	-2.5%	1,314,826	3.4%	1,320,106	0.4%	1,513,473	14.6%	4.0%
Supplies, textbooks & utilities	5,394,678	5,469,931	1.4%	5,819,673	6.4%	5,717,768	-1.8%	5,839,895	2.1%	2.1%
Equipment	983,018	1,111,108	13.0%	921,834	-17.0%	732,031	-20.6%	2,351,314	221.2%	34.8%
Total Expenditures & Encumbrances	80,533,353	83,185,426	3.3%	87,694,201	5.4%	91,198,856	4.0%	98,268,786	7.8%	5.5%
Other financing sources (uses)										
Operating transfer from Capital Outlay Fund to Maintenance & Operation Fund	417,238	154,795		1,942,385		0		0		
Excess (deficiency) of revenues and other sources (uses) over expenditures	77,709	90,506		2,030,891		912,094		2,068,441		
Other changes in reserved & designated fund balances	(77,709)	(90,506)		113,590		(1,500,711)		640		
Fund Balance Unreserved & Undesignated - July 1	0	1,900,090		1,900,090		4,044,571		3,455,954		
Fund Balances Unreserved & Undesignated - June 30	$ 0	$ 1,900,090		$ 4,044,571		$ 3,455,954		$ 5,525,035		

Budget Forecasts

(Criterion E-6)

Exhibit 5-16—Budget Forecast

GENERAL (OPERATING) FUND
EXPENDITURE BUDGET FORECAST BY OBJECT

	BUDGET 1999-00	BUDGET 2000-01	BUDGET 2000-02
REVENUE			
6000 Local Sources	$29,710,300	$30,980,300	$32,150,300
7000 State Sources	7,584,500	7,614,500	7,644,500
8000 Federal Sources	205,200	205,200	205,200
Total Revenue	$37,500,000	$38,800,000	$40,000,000
EXPENDITURES			
100 Salaries	$21,155,252	$21,789,910	$22,443,607
200 Benefits	5,921,628	6,196,713	6,350,954
300 Professional & Technical SVCS	857,734	874,889	892,387
400 Purchased Services	1,685,409	1,685,409	1,685,409
500 Other Purchased Services	3,655,116	3,728,218	3,802,782
600 Supplies	918,086	918,086	918,086
700 Equipment	144,750	144,750	144,750
800 Other Objects	337,025	337,025	337,025
900 Other Financing Uses	2,825,100	3,125,000	3,425,000
Total Expenditures	$37,500,100	$38,800,000	$40,000,000
Fund Balance - July 1	$ 1,080,000	$ 1,080,000	$ 1,080,000
Fund Balance - June 30	$ 1,080,000	$ 1,080,000	$ 1,080,000

Exhibit 5-17—Budget Forecast

Colorado Springs School District No. 11
GENERAL FUND
3 Year Projection Summary of Incremental Revenue & Expenditure Change
FY1997-98

	FY98-99	FY99-00	FY00-01	3 year total
Estimated Recurring Revenue Changes:				
Projected Increase in Students	311	308	283	902
Estimated Pupil Count	32,387	32,695	32,978	n/a
Estimated Charter School Pupil Count	1,213	1,513	1,753	n/a
Per Pupil Revenue Projected at **3.25%** Increase	$ 4,757.37	$ 4,911.98	$ 5,071.62	n/a
Estimated Growth Revenue	1,479,541	1,512,890	1,435,269	4,427,700
Inflation Adjustment in School Finance Act	4,849,877	5,055,119	5,264,589	15,169,585
Charter Schools - Buyback Revenue	51,000	102,000	81,600	234,600
Medicaid Reimbursements	-	-	-	-
Other Recurring & Non-Recurring	50,000	50,000	50,000	150,000
Total New Revenue	6,430,418	6,720,009	6,831,458	19,981,885
Reallocation Need				
Special Capital Account (.01% PERA)	100,000	100,000	100,000	300,000
Retirement Differential Savings	525,000	525,000	525,000	1,575,000
Other Required Reallocations *	250,000	150,000	150,000	550,000
Total Reallocation Need	875,000	775,000	775,000	2,425,000
Grand Total Resource Availability	$ 7,305,418	$ 7,495,009	$ 7,606,458	$ 22,406,885
New Demands for Recurring Resources:				
1) Mandatory/Statutory Requirements	$ 644,068	$ 622,191	$ 640,025	$ 1,906,284
% of Total Resource Availability	8.29%	8.01%	8.24%	8.51%
2) Strategic Plan - Student Achievement	2,063,034	2,239,792	2,075,066	$ 6,377,891
% of Total Resource Availability	28.24%	29.88%	27.28%	28.46%
3) Strategic Plan - Community Partnerships	170,000	130,000	90,000	$ 390,000
% of Total Resource Availability	2.33%	1.73%	1.18%	1.74%
4) Strategic Plan - Technology Plan	100,000	100,000	100,000	$ 300,000
% of Total Resource Availability	1.37%	1.33%	1.31%	1.34%
5) Strategic Plan - Capital Needs (M&O, Cap.Res.)	214,433	219,045	223,842	$ 657,320
% of Total Resource Availability	2.94%	2.92%	2.94%	2.93%
6) Other	2,275,500	1,922,500	1,322,500	$ 5,520,500
% of Total Resource Availability	31.15%	25.65%	17.39%	24.64%
7) Employee Compensation	4,125,000	4,253,691	4,309,860	$ 12,688,551
% of Total Resource Availability	56.46%	56.75%	56.66%	56.63%
Total Demands	9,592,035	9,487,218	8,761,293	27,840,546
Difference - Demands in Excess of Total Resource Availability	$ (2,286,617)	$(1,992,209)	$(1,154,835)	$ (5,433,661)

Exhibit 5-17 (continued)

Colorado Springs School District No. 11
GENERAL FUND
3 Year Projection Detail of Incremental Expenditure Change
FY1997-98

New Demands for Recurring Revenue:	FY1998-99	FY1999-00	FY2000-01	Total
1) Mandatory/Statutory Requirements				
Emergency Reserve	200,000	200,000	200,000	600,000
Increase instructional supplies	171,241	177,237	180,215	528,693
Increase Capital/Insurance funding	237,827	209,954	224,810	672,591
Other - New mandates, etc.	35,000	35,000	35,000	105,000
Total Mandatory Requirements	**644,068**	**622,191**	**640,025**	**1,906,284**
% of Annual Increase				
2) Strategic Plan - Student Achievement				
Charter Schools - Edison/GLOBE/CPS	764,832	1,661,142	1,458,724	3,884,698
ESL/PHLOTE implementation	160,000	20,000	20,000	200,000
Instruct. staffing increase/supplemental pay	406,042	410,010	383,974	1,200,026
Instruct. staffing Charter School Offsets	(195,840)	(399,360)	(325,632)	(920,832)
Staff Development	25,000	25,000	25,000	75,000
Special Ed staffing & contract services	88,000	88,000	88,000	264,000
Elementary Achievement Initiative	350,000	-	-	350,000
Middle School Implementation (class size)	200,000	200,000	200,000	600,000
Other Instructional Division	200,000	200,000	200,000	600,000
Other DPRE (Assessment)	65,000	35,000	25,000	125,000
Total Strategic Plan Goal #1	**2,063,034**	**2,239,792**	**2,075,066**	**6,377,891**
3) Strategic Plan - Community Partnerships				
Security	138,000	98,000	90,000	326,000
Staff development	32,000	32,000	-	64,000
Total Strategic Plan Goal #2	**170,000**	**130,000**	**90,000**	**390,000**
4) Strategic Plan - Technology Plan				
New resource need	100,000	100,000	100,000	300,000
Net new resource need	**100,000**	**100,000**	**100,000**	**300,000**
5) Strategic Plan - Capital (M&O, Cap RES.)				
Special Capital Account (.01% PERA)	100,000	100,000	100,000	300,000
Board Directed	114,433	119,045	123,842	357,320
Total Strategic Plan Goal #4	**214,433**	**219,045**	**223,842**	**657,320**
6) Other				
Athletics subsidy	25,000	25,000	25,000	75,000
Utilities increase @ 2%	50,000	50,000	50,000	150,000
Increase Sub Teacher/Sub Clerical base pay	50,000	25,000	25,000	100,000
School building supplies	35,000	35,000	35,000	105,000
Staffing (Comp Mgr, Reclasses,etc.)	25,000	25,000	25,000	75,000
County Treasurer Fees	12,500	12,500	12,500	37,500
Other Issues plus not yet identified	25,000	25,000	25,000	75,000
New School Overhead (3-ES, 1-MS, 1 Alt)	600,000	900,000	300,000	1,800,000
Transportation subsidy (3 tier maintain)	50,000	50,000	50,000	150,000
Transportation subsidy (2 tier) (net cost)	653,000	25,000	25,000	703,000
Replenish Contingency Reserve	150,000	150,000	150,000	450,000
Prior Year Recurring Charges (mismatch)	600,000	600,000	600,000	1,800,000
Total Other	**2,275,500**	**1,922,500**	**1,322,500**	**5,520,500**
7) Wage & Benefits @ 60% or $3.5 mill. min.	3,500,000	3,628,691	3,684,860	10,813,551
Health premium increase (5%/year) FYI only	*350,000*	*350,000*	*350,000*	*1,050,000*
Post employment benefits	100,000	100,000	100,000	300,000
Retirement Savings (35 per year @ $15,000)	525,000	525,000	525,000	1,575,000
Total Wage & Benefits Funding	**4,125,000**	**4,253,691**	**4,309,860**	**12,688,551**
8) Reallocation of Existing Budget				
Special Capital Account (.01% PERA)	(100,000)	(100,000)	(100,000)	(300,000)
Retirement savings rolled into salaries	(525,000)	(525,000)	(525,000)	(1,575,000)
Budget reallocation target/Reserve Utilization	(250,000)	(150,000)	(150,000)	(550,000)
Total Resource Reallocations	**(875,000)**	**(775,000)**	**(775,000)**	**(2,425,000)**

Exhibit 5-18—Budget Forecast

MSD of Washington Township, Indianapolis, Indiana
General Fund Forecasted Revenues and Expenditures
1998 Annual Budget

	Actual 1996[1]	Revised Estimate 1997[2]	% Growth	Budget 1998[2]	% Growth	Forecasted 1999	% Growth	Forecasted 2000	% Growth	Forecasted 2001	% Growth
Revenues											
Property Taxes	$ 23,021,338	$ 23,795,267	3.4%	$ 26,205,969	10.1%	$ 27,778,327	6.0%	$ 29,445,026	6.0%	$ 31,211,728	6.0%
Other Local Taxes	3,497,604	3,458,458	(1.1%)	3,685,407	6.6%	3,722,261	1.0%	3,759,483	1.0%	3,797,078	1.0%
State and Federal	21,115,167	21,173,716	0.3%	20,948,363	(1.1%)	20,738,880	(1.0%)	20,531,492	(1.0%)	20,326,178	(1.0%)
Interest on Investments	1,042,848	950,000	(8.9%)	850,000	(10.5%)	900,000	5.9%	950,000	5.6%	975,000	2.6%
Tuition and Fees	929,464	855,000	(8.0%)	730,000	(14.6%)	800,000	9.6%	850,000	6.3%	900,000	5.9%
Other	674,583	305,000	(54.8%)	382,500	25.4%	391,833	2.4%	392,504	0.2%	398,571	1.5%
Total Revenue	$ 50,281,004	$ 50,537,441	0.5%	$ 52,802,239	4.5%	$ 54,331,301	2.9%	$ 55,928,505	2.9%	$ 57,608,555	3.0%
Expenditures											
Instruction	$ 28,460,092	$ 32,609,316	14.6%	$ 31,820,856	(2.4%)	$ 32,775,481	3.0%	$ 33,758,746	3.0%	$ 34,771,508	3.0%
Support Services											
Pupils	1,494,176	1,448,091	(3.1%)	1,566,845	8.2%	1,621,684	3.5%	1,678,443	3.5%	1,712,011	2.0%
Instruction Staff	1,370,088	1,462,115	6.7%	1,452,844	(0.6%)	1,492,819	2.8%	1,534,617	2.8%	1,577,587	2.8%
General Administration	589,304	573,914	(2.6%)	622,311	8.4%	640,980	3.0%	660,209	3.0%	680,016	3.0%
School Administration	3,344,633	2,979,829	(10.9%)	3,110,274	4.4%	3,203,582	3.0%	3,299,689	3.0%	3,398,680	3.0%
Business	5,852,057	5,123,489	(12.4%)	5,294,949	3.3%	5,453,797	3.0%	5,617,411	3.0%	5,757,846	2.5%
Central	7,691,449	8,614,029	12.0%	8,581,369	(0.4%)	8,838,810	3.0%	9,103,974	3.0%	9,377,093	3.0%
Total Support Services	20,341,707	20,201,467	(0.7%)	20,628,592	2.1%	21,251,672	3.0%	21,894,343	3.0%	22,503,233	2.8%
Community Services	46,277	14,300	(69.1%)	142,000	893.0%	15,730	(88.9%)	15,730	0.0%	15,730	0.0%
Nonprogrammed Charges	1,023,711	1,038,500	1.4%	1,038,500	0.0%	1,040,000	0.1%	1,050,000	1.0%	1,060,000	1.0%
Debt Service	-	-		-							
Total Expenditures	$ 49,871,787	$ 53,863,583	8.0%	$ 53,629,948	(0.4%)	$ 55,082,883	2.7%	$ 56,718,819	3.0%	$ 58,350,471	2.9%
Excess (deficiency) of revenues over expenditures	$ 409,217	$ (3,326,142)		$ (827,709)		$ (751,582)		$ (790,314)		$ (741,916)	
Net Interfund Transfers In/(out) From Non-Taxable Funds	$ -	$ -		$ -		$ -		$ -		$ -	
Other Financing Sources (uses)	-										
Budgetary Reconciliation[3]		2,552,596		934,434		750,000		750,000		750,000	
Fund Balance, January 1	3,478,292	3,887,509		3,113,963		3,220,688		3,219,106		3,178,792	
Fund Balance, December 31	$ 3,887,509	$ 3,113,963		$ 3,220,688		$ 3,219,106		$ 3,178,792		$ 3,186,876	

[1] Source: Indiana Department of Education Calendar Financial Report.
[2] Source: State Board of Accounts, School Budget Forms 1, 1-S, 2 & 3.
[3] Refer to page 29 in the Financial Section for a detailed explanation.

Exhibit 5-19—Budget Forecast

SOUTH LYON COMMUNITY SCHOOLS
General Fund
1997-98 Budget With Comparative Information for Years 1993-94 Through 1996-97 and Forecasts for 1998-99 Through 2000-01
Fund Expenditure by Object

	1993-94 Actual	1994-95 Actual	1995-96 Actual	1996-97 Actual	1997-98 Budget	1998-99 Forecast	1999-00 Forecast	2000-01 Forecast
Revenues:								
Property taxes	$ 20,902,480	$ 3,670,798	$ 4,326,506	$ 4,606,738	$ 4,670,000	$ 4,987,934	$ 5,337,887	$ 5,712,393
Other local revenue	512,802	258,386	357,393	294,674	314,812	330,867	340,793	351,017
State of Michigan	773,746	20,751,770	22,337,347	24,696,752	26,426,498	28,225,614	30,205,923	32,325,171
Federal government	1,111	681	0	0	0	0	0	0
Other	328,633	229,579	351,797	769,851	385,888	405,568	417,735	430,267
Transfers from other funds	0	0	0	48,717	26,009	0	0	0
Total Revenues	$ 22,518,772	$ 24,911,214	$ 27,373,043	$ 30,416,732	$ 31,823,207	$ 33,949,983	$ 36,302,339	$ 38,818,848
Expenditures:								
Salaries	$ 13,515,206	$ 14,397,600	$ 15,797,366	$ 17,461,685	$ 18,898,002	$ 20,126,372	$ 21,423,517	$ 22,794,622
Employee benefits	4,281,243	5,673,229	6,001,276	6,441,590	6,952,438	7,623,348	8,324,696	9,090,568
Purchased services	526,350	868,193	1,223,519	1,437,462	1,592,830	1,664,507	1,820,971	1,919,303
Supplies, materials, other	1,950,853	1,899,654	2,222,479	2,401,940	2,280,747	2,383,381	2,607,418	2,748,219
Debt Service	193,375	180,165	183,323	250,872	385,053	402,380	440,204	463,975
Capital Outlay	492,322	370,540	518,743	938,674	646,369	675,456	738,948	778,852
Other expenditures	278,803	118,725	630,408	109,391	113,409	118,512	129,653	136,654
Transfer to other funds	226,121	231,748	604,017	1,145,564	774,253	809,094	885,149	932,947
Total Expenditures	$ 21,464,273	$ 23,739,854	$ 27,181,131	$ 30,187,178	$ 31,643,101	$ 33,803,051	$ 36,370,557	$ 38,865,141
Excess of revenues and other sources (uses) over expenditures:	$ 1,054,499	$ 1,171,360	$ 191,912	$ 229,554	$ 180,106	$ 146,932	$ (68,218)	$ (46,292)
Fund Balance July 1	(318,632)	735,867	1,907,227	2,099,139	1,752,038	1,932,144	2,079,076	2,010,858
Residual Equity Transfer	0	0	0	(576,655)	0	0	0	0
Fund Balance - June 30	$ 735,867	$ 1,907,227	$ 2,099,139	$ 1,752,038	$ 1,932,144	$ 2,079,076	$ 2,010,858	$ 1,964,566
Fund Balance:								
Designated for Bldg. Carryover	94,450	0	88,825	0	0	0	0	0
Designated for Capital Projects	0	0	576,655	242,679	349,989	388,924	192,330	21,309
Prepaid Expenditures	0	0	74,602	0	0	0	0	0
Undesignated	641,417	1,907,227	1,359,057	1,509,359	1,582,155	1,690,153	1,818,528	1,943,257

Exhibit 5-19 (continued)

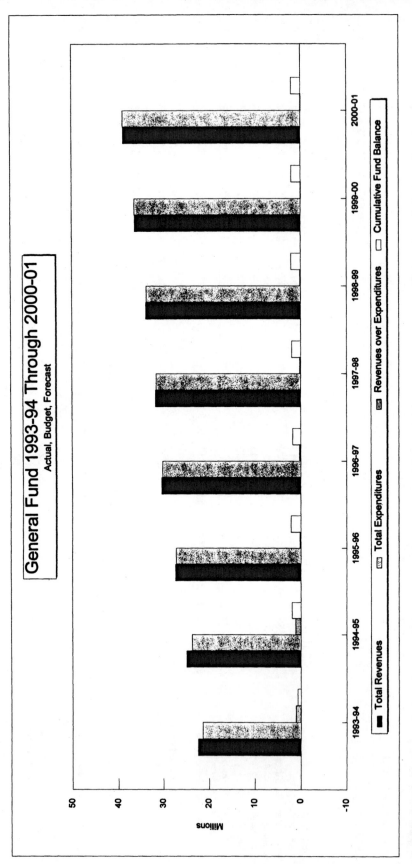

General Fund 1993-94 Through 2000-01
Actual, Budget, Forecast

■ Total Revenues   ▨ Total Expenditures   ▨ Revenues over Expenditures   ☐ Cumulative Fund Balance

This table contains a lot of information on what has happened to the School District financially in the past, as well as a view of what may happen given certain assumptions. Obviously, given the impact of unknowns, this forecast is more helpful in showing trends versus where the District will be in the next few years. Even a one or two percent deviation from the following assumptions will drastically impact the forecast:

Revenues:	1998-99	1999-00	2000-01		Expenditures	1998-99	1999-00	2000-01
Enrollment	4.0%	4.0%	4.0%		Salaries	6.5%	6.4%	6.4%
State Aid	2.7%	2.9%	2.9%		Benefits	9.7%	9.2%	9.2%
Other	5.1%	3.0%	3.0%		Other	4.5%	9.4%	5.4%

Salaries included new employees and step increases, other expenditures include new facility operating costs, CETA plan, and revised CIP plan.

Exhibit 5-19 (continued)

SOUTH LYON COMMUNITY SCHOOLS
Capital Projects Funds
1997-98 Budget With Comparative Information for Years 1993-94 Through 1996-97 and Forecasts for 1998-99 Through 2000-01
Fund Expenditure by Object

	1993-94 Actual	1994-95 Actual	1995-96 Actual	1996-97 Actual	1997-98 Budget	1998-99 Forecast	1999-00 Forecast	2000-01 Forecast
Revenues:								
Interest	$37,192	$124,181	$87,839	$75,000	$0	$0	$0	$0
Investment Income	82,421	0	0	0	0	0	0	0
Proceeds of long-term debt	0	3,470,137	4,100,000	0	0	0	0	0
Transfer From General Fund	0	0	360,250	803,433	474,821	358,937	356,467	298,608
Total Revenues	$119,613	$3,594,318	$4,548,089	$878,433	$474,821	$358,937	$356,467	$298,608
Expenditures:								
Capital Outlay	$8,024,198	$2,914,869	$1,112,527	$3,472,802	$1,974,821	$358,937	$356,467	$298,608
Dues and other fees	0	0	0	0	0	0	0	0
Bond Issuance Costs	0	48,703	72,535	0	0	0	0	0
Total Expenditures	$8,024,198	$2,963,572	$1,185,062	$3,472,802	$1,974,821	$358,937	$356,467	$298,608
Excess of revenues and other sources (uses) over expenditures:	(7,904,585)	630,746	3,363,027	(2,594,369)	(1,500,000)	0	0	0
Fund Balance July 1	8,095,826	191,241	821,987	4,185,014	2,167,300	667,300	667,300	667,300
Residual Equity Transfer	0	0	0	576,655	0	0	0	0
Fund Balance - June 30	$191,241	$821,987	$4,185,014	$2,167,300	$667,300	$667,300	$667,300	$667,300

The Capital Projects Fund type, previously called the Building and Site Fund, is comprised of two distinct funds. The 1996-97 costs associated with the technology project ($4,100,000 bond approved by voters) is accounted for in one fund. The other Capital Projects Fund is a generic fund that is financed by a transfer from the General Fund as opposed to a bond issue. It is used to identify primarily smaller projects over $1,000.

Exhibit 5-19 (continued)

II. CAPITAL IMPROVEMENT PROGRAM 1997-98 Through 2001-02

Definition of Capital Improvement: A capital improvement in South Lyon Community Schools is defined as any expenditure for building improvements, renovations or repairs in which the cost exceeds $1,000.

Capital Improvement Decision Process: The 1995-96 fiscal year is the first year that the Capital Improvement Program (CIP) had been part of the District's Annual Budget. The decision process for the CIP is incorporated into the district's annual budget process, similar to other budgets. Capital improvement needs can originate from the Shared Involvement Process, or from Board of Education, Administration and/or other employees of the District. Once a potential need is identified, it is evaluated by the District's Budget Committee. A final decision on the CIP is rendered at the time of budget adoption.

Functions of the CIP: The CIP allows for long-term financial planning for the District, although the five year plan is a flexible

planning tool. Each year revisions will be made to the plan that add, delete or modify anticipated projects based on changes in funding, project priority, safety issues, and unanticipated needs.

Funding of the CIP: The CIP will be 100% funded through transfers from the General Fund. Therefore, these costs will be isolated from other maintenance type costs and allow for easier identification of the project costs and funding in the District's budget and financial statements.

1997-98 Projects: The Budget includes $474,821 in capital improvement projects for 1997-98 that have been recommended by the Budget Committee. Due to the deficit in the Preliminary Budget, this amount was reduced from original requests that totaled in excess of $700,000. It is very likely that unforeseen situations may change this list of projects, although there is $10,000 in contingency to cover some of these situations.

Building	1997-98	1998-99	1999-00	2000-01	2001-02
High School	16,500	5,500	19,300	10,000	0
Middle School	44,400	15,500	21,000	11,000	0
Bartlett Elementary	11,500	2,500	2,500	2,500	2,500
Centennial Elementary	68,000	4,000	10,000	2,500	2,500
Dolsen Elementary	11,500	2,500	2,500	2,500	2,500
Salem Elementary	13,000	11,500	11,500	7,500	2,500
Sayre Elementary	13,000	2,500	22,500	2,500	2,500
Administration Building	213,721	149,737	147,467	147,908	146,283
Transportation Building	16,600	31,600	16,600	16,600	16,600
Warehouse	3,500	0	0	0	0
Maintenance Department	9,000	9,000	0	0	0
District Wide Projects	44,100	74,600	53,100	40,600	38,600
Contingency	10,000	50,000	50,000	50,000	50,000
Total	474,821	358,937	356,467	293,608	263,983

Exhibit 5-19 (continued)

II. CAPITAL IMPROVEMENT PROGRAM 1997-98 Through 2001-02

1997-98 Projects:

High School:

Project: *Install Fans In Pool Area* - Four fans will be installed in the seating area of the pool   **Cost:** $2,000   Operating Impact: Negligible

Project: *Refurbish Interior Gates* - These are the gates that are used to section the building   **Cost:** $3,500   Operating Impact: Negligible

Project: *Replace Ballasts / Outside Light Covers* - Fifteen ballasts will be replaced on the exterior of the building to fit the new light covers   **Cost:** $2,000   Operating Impact: Some savings due to energy efficiency

Project: *Replace Wallpaper with Paint* - Remove small section of wallpaper and match will washable paint   **Cost:** $2,000   Operating Impact: Negligible, however long-term savings on maintenance

Project: *Install New Paper Towel Holders* - Replace all old units   **Cost:** $1,500   Operating Impact: Negligible

Project: *Repair Roof Leaks* - Various leaks throughout the building   **Cost:** $2,500   Operating Impact: leak damage has been up to $2,000 in the past

Project: *Inspect Outside Bleachers* - Football and baseball bleachers   **Cost:** $3,000   Operating Impact: Will reduce liability and improve safety

Middle School:

Project: *Hook Up Heating Unit in Room 104* - To increase heating   **Cost:** $4,000   Operating Impact: Negligible

Project: *Install Backflow Preventers* - In main water line to improve quality of water   **Cost:** $4,000   Operating Impact: Negligible

Project: *Install Ceiling Fans* - Various classrooms to increase airflow   **Cost:** $1,500   Operating Impact: Negligible

Project: *Demolish Old Press Box / Build New One* - On soccer field bleachers   **Cost:** $5,000   Operating Impact: Negligible

Project: *Room 216 Painting* - Paint back wall only   **Cost:** $1,200   Operating Impact: Negligible

Project: *Repair Kitchen Drains* - Repair leaks   **Cost:** $5,000   Operating Impact: Negligible

Project: *Install Baseboard in Cafe* - Aesthetically pleasing as well as easier to clean   **Cost:** $2,000   Operating Impact: Negligible

Project: *Replace Ventilator Inlet Diffusers* - In gymnasium, old one bent   **Cost:** $1,500   Operating Impact: Negligible

Project: *Add Phone Line to Elevator* - Currently there is no phone   **Cost:** $1,500   Operating Impact: Improve safety

Project: *Install Fencing for Grounds Area* - Paint interior of building   **Building:** Sayre Elementary   **Cost:** $3,000   Operating Impact: Negligible

Project: *Repair Track* - General repair of cracks   **Cost:** $1,000   Operating Impact: Will increase longevity of track

Project: *Waiting Room Office Remodeling* - To allow for segregation of students and staff   **Cost:** $3,000   Operating Impact: Negligible

---

Project: *Repair Gymnasium Bleachers* - Inspection showed need for upgrade and repair   **Cost:** $10,000   Operating Impact: Improve safety, reduce liability

Project: *Replace Grating in Gymnasium Air Handler* - Old unit needed replacing   **Cost:** $1,000   Operating Impact: Negligible, however there will be some increase in unit efficiency

Project: *Replace Gymnasium Padding under Backstops* - Old padding was torn   **Cost:** $1,500   Operating Impact: Improve safety, reduce liability

Project: *Build Storage under Bleachers* - For grounds equipment   **Cost:** $3,000   Operating Impact: Increase life of grounds equipment

Bartlett Elementary:

Project: *Inspect Outside Bleachers* - To determine the safety of bleachers   **Cost:** $1,500   Operating Impact: Improve safety, reduce liability

Project: *Install NCA Sign* - Carryover project for all elementaries and Middle School   **Cost:** $2,500   Operating Impact: None

Project: *Replace Bushes* - Replace dead bushes in front of building   **Cost:** $1,500   Operating Impact: Negligible

Project: *Site Work / Old Community Ed Area* - New grass as well as children's walkway improvements   **Cost:** $3,500   Operating Impact: Improve safety, reduce liability

Project: *Playground Equipment Match* - To assist PTO in upgrading playgrounds   **Cost:** $2,500   Operating Impact: Improve safety, reduce liability

Centennial Elementary:

Project: *Install New Firmed Doors in Supply Rooms* - To allow for more airflow into Kids Club area   **Cost:** $1,500   Operating Impact: Negligible

Project: *HVAC Upgrades* - To increase airflow throughout the entire building   **Cost:** $60,000   Operating Impact: Will increase utility costs by 10%

Project: *Install NCA Sign* - Carryover project for all elementaries and Middle School   **Cost:** $2,500   Operating Impact: None

Project: *Additional Repair Work to Soccer Fields* - To improve new soccer fields install in 1996   **Cost:** $1,500   Operating Impact: Negligible

Project: *Playground Equipment Match* - To assist PTO in upgrading playgrounds   **Cost:** $2,500   Operating Impact: Improve safety, reduce liability

Dolsen Elementary:

Project: *Install NCA Sign* - Carryover project for all elementaries and Middle School   **Cost:** $2,500   Operating Impact: None

Project: *Install Paper Towel Dispensers* - Replacements as well as additional units throughout building   **Cost:** $2,000   Operating Impact: Negligible increase in supplies

Project: *New School Sign* - Exterior of building   **Cost:** $1,000   Operating Impact: None

Project: *Playground Site Work* - To level playground area and allow for proper drainage   **Cost:** $2,500   Operating Impact: Improve safety, reduce liability

Project: *Replace Exterior Door / Room 114B* - Replace old wooden door with steel for safety and security   **Cost:** $1,000   Operating Impact: Negligible

Exhibit 5-19 (continued)

II. CAPITAL IMPROVEMENT PROGRAM 1997-98 Through 2001-02

Project: *Annual Debt Retirement* - New building   Cost: $148,721   Operating Impact: Debt retirement for 15 years

Transportation Building:

Project: *Parking Lot Expansion* - Adds 16 spaces for additional buses   Cost: $16,600   Operating Impact: Negligible

Warehouse:

Project: *Clean Up Behind Warehouse* - Construction debris   Cost: $1,500   Operating Impact: Improve safety, reduce liability

Project: *Install Alarms* - No alarm currently   Cost: $2,000   Operating Impact: Improve safety, reduce liability $260 annual cost

District Wide Projects:

Project: *Phone System* - Current systems are over 15 years old   Cost: $35,600   Operating Impact: This will be financed over five years

Project: *Fencing Repairs on Ball Fields* - Throughout district   Cost: $1,500   Operating Impact: Improve safety, reduce liability

Project: *Additional Pea Gravel for Playgrounds* - To improve depth of gravel   Cost: $4,000   Operating Impact: Improve safety, reduce liability

Project: *Install Crusher Dust on Fields* - To improve field playability   Cost: $3,000   Operating Impact: Improve safety, reduce liability, and a negligible reduction in grounds maintenance

Maintenance Department:

Project: *Boiler Stack Gas Tests* - All building boilers   Cost: $3,000   Operating Impact: Improve safety, reduce liability and reduce boiler utility cost from 4%-10%

Project: *Electrical Stock Items* - To provide ready inventory   Cost: $1,500   Operating Impact: Reduction in travel costs

Project: *Nuts/Bolts Stock Setup* - To provide ready inventory   Cost: $3,000   Operating Impact: Reduction in travel costs

Project: *Plumbing Parts Stock Items* - To provide ready inventory   Cost: $1,500   Operating Impact: Reduction in travel costs

Contingency:

Project: *Contingency / Next Year Project Costs* - For cost overruns and unseen projects   Cost: $10,000   Operating Impact: None

---

Project: *Playground Equipment Match* - To assist PTO in upgrading playgrounds   Cost: $2,500   Operating Impact: Improve safety, reduce liability

Salem Elementary:

Project: *Playground Upgrades* - Due impact of new track and grant project   Cost: $2,500   Operating Impact: Improve safety, reduce liability

Project: *Redo Communications with AHU in Classrooms* - To improve computer control of air handling units   Cost: $3,000   Operating Impact: 2%-5% savings in utilities

Project: *Install NCA Sign* - Carryover project for all elementaries and Middle School   Cost: $2,500   Operating Impact: None

Project: *Repair Carpet* - Old carpet torn   Cost: $1,500   Operating Impact: Improve safety, reduce liability

Project: *Replace Plexiglass with Tempered* - In main hallway   Cost: $1,000   Operating Impact: None

Project: *Playground Equipment Match* - To assist PTO in upgrading playgrounds   Cost: $2,500   Operating Impact: Improve safety, reduce liability

Sayre Elementary:

Project: *Build Bell Stand* - To house old school bell and time capsule that was at Community Ed Building   Cost: $2,000   Operating Impact: None

Project: *Enlarge AV Room for Classroom* - Due to increased student enrollment   Cost: $2,500   Operating Impact: Negligible increase in utilities and custodial

Project: *Install NCA Sign* - Carryover project for all elementaries and Middle School   Cost: $2,500   Operating Impact: None

Project: *Repair/Replace Water Tank* - Old tank was at least 20 years old   Cost: $1,500   Operating Impact: Some savings of hot water heat

Project: *Replace Base Cove* - Throughout school   Cost: $2,000   Operating Impact: Negligible savings in cleaning

Project: *Playground Equipment Match* - To assist PTO in upgrading playgrounds   Cost: $2,500   Operating Impact: Improve safety, reduce liability

Administration Building:

Project: *Remove AC Unit for Kids Club* - When old building is torn down   Cost: $5,000   Operating Impact: Savings of $10,000 versus buying new unit

Project: *New Building Technology* - For new administration building   Cost: $60,000   Operating Impact: Some increase in utility cost as well as technical support

Exhibit 5-19 (continued)

CAPITAL IMPROVEMENT PROGRAM

Building	Contractor (C)/ Staff (S)/ Both (B)	Task Description	1997-98	1998-99	1999-00	2000-01	2001-02
ADMIN	C	REMOVE AC UNIT ON ADMIN AND MOVE TO CENTENNIAL FOR KIDS CLUB	5,000				
ADMIN	C	NEW BUILDING TECHNOLOGY	60,000				
ADMIN	N/A	ANNUAL DEBT RETIREMENT	148,721	149,737	147,467	147,908	146,283
VARIOUS	C	DISTRICT WIDE PHONE SYSTEM	35,600	35,600	35,600	35,600	35,600
VARIOUS	C	DISPOSE OF CHEMICALS MAINTENANCE		25,000			
VARIOUS	C	FENCING REPAIRS ON BALL FIELDS	1,500				
VARIOUS	S	FINISH PEA GRAVEL ALL PLAYGROUNDS	4,000	4,000	4,500		
VARIOUS	S	INSTALL CRUSHER DUST ON FIELDS	3,000	3,000	3,000	3,000	3,000
VARIOUS	S	REPLENISH STONES AT ALL SCHOOLS		2,000			
VARIOUS	B	INSTALL CURBS TO KEEP PEOPLE OFF OF THE GRASS		3,000			
VARIOUS	C	FENCING REPAIRS THROUGHOUT DISTRICT		2,000		2,000	
VARIOUS	C	INSTALL ALARMS TO FREEZERS			10,000		
BARTLETT	C	INSPECT OUTSIDE BLEACHERS	1,500				
BARTLETT	B	INSTALL NCA SIGN	2,500				
BARTLETT	S	REPLACE BUSHES	1,500				
BARTLETT	B	COMMUNITY ED OLD SITE WORK	3,500				
BARTLETT	C	PLAYGROUND EQUIPMENT MATCH	2,500	2,500	2,500	2,500	2,500
BUS GARAGE	C	PARKING LOT EXPANSION	16,600	16,600	16,600	16,600	16,600
BUS GARAGE	C	TANK REMOVAL		15,000			
CENTENNIAL	S	INSTALL NEW FINNED DOORS IN SUPPLY ROOMS	1,500				
CENTENNIAL	C	HVAC UPGRADES	60,000				
CENTENNIAL	B	INSTALL NCA SIGN	2,500				
CENTENNIAL	B	REWIRE SUMP PUMPS AND INSTALL ALARMS		1,500			
CENTENNIAL	B	ADDITIONAL REPAIR / WORK TO SOCCER FIELDS	1,500				
CENTENNIAL	C	PLAYGROUND EQUIPMENT MATCH	2,500	2,500	2,500	2,500	2,500
CENTENNIAL	B	REPLACE STAGE FLOOR			3,000		
CENTENNIAL	S	UPGRADE PLUMBING FIXTURES			3,000		
CENTENNIAL	S	REMOVE BASEBALL BACKSTOP TOWARD CENTENNIAL			1,500		
DOLSEN	B	INSTALL NCA SIGN	2,500				
DOLSEN	S	INSTALL PAPER TOWEL DISPENSERS IN BATHROOMS/CLASSROOMS	2,000				
DOLSEN	C	NEW SCHOOL SIGN	1,000				
DOLSEN	S	PLAYGROUND SITE WORK	2,500				
DOLSEN	S	REPLACE RM 114B EXTERIOR DOOR	1,000				
DOLSEN	C	PLAYGROUND EQUIPMENT MATCH	2,500	2,500	2,500	2,500	2,500
HIGH SCHOOL	C	INSTALL FANS IN POOL CEILING	2,000				
HIGH SCHOOL	C	REFIRBISH INTERIOR GATES /REPAIR	3,500				
HIGH SCHOOL	S	REPLACE BALLESTS FOR OUTSIDE LIGHTS / COVERS	2,000				
HIGH SCHOOL	B	REPLACE WALLPAPER WITH PAINT	2,000				
HIGH SCHOOL	S	INSTALL NEW PAPER TOWEL HOLDERS THROUGHOUT	1,500				
HIGH SCHOOL	C	REPAIR ROOF LEAKS	2,500	2,500			
HIGH SCHOOL	C	INSPECT OUTSIDE BLEACHERS	3,000	3,000			
HIGH SCHOOL	S	INSTALL ELECTRICITY TO SOFTBALL			1,300		
HIGH SCHOOL	C	RESURFACE AND PAINT GYM FLOOR			8,000		
HIGH SCHOOL	C	REPLACE QUARY TILE			10,000		
HIGH SCHOOL	C	PAINT LOCKERS				15,000	
MAINTENANCE	C	BOILER STACK GAS TESTS	3,000	3,000			
MAINTENANCE	C	ELECTRICAL STOCK ITEMS	1,500	1,500			
MAINTENANCE	C	NUTS/BOLTS STOCK SETUP	3,000	3,000			
MAINTENANCE	C	PLUMBING PARTS ITEMS	1,500	1,500			
MIDDLE SCHOOL	S	HOOK UP HEATING UNIT IN RM 134	1,200				
MIDDLE SCHOOL	C	INSTALL BACKFLOW PREVENTERS	4,000				
MIDDLE SCHOOL	S	INSTALL FANS IN CEILINGS VARIOUS CLASSROOMS	1,500				
MIDDLE SCHOOL	C	CONNECT AUDIBLE ALARM FOR PUMP ROOM	0	1,000			
MIDDLE SCHOOL	B	MOVE PRESS BOX DOWN AND BUILD NEW ONE	5,000				

Exhibit 5-19 (continued)

CAPITAL IMPROVEMENT PROGRAM

MIDDLE SCHOOL	S	NEED HOLES PATCHED AND PAINTED RM 216	1,200				
MIDDLE SCHOOL	C	REPAIR KITCHEN DRAINS	5,000				
MIDDLE SCHOOL	C	REPIPE DRAINS FROM SOFTENER TO PUMP ROOM	0	2,000			
MIDDLE SCHOOL	S	INSTALL BASEBOARD IN CAFÉ	2,000				
MIDDLE SCHOOL	C	REPAIR WATER LEAK ON MAIN IN TUNNEL	0	2,000			
MIDDLE SCHOOL	S	REPLACE VENTILATOR INLET DIFUSERS	1,500				
MIDDLE SCHOOL	C	ADD PHONE LINE TO ELEVATOR	1,500				
MIDDLE SCHOOL	C	INSTALL FENCING M/S FOR GROUNDS AREA	2,000				
MIDDLE SCHOOL	S	REPAIR MIDDLE SCHOOL TRACK	1,000				
MIDDLE SCHOOL	B	WAITING ROOM / OFFICE REMODELING	3,000				
MIDDLE SCHOOL	C	REPAIR GYMNASIUM BLEACHERS	10,000				
MIDDLE SCHOOL	C	REPLACE CHAIN LINK FENCING IN BALCONY	0	1,500			
MIDDLE SCHOOL	C	REPLACE GRATING IN GYM AIR HANDLER	1,000				
MIDDLE SCHOOL	C	REPLACE GYM PADDING UNDER BACKSTOPS	1,500				
MIDDLE SCHOOL	S	BUILD STORAGE UNDER BLEACHERS	3,000		3,000		
MIDDLE SCHOOL	S	REMOVE CHAIN LINK FENCING AT BOTTOM OF STAIRWELLS		1,000			
MIDDLE SCHOOL	C	REPAIR GYM FLOOR		2,000			
MIDDLE SCHOOL	C	CONNECT UNITS NOT IN CLASSROOMS TO COMPUTER CONTROLS		2,000	2,000		
MIDDLE SCHOOL	B	PAINTING OF CLASSROOMS UPSTAIRS		4,000	4,000		
MIDDLE SCHOOL	C	MOVE AUDIBLE ALARM TO HALLWAY			1,000		
MIDDLE SCHOOL	C	RESURFACE AND PAINT GYM FLOOR			6,000		
MIDDLE SCHOOL	B	PAINTING OF CLASSROOMS DOWNSTAIRS			5,000	5,000	
MIDDLE SCHOOL	S	PAINT BUILDING EXTERIOR				4,000	
MIDDLE SCHOOL	C	INSTALL LIGHT ON SCHOOL SIGN				2,000	
SALEM	S	PLAYGROUND UPGRADES	2,500				
SALEM	B	REDO COMMUNICATIONS WITH AHU IN CLASSROOMS	3,000				
SALEM	B	INSTALL NCA SIGN	2,500				
SALEM	C	REPAIR CARPET	1,500				
SALEM	S	REPLACE PLEXIGLASS WITH TEMPERED	1,000				
SALEM	C	PLAYGROUND EQUIPMENT MATCH	2,500	2,500	2,500	2,500	2,500
SALEM	C	RETILE THREE CLASSROOMS		4,000	4,000		
SALEM	C	REPLACE CARPET THREE CLASSROOMS		5,000	5,000	5,000	
SAYRE	C	BUILD BELL STAND	2,000				
SAYRE	S	ENLARGE AV ROOM FOR CLASSROOM	2,500				
SAYRE	B	INSTALL NCA SIGN	2,500				
SAYRE	C	REPAIR / REPLACE WATER TANK	1,500				
SAYRE	S	REPLACE BASE COVE - REST OF SCHOOL	2,000				
SAYRE	C	PLAYGROUND EQUIPMENT MATCH	2,500	2,500	2,500	2,500	2,500
SAYRE	S	PAINT CLASSROOMS			10,000		
SAYRE	B	CLEAN UP BACK DUMP SITE NORTH			5,000		
SAYRE	B	CLEAN UP BACK DUMP SITE EAST			5,000		
WAREHOUSE	S	CLEAN UP BEHIND WAREHOUSE	1,500				
WAREHOUSE	C	INSTALL ALARMS	2,000				
CONTINENCY	B	CONTINGENCY / NEXT YEAR PREP FEES	10,000	50,000	50,000	50,000	50,000
		TOTALS	474,821	358,937	356,467	298,608	263,983

Student Enrollment History and Forecasts

(Criterion E-7)

Exhibit 5-20

Exhibit 5-21

Exhibit 5-22

Exhibit 5-20—Student Enrollment History and Forecast

PRINCE WILLIAM COUNTY PUBLIC SCHOOLS

STUDENT MEMBERSHIP SUMMARY AND PROJECTION

Grade Level	Sept 1994 Actual	Sept 1995 Actual	Sept 1996 Actual	Sept 1996 Estimate	Sept 1997 Estimate	Projected Increase (Decrease)	Sept 1998 Projection	Sept 1999 Projection	Sept 2000 Projection
Pre-K	454	460	324	0	0	0	0	0	0
K	3,447	3,677	3,611	3,744	3,580	(31)	3,650	3,720	3,790
T-1	0	0	0	0	0	0	0	0	0
1	3,551	3,818	4,051	3,984	3,979	(72)	3,945	4,022	4,099
2	3,715	3,682	3,884	3,900	4,127	243	4,054	4,019	4,098
3	3,665	3,737	3,781	3,646	3,912	131	4,156	4,083	4,048
4	3,684	3,752	3,775	3,793	3,831	56	3,963	4,210	4,137
5	3,764	3,807	3,784	3,828	3,857	73	3,914	4,049	4,301
6	3,625	3,782	3,790	3,652	3,817	27	3,868	3,925	4,060
7	3,624	3,666	3,857	3,880	3,829	(28)	3,837	3,911	3,968
8	3,484	3,637	3,680	3,730	3,831	151	3,825	3,830	3,904
9	3,996	4,281	4,328	4,305	4,369	41	4,567	4,537	4,543
10	3,135	3,304	3,511	3,527	3,529	18	3,577	4,129	4,102
11	2,821	2,867	2,980	2,999	3,189	209	3,206	3,234	3,733
12	2,870	2,877	3,009	2,942	3,088	79	3,292	3,326	3,355
Special Schools	311	244	150	188	200	50	200	200	200
TJHS Students	135	117	133	117	133	0	117	117	117
Total excluding Pre-K Students	45,827	47,248	48,324	48,235	49,271	947	50,171	51,312	52,455

This chart shows that the September 1996 estimate anticipated 89 fewer students than actually enrolled in Prince William County Schools. The September 1996 Actual membership of 48,324 students is expected to increase by an estimated 947 students to 49,271 in September 1997.

The Prince William County School Division does not receive state Basic Aid funding for pre-kindergarten students.

Source of out-year projections is the Capital Improvements Program as approved March 22, 1997.

Exhibit 5-20 (continued)

Student Enrollment Forecasting Methodology

The forecasting methodology used to predict the number of students who will be attending Prince William County Schools for the next six years is a combination of methods and analyses. These methods include a birth to kindergarten analysis, the cohort survival method for grades 1 through 12 for one year ahead, the generation factor analysis for all projections more than one year ahead, and judgmental adjustments to fine-tune the forecasts. This combination of methods is used because it provides for accurate forecasts and at the same time is relatively inexpensive to produce.

Phase I - First Year Out Forecasts

The year out forecasts are created using a birth to kindergarten analysis and the cohort progression method, on a school by grade basis, for first through twelfth grades. These forecasts are then used as a baseline for calculating the forecasts for the out years.

The *Birth to Kindergarten* method used to forecast incoming kindergartners is a modified cohort procedure. Instead of using the grade to grade progression used in the standard cohort progression method, births county-wide are used to forecast kindergarten enrollment five years later.

The *Cohort Progression* method is, in basic terms, the application of an average growth rate over time to the current year's enrollment by grade progression. This growth rate can be taken from the previous year or from an average of several previous years. The resulting ratio or growth rate is then applied to the current year's enrollment to project the next year's enrollment.

Phase II - Out Year Forecasts

The out year forecasts are created using the *Generation Factor* method and are built using the first year (from Phase I) as a baseline. This is a rather simple but effective method that can, with accurate data, provide highly accurate forecasts of future enrollments.

Generation factors are created by calculating the number of students per housing unit of each type within the county. This ratio is then applied to the number of projected housing units to produce the projected number of new students in Prince William County Schools. To more accurately project student growth using the generation method, the type of housing unit and school level must be taken into consideration. What results is a matrix of nine generation factors for single family, townhouse, and apartment units for each of the three school levels (elementary, middle, and high). Where appropriate, judgmental adjustments are made.

The accuracy of this forecasting method has resulted in an average error margin of less than 0.4% for county-wide forecasts. Success at the school level has not been as great, but the forecasts have been well within the acceptable range. County-wide forecasts have been more successful than the school level forecasts because the population being forecasted is much larger. This phenomenon is common to all forecasting methodologies and is therefore expected.

Exhibit 5-20 (continued)

II. Enrollment

ENROLLMENT HISTORY and TRENDS

Enrollment has grown steadily over the years as Jordan District has changed from a rural farming community to one of the state's prime residential and commercial areas. Currently, the population is shifting as housing matures in the District's northeast section and residential development continues at an accelerated rate in the west and far south sections. Enrollment growth is expected to continue for at least 20 more years.

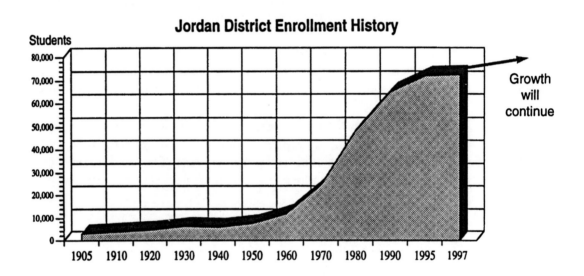

ENROLLMENT HISTORY and PROJECTIONS

In January 1997, A/P Associates, an outside consulting firm, was hired to update Jordan District's enrollment projections. Working in consultation with the Bureau of Economic and Business Research, David Eccles School of Business, University of Utah, and with assistance from city planners in each of the municipalities, the firm projected enrollments by area through the year 2006. The graph below shows the A/P Associates' 10-year total enrollment projections:

10-year Total District Enrollment Projections

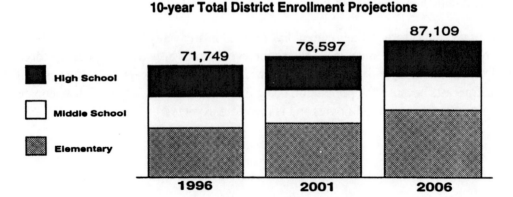

Exhibit 5-20 (continued)

METHODOLOGY USED FOR ENROLLMENT ESTIMATES

Each year, as part of the annual planning cycle, an estimate is made of Jordan District's mid-year enrollment by school, grade level, and total district. Because the enrollment estimates are used for hiring, they are conservative by design. The 1997-98 enrollment estimates are based on the following factors:

1. The current enrollment trend as shown by a 4-year enrollment history by school.
2. The number of students who continue in the system from one year to the next.
3. The number as the continuing students move forward one grade.
4. The number of students transferring to other Districts on group permits.
5. The number of housing starts within each geographic area and the estimated number of students per new household.
6. The number of students that are expected to move away or drop out of school by mid-year.

Based upon these factors, the estimated enrollment used for developing the 1997-98 budget is 72,693. This is 333 more students than the District enrolled at the first of the 1996-97 school year and represents a growth rate of 0.46%. Most of the additional students will be at the elementary level. Major enrollment increases will occur in schools west of the Jordan River; however, much of these increases will be countered by enrollment declines in the District's Northeast area. (See the school by school enrollment estimates on pages 113, 114, and 115.)

Exhibit 5-21—Student Enrollment History and Forecast

JORDAN SCHOOL DISTRICT
ELEMENTARY ENROLLMENT

* Year-round Schedule

Northeast Area

	Actual Oct. 1996	Est. 1997-98	Difference
Bella Vista	449	433	-16
Brookwood	524	481	-43
Butler	630	628	-2
Canyon View	597	560	-37
Copperview	593	582	-11
Cottonwood Heights	537	523	-14
East Midvale	506	504	-2
East Sandy	727	723	-4
Granite	756	741	-18
Midvale	617	590	-27
Midvalley	676	666	-10
Mountview	567	540	-27
Oakdale	616	598	-18
Peruvian Park	686	664	-22
Quail Hollow	818	806	-12
Ridgecrest	511	501	-10
Silver Mesa	655	639	-16
17 Schools	**10,468**	**10,179**	**-289**

Southeast Area

	Actual Oct. 1996	Est. 1997-98	Difference
Altara*	1,063	1,056	-7
Alta View	593	576	-17
Bell View	529	538	+9
Crescent*	1,044	1,036	-8
Draper*	1,002	1,053	+51
Edgemont	740	747	+7
Lone Peak*	1,012	1,034	+22
Park Lane*	855	845	-10
Sandy	669	669	—
Sprucewood*	1,029	1,074	+45
Sunrise*	953	934	-19
Willow Canyon*	808	782	-26
12 Schools	**10,297**	**10,344**	**+47**

Northwest Area

	Actual Oct. 1996	Est. 1997-98	Difference
Columbia*	1,032	1,106	+74
Heartland	657	647	-10
Majestic	464	440	-24
Mtn. Shadows*	1,154	1,239	+85
Oquirrh*	867	856	-11
Riverside*	991	1,030	+39
Terra Linda*	1,107	1,166	+59
West Jordan*	840	818	-22
Westland*	787	761	-26
Westvale*	1,018	1,042	+24
10 Schools	**8,917**	**9,105**	**+188**

Southwest Area

	Actual Oct. 1996	Est. 1997-98	Difference
Bluffdale*	1,020	1,103	+83
Jordan Ridge*	1,082	1,129	+47
Monte Vista*	1,214	1,064	-150
Riverton*	884	897	+13
Rosamond*	1,012	1,014	+2
South Jordan*	1,044	1,082	+38
Southland*	1,003	1,110	+107
Welby*	1,023	1,194	+171
8 Schools	**8,282**	**8,593**	**+311**

TOTAL ELEMENTARY ENROLLMENT (47 Schools)

Actual Oct. 1996	Est. 1997-98	Difference
37,964	38,221	+257

Exhibit 5-21 (continued)

MIDDLE SCHOOL ENROLLMENT

Northeast Area	Actual Oct. 1996	Est. 1997-98	Difference
Albion	1,207	1,205	-2
Butler	1,382	1,313	-69
Midvale	750	703	-47
Union	1,289	1,224	-65
4 Schools	4,628	4,445	-183

Southeast Area	Actual Oct. 1996	Est. 1997-98	Difference
Crescent View	1,338	1,354	+16
Eastmont	1,194	1,156	-38
Indian Hills	1,451	1,395	-56
Mt. Jordan	922	889	-33
4 Schools	4,905	4,794	-111

Northwest Area	Actual Oct. 1996	Est. 1997-98	Difference
Joel P. Jensen	1,312	1,254	-58
West Hills	766	866	+100
West Jordan	1,343	1,298	-45
3 Schools	3,421	3,418	-3

Southwest Area	Actual Oct. 1996	Est. 1997-98	Difference
Elk Ridge	1,286	1,495	+209
Oquirrh Hills	1,632	1,567	-65
South Jordan	1,562	1,600	+38
3 Schools	4,480	4,662	+182

Total Middle School Enrollment (14 Schools)

Actual Oct. 1996	Est. 1997-98	Difference
17,434	17,319	-115

HIGH SCHOOL ENROLLMENT

Northeast Area	Actual Oct. 1996	Est. 1997-98	Difference
Brighton	2,449	2,395	-54
Hillcrest	2,197	2,066	-131
2 Schools	4,646	4,461	-185

Southeast Area	Actual Oct. 1996	Est. 1997-98	Difference
Alta	2,564	2,456	-108
Jordan	2,331	2,527	+196
2 Schools	4,895	4,983	+88

Northwest Area	Actual Oct. 1996	Est. 1997-98	Difference
Copper Hills	1,777	1,900	+123
West Jordan	2,240	2,201	-39
2 Schools	4,017	4,101	+84

Southwest Area	Actual Oct. 1996	Est. 1997-98	Difference
Bingham	2,778	2,902	+124
1 School	2,778	2,902	+124

Total High School Enrollment (7 Schools)

Actual Oct. 1996	Est. 1997-98	Difference
16,995	17,186	+ 191

Exhibit 5-21 (continued)

ENROLLMENT IN SCHOOLS SERVING SPECIAL POPULATIONS DISTRICT WIDE

	Actual Oct. 1996	Est. 1997-98	Difference
Alternative High School			
Valley High	656	739	+83
Odyssey House	3	0	—
Special Education Schools			
Jordan Resource	21	21	—
Jordan Valley	81	81	—
South Valley	81	81	—
Utah State Prison			
South Park Academy	28	28	—

TOTAL DISTRICT ENROLLMENT

	Actual Oct. 1996	Est. 1997-98	Difference
Elementary Enrollment	37,964	38,221	+257
Middle School Enrollment	17,434	17,319	-115
High School Enrollment	16,995	17,186	+191
Valley High	656	739	+83
Special Education	183	183	—
South Park Academy	28	28	—
TOTAL	72,693	73,026	+333

Exhibit 5-22—Student Enrollment History and Forecast

Mt. Lebanon School District
1997-98 Budget

ENROLLMENT STATISTICS

Enrollment forecasts are the basic planning tool for all school districts. They are the prime indicator of future trends for staff, programs and services.

This enrollment projection is based upon the cohort survival and grade progression methods of enrollment forecasting. This method assumes that grade one becomes grade two in the following year and that migration patterns affecting this process continue from one year to the next. The federal government, Commonwealth of Pennsylvania and the Department of Education had all been predicting gradual increases in the number of live births during past years. We have seen this trend materialize in Mt. Lebanon.

School district enrollment projections have been quite accurate. Next year's kindergarten was born four years ago and our annual census provides us with the identity of members of next year's kindergarten class. The discrepancies, when they occur, are usually the result of changes in migration patterns.

POPULATION AGES 3-17 FROM 1990-1996

AGE	1990	1991	1992	1993	1994	1995	1996
3	380	443	410	527	419	438	402
4	437	395	454	481	496	434	443
5	468	493	455	523	468	508	485
6	489	435	466	452	487	470	510
7	447	486	451	491	466	486	476
8	452	469	468	460	520	474	492
9	461	445	458	479	472	531	494
10	409	456	453	451	487	483	544
11	391	402	463	460	460	494	494
12	371	396	392	445	469	477	511
13	385	363	387	391	456	486	490
14	362	377	368	391	419	462	508
15	374	371	380	360	385	421	475
16	402	384	371	383	365	377	414
17	304	376	363	366	324	314	337

Exhibit 5-22 (continued)

Mt. Lebanon School District
1997-98 Budget

ENROLLMENT STATISTICS
(Continued)

Each October the Office of Civil Rights requires the school district to enumerate minority races enrolled in the public schools. The following is a comparison of prior years.

MINORITY ENROLLMENT

	1972	1982	1992	1996
American Indian or Alaskan Native	2	1	1	0
Black	14	35	47	49
Asian or Pacific Islander	23	95	138	136
Hispanic	0	4	20	33

In August we conduct a census of students enrolled in the Mt. Lebanon School District by street and house number. In 1996-97 our 5,546 students lived in 3,620 homes.

STUDENT-DWELLING RATIO

	1970	1981	1996
Single family dwelling units	10,207	10,455	10,811
Two family and multifamily dwelling units	2,287	3,077	3,364
Total dwelling units	12,494	13,532	14,075
Enrollment in all public schools K-12	8,667	5,864	5,546
Dwelling units sending students	4,492	3,437	3,620
Students per average dwelling unit	0.69	0.43	0.39
Students per home sending students	1.93	1.71	1.53
Dwelling units not sending students	8,002	10,095	10,455
Percent of dwelling units not sending students to Mt. Lebanon	64%	75%	74%
Percent of dwelling units sending students to Mt. Lebanon Schools	36%	25%	26%

Exhibit 5-22 (continued)

Mt. Lebanon School District
1997-98 Budget

ENROLLMENT PROJECTIONS

DISTRICT WIDE ENROLLMENTS AND PROJECTIONS

GRADE	ACTUAL*					PROJECTIONS*				
	1992	1993	1994	1995	1996	1997	1998	1999	2000	2001
K	387	415	426	416	395	434	412	376	400	400
1	457	422	427	436	447	412	453	435	395	421
2	413	460	423	423	436	446	411	452	434	395
3	419	424	463	420	415	434	443	407	449	431
4	429	436	433	469	435	425	444	457	419	462
5	415	435	440	439	469	438	427	447	460	422
6	419	444	447	464	457	488	458	449	467	482
7	364	417	430	447	451	448	480	448	440	458
8	335	355	426	425	436	449	442	473	443	434
9	348	364	378	431	447	455	465	461	492	461
10	356	330	363	366	434	443	450	463	457	488
11	372	363	335	357	360	431	437	444	458	451
12	326	364	373	342	364	368	440	446	453	467
TOTAL	5,040	5,229	5,364	5,435	5,546	5,671	5,762	5,758	5,767	5,772

TOTALS BY CATEGORY

GRADE	ACTUAL**					PROJECTIONS**				
	1992	1993	1994	1995	1996	1997	1998	1999	2000	2001
Elementary	2,939	3,036	3,059	3,067	3,054	3,077	3,048	3,023	3,024	3,013
Secondary	2,101	2,193	2,305	2,368	2,498	2,612	2,734	2,775	2,810	2,759

* Reflects the school year beginning September

Exhibit 5-22 (continued)

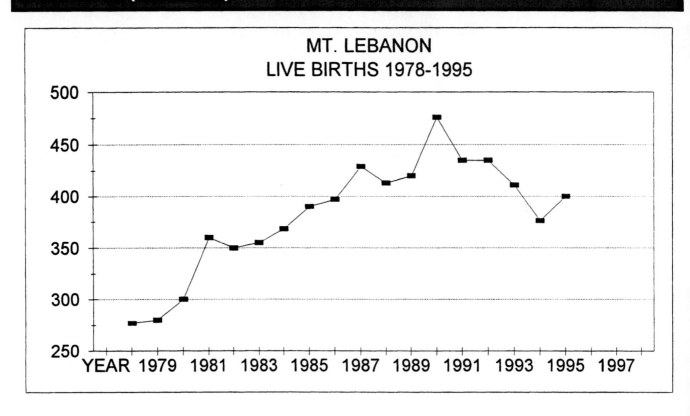

MT. LEBANON
LIVE BIRTHS 1978-1995

LIVE BIRTHS 1988-1995
MT. LEBANON AND ALLEGHENY COUNTY

	1988	1989	1990	1991	1992	1993	1994	1995
Mt. Lebanon	413	420	476	435	435	411	376	400
Allegheny County	17,356	17,822	18,068	17,441	17,583	16,638	16,128	15,506

Source: Allegheny County Health Department

Personnel Resource Allocations

(Criterion E-8)

Exhibit 5-23

Exhibit 5-24

Exhibit 5-25

Exhibit 5-26

Exhibit 5-27

Exhibit 5-28

Exhibit 5-23—Personnel Resource Allocations

Prince William County Public Schools
FY 1998 Approved Budget

Personnel Position History

	FY 1993	FY 1994	FY 1995	FY 1996	FY 1997	FY 1998
School Board Member	8.00	8.00	8.00	8.00	8.00	8.00
Superintendent	1.00	1.00	1.00	1.00	1.00	1.00
Associate Superintendent	6.00	6.00	6.00	6.00	6.00	6.00
Director	8.00	9.00	9.00	9.00	9.00	9.00
Associate Director	1.00	0.00	0.00	0.00	0.00	0.00
Supervisor	61.41	48.65	48.88	46.00	44.00	46.00
Project Manager	0.00	0.00	0.00	0.00	2.00	2.00
Principal	61.00	62.25	65.50	66.00	66.00	67.00
Assistant Principal	59.00	60.00	61.00	60.00	60.00	58.67
Teacher, Admin Assignment	27.95	49.15	50.35	53.85	58.07	65.05
Teacher, Classroom	2,696.91	2,779.26	2,818.37	2,860.86	2,959.47	3,037.81
Librarian	69.50	70.00	69.50	70.50	72.00	73.00
Counselor	131.90	132.55	135.45	137.01	135.29	142.56
Visiting Teacher	21.00	21.00	22.00	21.80	22.00	23.50
Psychologist	21.00	23.60	22.60	24.10	23.60	24.60
School Nurse	1.00	1.50	0.50	1.00	1.00	1.00
Diagnostician	5.00	5.22	7.00	10.00	9.50	10.50
Behavior Specialist	0.00	0.00	0.00	10.20	6.00	5.00
Teacher Assistant	313.73	328.50	320.00	340.86	372.46	374.21
Student Attendant	10.00	11.50	9.00	7.50	7.00	23.50
Cafeteria Aide	53.00	60.00	58.50	56.00	63.50	62.50
Bus Aide	91.00	91.00	91.00	91.00	93.00	97.00
Attendance Personnel	8.00	8.00	6.00	6.00	6.00	6.00
Technologist/Technician	16.00	19.00	35.00	43.19	45.00	51.00
Home/Community Specialist	1.50	3.00	3.00	3.50	3.70	3.70
Coordinator	12.00	12.00	12.00	12.00	13.00	12.00
Specialist	48.50	51.00	63.50	67.80	84.99	91.00
Secretary/Clerical	370.13	364.06	362.31	373.41	385.51	394.33
Maintenance Personnel	133.00	134.00	134.00	134.00	132.00	132.00
Bus Driver	417.00	417.00	417.00	413.00	421.00	431.00
Garage Employee	31.00	31.00	31.00	32.00	32.00	32.00
Bus Service Attendant	13.00	13.00	13.00	13.00	13.00	13.00
Custodian	320.50	314.25	314.00	315.50	317.80	320.55
Warehouseman	22.00	22.00	21.00	21.00	21.00	21.00
Total	5,040.03	5,156.49	5,215.46	5,315.08	5,493.89	5,645.48

Exhibit 5-24—Personnel Resource Allocations

DeSoto Parish School Board
Mansfield, Louisiana

Total Personnel Roster (1)

	Actual 1988-89	Actual 1989-90	Actual 1990-91	Actual 1991-92	Actual 1992-93	Actual 1993-94	Actual 1994-95	Actual 1995-96	Budget 1996-97	Budget 1997-98
Instruction:										
Principals	11.0	11.0	11.0	11.0	9.0	9.0	11.0	12.0	12.0	12.0
Assistant Principals	6.0	6.0	8.0	8.0	8.0	8.0	7.0	10.0	12.0	12.0
Teachers	315.0	324.0	322.0	322.0	326.0	339.0	349.0	359.5	359.0	356.0
Librarians	9.0	10.0	10.0	10.0	10.0	10.0	10.0	11.0	11.0	11.0
Aides	52.0	55.0	55.5	60.5	72.5	76.5	80.5	82.5	83.0	84.0
Support Services:										
Superintendent	1.0	1.0	1.0	1.0	1.0	1.0	1.0	1.0	1.0	1.0
Administrators	10.0	10.0	11.0	12.0	12.0	12.5	12.5	12.5	11.5	11.5
Other Professional	4.0	5.5	6.0	6.0	6.0	7.0	6.5	7.5	7.5	7.5
Psychologist	2.0	2.0	2.0	2.0	2.0	2.0	2.0	2.0	2.0	2.0
Counselors	5.0	5.0	5.0	5.0	5.0	7.0	8.0	5.0	5.0	5.0
Nurses	1.0	1.0	1.0	1.0	1.0	2.0	3.0	3.0	3.0	3.0
Clerical/Secretarial	30.5	32.5	36.0	37.0	36.5	37.5	39.0	37.0	37.5	37.5
Maintenance	11.0	11.0	11.0	11.0	12.0	12.0	12.0	11.0	20.0	20.0
Custodial	30.5	29.0	30.0	32.5	34.5	36.0	46.5	46.5	46.5	46.5
Bus Drivers	75.0	74.0	74.0	73.0	74.0	74.0	74.0	75.0	76.0	76.0
Bus Aides	3.0	4.0	4.0	5.0	5.0	5.0	5.0	6.0	6.0	6.0
Food Service	56	56	56	57	58	58	58	59	59	59
Grand Total	622.0	637.0	643.5	654.0	672.5	696.5	725.0	740.5	752.0	750.0

Notes:
(1) A position of .5 indicates that this position is part-time.

Exhibit 5-25—Personnel Resource Allocations

SOUTH LYON COMMUNITY SCHOOLS

District Staffing Levels
1992-93 through 1997-98

	1992-93	1993-94	1994-95	1995-96	1996-97	1997-98
Teachers	207.0	214.0	219.0	235.0	251.6	261.8
Supervisors	4.0	4.0	4.0	3.0	3.0	4.0
Principals & Asst. Principals	10.0	11.0	11.0	11.0	12.0	12.5
Superintendent, Assistants, and Personnel Director	4.0	4.0	4.0	4.0	4.0	4.0
Guidance Counselors	7.0	6.0	6.0	6.0	7.0	8.0
Librarians	7.0	7.0	7.0	7.0	7.0	7.0
Clerical Staff / Aides	32.0	41.0	42.0	42.0	43.0	45.1
Transportation	11.0	39.0	38.0	38.0	38.5	39.5
Custodians, Maintenance & Grounds	39.5	39.5	38.5	42.5	42.5	43.0
Food Service Staff	32.0	30.0	31.0	31.0	31.0	31.0
Community Education	34.0	35.0	35.0	36.0	36.0	36.0
Other	2.0	2.0	2.5	2.8	3.0	3.0
	389.5	432.5	438.0	458.3	478.6	494.9

(1) Other staff includes: technology staff, Athletic Director

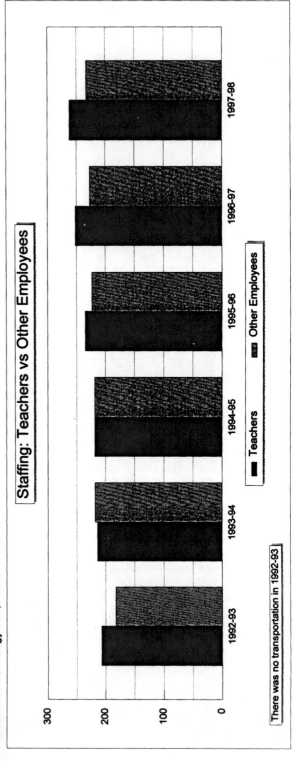

Staffing: Teachers vs Other Employees

■ Teachers ▨ Other Employees

There was no transportation in 1992-93

Exhibit 5-25 (continued)

SOUTH LYON COMMUNITY SCHOOLS

Staffing Ratios versus student enrollment: 1992-93 through 1997-98

	1992-93	1993-94	1994-95	1995-96	1996-97	1997-98
Teachers	21.9	21.1	21.3	21.3	20.6	19.8
Supervisors	1,131.8	1,130.0	1,168.5	1,664.7	1,729.0	1,296.8
Principals & Asst. Principals	452.7	410.9	424.9	454.0	432.3	415.0
Superintendent, Assistants, and Personnel Director	1,131.8	1,130.0	1,168.5	1,248.5	1,296.8	1,296.8

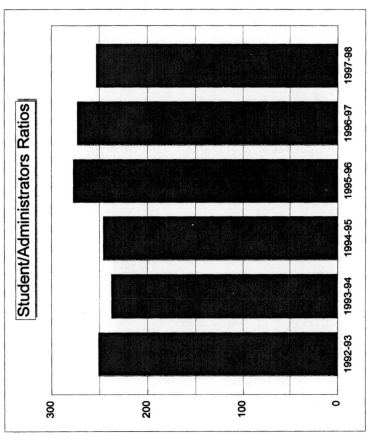

Student/Administrators Ratios

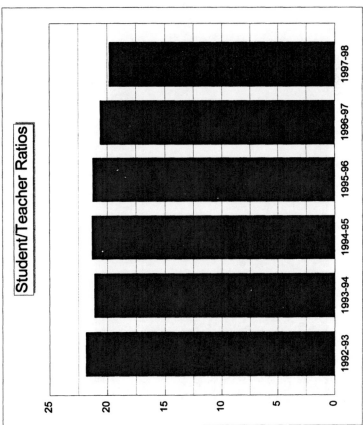

Student/Teacher Ratios

Exhibit 5-25 (continued)

SOUTH LYON COMMUNITY SCHOOLS

Staffing Ratios versus student enrollment (continued):
1992-93 through 1997-98

	1992-93	1993-94	1994-95	1995-96	1996-97	1997-98
Guidance Counselors	646.7	753.3	779.0	832.3	741.0	648.4
Librarians	646.7	645.7	667.7	713.4	741.0	741.0
Clerical Staff	141.5	110.2	111.3	118.9	120.6	115.0
Bus Drivers	411.5	115.9	123.0	131.4	134.7	131.3
Custodians, Maintenance & Grounds	114.6	114.4	121.4	117.5	122.0	120.6
Food Service Staff	141.5	150.7	150.8	161.1	167.3	167.3
Community Education	133.1	129.1	133.5	138.7	144.1	144.1
Other	2,263.5	2,260.0	1,869.6	1,783.6	1,729.0	1,729.0

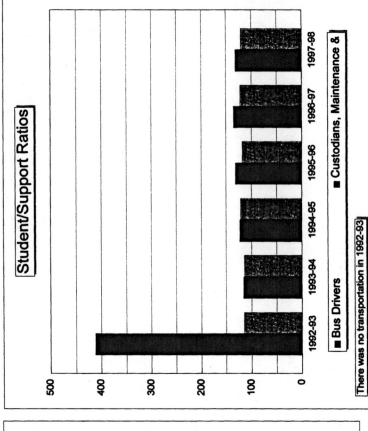

Student/Support Ratios

■ Bus Drivers   ■ Custodians, Maintenance &

There was no transportation in 1992-93

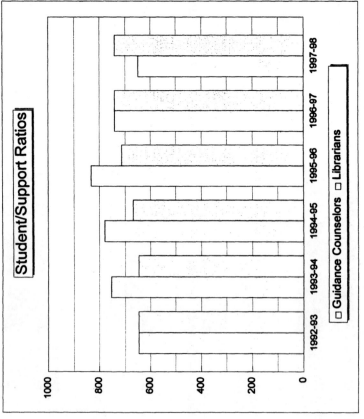

Student/Support Ratios

□ Guidance Counselors   □ Librarians

Exhibit 5-26—Personnel Resource Allocations

Staffing Summary - Souderton Area School District

Instructional Staff	Acct Code	# of Staff 92/93	# of Staff 93/94	# of Staff 94/95	# of Staff 95/96	# of Staff 96/97	# of Staff 97/98
Teachers - Reg & Spec Ed.	1100-1400	301.25	307.25	318.75	328.75	348	375
Inst. Assistants - Reg. & Spec Ed.	1100-1400	46	46	51	53	75	46
Special Education Supervisor	1200	1	1	1	1	1	1
Speech Therapists	1200	4	4	4	4	5	5
Special Education Secretary	1200	1	1	1	1	1	1
Pupil Services Staff							
Guidance Counselors	2120	12	12	12	12	12	14
Home & School Visitor	2130	1	1	1	1	1	1
Psychologists	2140	2	2	3	3	3	3
Secretaries	2100	3	3	3	4	3	3
Instructional Support Staff							
Federal Pgm Coordinator	2210	1	1	1	1	1	1
Subject Area Coordinators (FTE)	2210	0	0	0	4	4	4
District Media Specialist	2220	0.6	0.6	0.6	1	1	1
Technology Coordinator	2220	0.5	0.5	0.5	1	1	1
Hardware/Software Technician	2220	0	0	0	0	1	1
Librarians	2250	7	7	8	8	8	9
Library Aides	2250	2	2	2	2	2	2
Director-Staff Dev/Curriculum	2260	1	1	1	1	1	1
Secretary - Curriculum	2260	1	1	1	1	1	1
Staff Development Coordinators	2270	0	0	0	2	2	2
Administrative Staff							
Tax Collectors	2330	6	6	6	6	6	6
Superintendent	2360	1	1	1	1	1	1
Community Relations Specialist	2370	1	1	1	1	1	1
Building Principals/Assistants	2380	14	14	14	14	14	14
Secretaries - Administration	2300	17	17	17	17	21	21
Pupil Health Services							
Certified School Nurses	2400	4	4	4	4	4.4	4.5
Medical Assistants	2400	5	5	6	6	4.6	4.5
Medical Clerk	2400	1.5	1.5	1.5	1.5	1.5	1.5
Business Services Staff							
Director of Business Affairs	2500	1	1	1	1	1	1
Secretary - Dir of Business Affairs	2500	1	1	1	1	1	1
Supervisor of Accounting	2500	0	0	0	1	1	1
Payroll/Accts Payable Bookkeepers	2500	2	2	2	2	2	2
Operations & Maintenance Staff							
Supervisors-Oper/Maint/Bldgs	2600	2	2	2	2	2	2
Secretaries-Oper/Maint/Bldgs	2600	2	2	2	2	2	2
Maintenance	2600	5	5	5	5	5	6
Building Facility Managers	2600	9	9	9	9	9	9
Custodians (FTE)	2600	38	38	38	38	35	38
Transportation Staff							
Van Driver	2700	1	1	1	1	1	1
Central Support Staff							
Assistant to Superintendent	2830	1	1	1	1	1	1
Secretary-Assist. to Superintendent	2830	1	1	1	1	1	1
Data Processing Specialist	2840	1	1	1	1	1	1
TOTAL		497.85	503.85	523.35	544.25	586.50	591.50

NOTE: Above represents full time equivalents (FTE) and does not include coaches, activity sponsors
and other "temporary type" personnel.

June 12, 1997

Exhibit 5-27—Personnel Resource Allocations

PERSONNEL INFORMATION

Staffing for 1992-93 through 1996-97 is shown on the following table. The table reports staffing by purpose and classification.

	ACTUAL 1992-93	ACTUAL 1993-94	ACTUAL 1994-95	ACTUAL 1995-96	CHANGE FOR 1996-97	BUDGET 1996-97
Student Enrollment	3852	3877	4006	4067	94	4161
PURPOSE						
Instruction						
Certified Teaching Staff	255.705	262.950	263.247	264.240	0.160	264.400
Instructional Assistants	53.480	51.820	51.340	53.820	0.920	54.740
Total Instruction	309.185	314.770	314.587	318.060	1.080	319.140
Athletic & Activities Director	1.000	1.000	1.000	1.000	0.090	1.090
Instructional and Staff Support	38.180	36.680	40.160	42.840	2.000	44.840
Pupil Services	21.650	21.280	21.280	22.540	-0.250	22.290
Business Services	7.500	7.500	7.250	7.750	0.000	7.750
Facility Services	27.270	26.270	26.520	26.500	1.000	27.500
Auxiliary Services (Food Service)	16.671	16.071	16.151	16.790	0.000	16.910
District Operations	2.500	2.500	2.500	2.000	0.000	2.000
Community Services	1.750	1.750	2.500	2.500	0.250	2.750
TOTAL STAFF	425.706	427.821	431.948	439.980	4.170	444.270
CLASSIFICATION						
Certified Instructional & Support						
Daily Classroom Instruction	251.555	258.710	258.692	259.220	-1.840	257.380
Resource & Direct Instruction	6.160	5.920	6.215	8.860	3.000	11.860
Certified Librarians	6.170	6.000	6.500	6.000	0.000	6.000
Certified Pupil Services	13.000	12.500	12.500	13.250	0.000	13.250
Sabbatical	0.500	0.000	0.500	0.000	0.000	0.000
Athletic & Activities Director	1.000	1.000	1.000	1.000	-0.660	0.340
Nursing and AODA	5.650	5.780	5.530	6.040	-0.250	5.790
Instructional Assistants	53.480	51.820	51.340	53.820	0.920	54.740
Secretarial & Clerical	27.000	26.500	27.000	27.000	-0.120	27.000
Administrative Assistant	4.000	4.000	4.000	4.000	0.000	4.000
Administrators	15.000	15.000	16.000	16.000	1.000	17.000
Supervisory	1.750	1.750	2.000	2.000	0.000	2.000
Custodial & Maintenance	25.270	24.270	24.520	24.500	1.000	25.500
Food Service	15.171	14.571	14.651	15.290	0.120	15.410
Technical	0.000	0.000	1.500	3.000	1.000	4.000
	425.706	427.821	431.948	439.980	4.170	444.270

Exhibit 5-27 (continued)

The following shows that staffing levels are relatively stable over the 4 year period illustrated. Total certified non-administrative staff (mostly classroom teachers) has increased as student enrollment increased. Administration and Instructional Assistants have not been increased on the same basis.

Total Staff

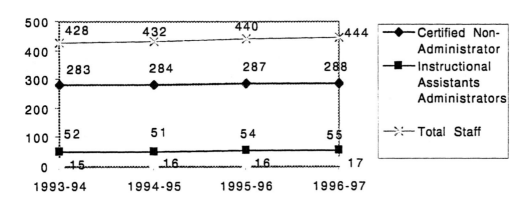

The district increased the number of students to teachers for just less than 15 to 1 to just over 16 to 1, as shown on the following chart.

Certified Teaching Staff

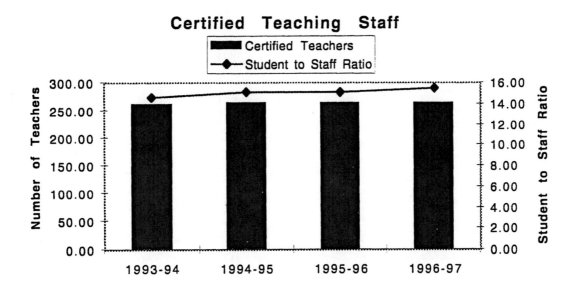

Exhibit 5-28—Personnel Resource Allocations

V. Staffing Levels

JORDAN SCHOOL DISTRICT

FTE REPORT
1996-97 SCHOOL YEAR

		Actual 1993-94	Actual 1994-95	Actual 1995-96	Final Amended 1996-97	Proposed 1997-98	Difference
1000	**Instruction**						
	Teachers	3,224.27	3,283.03	3,348.47	3,524.46	3,569.46	45.00
	Teacher Aides/Paraprofessionals	533.09	566.66	576.44	681.49	696.49	15.00
	Subtotal - Certificated	3,224.27	3,283.03	3,348.47	3,524.46	3,569.46	45.00
	Subtotal - Classified	533.09	566.66	576.44	681.49	696.49	15.00
	Total	3,757.36	3,849.69	3,924.91	4,205.95	4,265.95	60.00
2100	**Student Support Services**						
	Director				1.00	1.00	0.00
	Social Workers	12.50	10.50	6.00	6.00	6.00	0.00
	Counselors/Guidance Personnel	60.67	60.28	55.00	59.00	62.00	3.00
	Psychologists	45.00	47.10	56.50	56.50	56.50	0.00
	Other (Audiologists, etc.)	2.50	2.90	2.50	3.50	3.50	0.00
	Secretarial/Clerical	4.43	4.50	27.93	3.00	3.00	0.00
	Teacher Assistants	5.50	6.00	6.50	7.88	7.88	0.00
	Subtotal - Certificated	120.67	120.78	120.00	126.00	129.00	3.00
	Subtotal - Classified	9.93	10.50	34.43	10.88	10.88	0.00
	Total	130.60	131.28	154.43	136.88	139.88	3.00
2200	**Instr. Support Services**						
	Assistant Superintendent	0.00	0.00	0.00	1.00	1.00	0.00
	Supervisors/Directors	17.00	18.00	18.00	6.50	7.50	1.00
	Consultants/Specialists	21.97	21.44	21.77	6.00	7.00	1.00
	Media Coordinators	22.00	22.00	24.00	24.00	24.00	0.00
	Secretarial/Clerical	42.45	40.98	29.86	23.50	23.50	0.00
	Media Aides/Paraprofessionals	60.63	59.33	111.12	58.48	58.48	0.00
	Other (Printers, Graphics, etc.)	0.00	0.00	0.00	14.00	14.00	0.00
	Subtotal - Certificated	60.97	61.44	63.77	37.50	39.50	2.00
	Subtotal - Classified	103.08	100.31	140.98	95.98	95.98	0.00
	Total	164.05	161.75	204.75	133.48	135.48	2.00
2300	**General District Admin.**						
	Superintendent	1.00	1.00	1.00	1.00	1.00	0.00
	Asst. Superintendents	3.00	3.00	4.00	4.00	4.00	0.00
	Supervisors/Directors	0.00	0.00	0.00	0.00	0.00	0.00
	Secretarial/Clerical	2.00	4.00	5.00	5.00	5.00	0.00
	Subtotal - Certificated	4.00	4.00	5.00	5.00	5.00	0.00
	Subtotal - Classified	2.00	4.00	5.00	5.00	5.00	0.00
	Total	6.00	8.00	10.00	10.00	10.00	0.00
2400	**School Administration**						
	Principals	70.00	71.00	73.00	73.00	73.00	0.00
	Assistant Principals	38.95	40.50	40.50	34.00	43.00	9.00
	Secretarial/Clerical	189.68	210.05	189.36	174.42	175.42	1.00
	Subtotal - Certificated	108.95	111.50	113.50	107.00	116.00	9.00
	Subtotal - Classified	189.68	210.05	189.36	174.42	175.42	1.00
	Total	298.63	321.55	302.86	281.42	291.42	10.00
2500	**Business Administration**						
	Business Administrator	1.00	1.00	1.00	1.00	1.00	0.00
	Supervisors/Directors	3.00	3.00	3.00	3.00	3.00	0.00
	Accounting/Personnel	3.00	3.00	3.00	3.00	3.00	0.00
	Secretarial/Clerical	22.01	24.15	25.15	26.15	27.01	0.86
	Subtotal - Certificated	1.00	1.00	1.00	1.00	1.00	0.00
	Subtotal - Classified	28.01	30.15	31.15	32.15	33.01	0.86
	Total	29.01	31.15	32.15	33.15	34.01	0.86

Exhibit 5-28 (continued)

		Actual 1993-94	Actual 1994-95	Actual 1995-96	Final Amended 1996-97	Proposed 1997-98	Difference
2600	**Oper. & Maint. of Schools**						
	Assistant Superintendent	0.00	0.00	0.00	1.00	1.00	0.00
	Supervisors	4.50	7.50	14.50	8.00	8.00	0.00
	Custodial/Maintenance Personnel	307.12	294.43	301.00	312.96	312.96	0.00
	Secretarial/Clerical	9.50	8.43	6.00	9.00	9.00	0.00
	Subtotal - Certificated	0.00	0.00	0.00	1.00	1.00	0.00
	Subtotal - Classified	321.12	310.36	321.50	329.96	329.96	0.00
	Total	321.12	310.36	321.50	330.96	330.96	0.00
2700	**Student Transportation**						
	Supervisors	5.50	5.50	4.50	6.00	6.00	0.00
	Secretarial/Clerical	6.00	7.00	9.75	8.22	8.65	0.43
	Bus Drivers	143.00	144.91	204.14	118.84	126.84	8.00
	Mechanics/Garage Personnel	14.00	15.00	14.00	14.00	14.00	0.00
	Subtotal - Certificated	0.00	0.00	0.00	0.00	0.00	0.00
	Subtotal - Classified	168.50	172.41	232.39	147.06	155.49	8.43
	Total	168.50	172.41	232.39	147.06	155.49	8.43
2800	**Support Services - Central**						
	Assistant Superintendent	0.00	0.00	0.00	2.00	2.00	0.00
	Supervisors/Directors	15.25	14.50	14.50	9.00	9.00	0.00
	Secretarial/Clerical	29.13	31.66	32.62	33.58	33.58	0.00
	Other	0.00	0.00	9.00	9.00	9.00	0.00
	Subtotal - Certificated	15.25	14.50	14.50	11.00	11.00	0.00
	Subtotal - Classified	29.13	31.66	41.62	42.58	42.58	0.00
	Total	44.38	46.16	56.12	53.58	53.58	0.00
3100	**School Food Service**						
	Supervisors/Directors	5.00	5.00	5.00	5.00	5.00	0.00
	Secretarial/Clerical	5.00	4.00	4.00	5.00	5.00	0.00
	Food Service Personnel	323.49	338.17	324.42	338.41	345.41	7.00
	Subtotal - Certificated	0.00	0.00	0.00	0.00	0.00	0.00
	Subtotal - Classified	333.49	347.17	333.42	348.41	355.41	7.00
	Total	333.49	347.17	333.42	348.41	355.41	7.00
3300	**Community Service**						
	Principal	1.00	1.00	1.00	1.00	1.00	0.00
	Directors/Coordinators	1.50	1.50	1.50	1.50	1.50	0.00
	Teachers	13.00	15.00	18.00	18.00	18.00	0.00
	Guidance	2.00	2.00	2.00	2.00	2.00	0.00
	Speech Therapists	8.83	8.83	8.83	9.83	9.83	0.00
	Nurses	4.00	5.50	6.50	7.50	7.50	0.00
	Secretarial/Clerical	10.50	10.50	12.00	14.50	14.50	0.00
	Subtotal - Certificated	30.33	33.83	37.83	39.83	39.83	0.00
	Subtotal - Classified	10.50	10.50	12.00	14.50	14.50	0.00
	Total	40.83	44.33	49.83	54.33	54.33	0.00
4000	**Facility Acq./Construction**						
	Supervisors/Directors	1.00	1.00	1.00	1.00	1.00	0.00
	Secretarial/Clerical	1.00	1.00	1.00	1.00	1.00	0.00
	Other Personnel	6.00	5.00	4.00	4.00	4.00	0.00
	Subtotal - Certificated	0.00	0.00	0.00	0.00	0.00	0.00
	Subtotal - Classified	8.00	7.00	6.00	6.00	6.00	0.00
	Total	8.00	7.00	6.00	6.00	6.00	0.00
*	Subtotal - Certificated	3,565.44	3,630.08	3,704.07	3,852.79	3,911.79	59.00
*	Subtotal - Classified	1,736.53	1,800.77	1,924.29	1,888.43	1,920.72	32.29
***	**TOTAL FTE**	5,301.97	5,430.85	5,628.36	5,741.22	5,832.51	91.29

Bond Amortization Schedules

(Criterion E-9)

Exhibit 5-29

Exhibit 5-30

Exhibit 5-29—Bond Amortization Schedule

MSD of Washington Township, Indianapolis, Indiana
North Central Campus School Building Corporation Lease Payments[2]
1998 Annual Budget

Lease Payment Schedule
North Central Campus School Building Corporation Dated May 15, 1993

Date	Amount	Interest Payment	Total Payment	Total Amount Lease Payment
1/15/94	$ 915,000	$ 856,258 [1]	$ 1,771,258	$ 1,800,000
7/15/94	170,000	619,319	789,319	
1/15/95	180,000	615,069	795,069	1,800,000
7/15/95	180,000	610,569	790,569	
1/15/96	190,000	606,069	796,069	1,800,000
7/15/96	605,000	601,319	1,206,319	
1/15/97	625,000	586,194	1,211,194	2,422,000
7/15/97	640,000	570,569	1,210,569	
1/15/98	665,000	554,569	1,219,569	2,435,000
7/15/98	680,000	537,944	1,217,944	
1/15/99	705,000	520,944	1,225,944	2,448,000
7/15/99	725,000	503,319	1,228,319	
1/15/00	745,000	485,194	1,230,194	2,463,000
7/15/00	765,000	466,569	1,231,569	
1/15/01	795,000	447,444	1,242,444	2,479,000
7/15/01	815,000	427,171	1,242,171	
1/15/02	840,000	406,389	1,246,389	2,493,000
7/15/02	865,000	384,969	1,249,969	
1/15/03	890,000	362,911	1,252,911	2,507,000
7/15/03	915,000	340,216	1,255,216	
1/15/04	945,000	316,884	1,261,884	2,522,000
7/15/04	970,000	292,314	1,262,314	
1/15/05	1,005,000	267,094	1,272,094	2,539,000
7/15/05	1,030,000	240,713	1,270,713	
1/15/06	1,065,000	213,675	1,278,675	2,555,000
7/15/06	1,095,000	185,719	1,280,719	
1/15/07	1,125,000	156,975	1,281,975	2,567,000
7/15/07	1,160,000	127,444	1,287,444	
1/15/08	1,195,000	96,994	1,291,994	2,584,000
7/15/08	1,230,000	65,625	1,295,625	
1/15/09	1,270,000	33,338	1,303,338	2,603,000
	$ 25,000,000	$ 12,499,775	$ 37,499,775	$ 38,017,000

[1] For the Period 5/15/93 through 1/15/94.

[2] MSD Washington Township is required to pay the lease payments only.

Exhibit 5-30—Bond Amortization Schedule

OUTSTANDING BONDED DEBT SCHEDULE

Year Ended	1996	1994	1992	1988	1974	1968/69	Total Outstanding Debt
1992	0	0	0	$30,696,139	$1,700,000	$348,576	$32,744,715
1993	0	0	10,000,000	29,715,000	1,525,000	240,676	41,480,676
1994	0	0	10,000,000	28,905,000	1,350,000	138,350	40,393,350
1995	0	3,500,000	10,000,000	28,010,000	1,175,000	41,600	42,726,600
1996	0	3,500,000	10,000,000	26,985,000	1,000,000	0	41,485,000
1997	4,100,000	3,500,000	9,775,000	25,850,000	800,000	0	44,025,000
1998	3,845,000	3,425,000	9,550,000	24,605,000	600,000	0	42,025,000
1999	3,305,000	3,300,000	9,325,000	23,255,000	400,000	0	39,585,000
2000	2,530,000	3,150,000	9,100,000	21,795,000	200,000	0	36,775,000
2001	1,475,000	3,000,000	8,800,000	20,310,000	0		33,585,000
2002	0	2,850,000	8,325,000	18,830,000	0		30,005,000
2003	0	2,700,000	7,850,000	17,350,000	0		27,900,000
2004	0	2,550,000	7,375,000	15,880,000	0		25,805,000
2005	0	2,400,000	6,900,000	14,415,000	0		23,715,000
2006	0	2,250,000	6,425,000	12,955,000	0		21,630,000
2007	0	2,100,000	5,950,000	11,475,000	0		19,525,000
2008	0	1,950,000	5,475,000	9,925,000	0		17,350,000
2009	0	1,800,000	5,000,000	8,385,000	0		15,185,000
2010	0	1,650,000	4,500,000	6,855,000	0		13,005,000
2011	0	1,500,000	4,000,000	5,340,000	0		10,840,000
2012	0	1,350,000	3,500,000	3,840,000	0		8,690,000
2013	0	1,200,000	3,000,000	2,355,000	0		6,555,000
2014	0	1,050,000	2,500,000	885,000	0		4,435,000
2015	0	900,000	2,000,000	0	0		2,900,000
2016	0	750,000	1,500,000	0	0		2,250,000
2017	0	600,000	1,000,000	0	0		1,600,000
2018	0	450,000	500,000	0	0		950,000
2019	0	300,000	0	0	0		300,000
2020	0	150,000	0	0	0		150,000

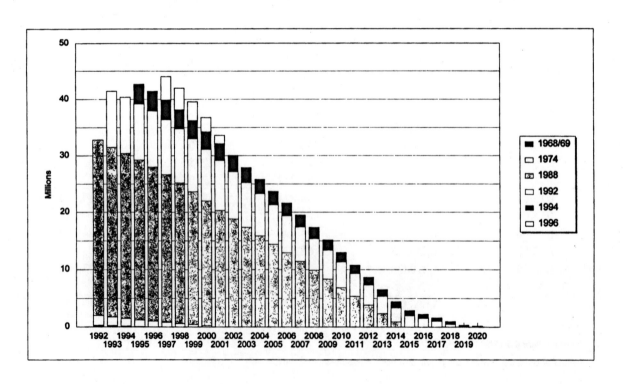

Exhibit 5-30 (continued)

BOND AMORTIZATION SCHEDULE

Fiscal Year Ended 6-30	1996 General Obligation Bonds $4,100,000 Technology Project - District Wide			1994 General Obligation Bonds $3,500,000 6th Grade Wing - Middle School			1992 General Obligation Bonds $10,000,000 Elementary Additions/Remodel			1988 General Obligation Bonds $28,980,000 New High School			1974 General Obligation Bonds $4,070,000 Centennial Elementary			G.O.Bonds 1968,1969 P & I $1,900,000	Grand Total
	Interest	Principal	Total	Interest	Principal	Total	Interest	Principal	Total	Interest	Principal	Total	Interest	Principal	Total		
1992										1,901,005	981,139	2,882,144	110,350	175,000	285,350	107,900	3,275,394
1993							328,828	0	328,828	1,942,750	810,000	2,752,750	98,975	175,000	273,975	102,326	3,457,879
1994							657,656	0	657,656	1,865,193	895,000	2,760,193	87,425	175,000	262,425	96,750	3,777,024
1995				154,097	0	154,097	657,656	0	657,656	1,778,830	1,025,000	2,803,830	75,700	175,000	250,700	41,600	3,907,883
1996				205,462	0	205,462	657,656	225,000	882,656	1,712,756	1,135,000	2,847,756	63,800	200,000	263,800		4,199,674
1997	196,647	255,000	451,647	205,462	75,000	280,462	638,532	225,000	863,532	1,637,416	1,245,000	2,882,416	50,000	200,000	250,000		4,728,057
1998	148,648	540,000	688,648	199,728	125,000	324,726	619,406	225,000	844,406	1,553,466	1,350,000	2,903,466	36,000	200,000	236,000		4,997,246
1999	129,208	775,000	904,208	189,976	150,000	339,976	600,282	225,000	825,282	1,460,978	1,460,000	2,920,978	22,000	200,000	222,000		5,212,444
2000	100,145	1,055,000	1,155,145	180,600	150,000	330,600	581,156	300,000	881,156	1,373,376	1,485,000	2,858,376	13,000	200,000	213,000		5,438,279
2001	59,000	1,475,000	1,534,000	172,650	150,000	322,650	555,656	475,000	1,030,656	1,282,792	1,480,000	2,762,792					5,650,098
2002				164,700	150,000	314,700	525,376	475,000	1,000,376	1,191,032	1,480,000	2,671,032					3,986,108
2003				156,750	150,000	306,750	496,876	475,000	971,876	1,098,532	1,470,000	2,568,532					3,847,158
2004				148,800	150,000	298,800	468,332	475,000	943,332	1,005,922	1,465,000	2,470,922					3,713,054
2005				140,850	150,000	290,850	439,162	475,000	914,162	912,162	1,460,000	2,372,162					3,577,174
2006				132,750	150,000	282,750	409,476	475,000	884,476	817,262	1,480,000	2,297,262					3,464,488
2007				124,500	150,000	274,500	379,312	475,000	854,312	721,062	1,550,000	2,271,062					3,399,874
2008				116,100	150,000	266,100	349,032	475,000	824,032	620,312	1,540,000	2,160,312					3,250,444
2009				107,550	150,000	257,550	318,750	500,000	818,750	524,062	1,530,000	2,054,062					3,130,362
2010				98,850	150,000	248,850	286,876	500,000	786,876	428,438	1,515,000	1,943,438					2,979,184
2011				90,000	150,000	240,000	255,000	500,000	755,000	333,750	1,500,000	1,833,750					2,828,750
2012				81,000	150,000	231,000	223,126	500,000	723,126	240,000	1,485,000	1,725,000					2,679,126
2013				72,000	150,000	222,000	191,250	500,000	691,250	147,188	1,470,000	1,617,188					2,530,438
2014				63,000	150,000	213,000	159,376	500,000	659,376	55,312	885,000	940,312					1,812,688
2015				54,000	150,000	204,000	127,500	500,000	627,500								831,500
2016				45,000	150,000	195,000	95,626	500,000	595,626								790,626
2017				36,000	150,000	186,000	63,750	500,000	563,750								749,750
2018				27,000	150,000	177,000	31,876	500,000	531,876								708,876
2019				18,000	150,000	168,000											168,000
2020				9,000	150,000	159,000											159,000

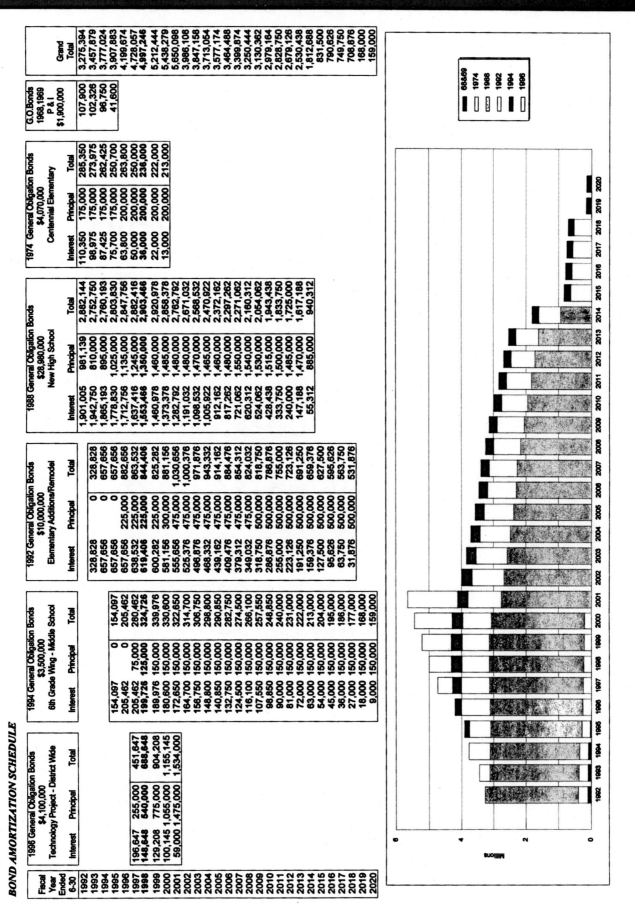

Legend: 68&69 | 1974 | 1988 | 1992 | 1994 | 1996

Performance Measurements

(Criterion E-10)

Exhibit 5-31—Performance Measurements

PERFORMANCE REPORT

The school district regularly evaluates various measures of performance to assure parents and taxpayers are receiving a quality education. Reports are made to taxpayers as part of the budget presentation at both the annual pre-budget hearing and the required Annual Meeting.

The State of Wisconsin initiated a required reporting standard for public school districts beginning with the school year 1991-92. According to this standard, districts will annually publish performance results on specified measures. Through this reporting mechanism the School District of Kettle Moraine is able to make comparisons to state wide averages. In future years the district will be able to make comparisons to other school districts serving taxpayers in Waukesha County.

Results from the last three years are shown in the following graphs. In each graph Kettle Moraine results are shown in the striped (red) bar. State of Wisconsin averages are shown in the solid (blue) bar. A complete listing of the state mandated performance standards follows the graphs. Data for the most recently completed school year, 1995-96, is not available until December, 1996. The district provides a complete report on all measures to all taxpayers of the district.

Kettle Moraine had a higher graduation rate than the state wide average for 1992-93. The 1993-94 and 1994-95 the district's graduation rate is below the state average. The district has begun to explore options to address the graduation rate disparity.

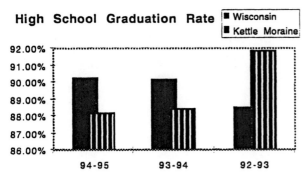

Graduation rate is the number of graduates divided by the number of 12th graders enrolled.

Exhibit 5-31 (continued)

The State of Wisconsin traditionally performs better on the ACT Composite Score than the national average. Kettle Moraine typically outperforms the state average. Comparisons for English, Math, Reading and Science scores are shown on the table following these charts.

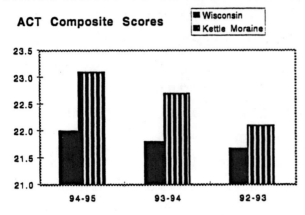

Information is from the number of each year's graduating class that took the ACT test as juniors. Additional information is provided in the table that follows.

Kettle Moraine students have a higher percentage of students who score above the standard on the state wide Third Grade Reading Test than the state average.

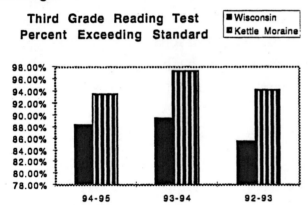

This chart shows the number of students who scored above the standard on the statewide Third Grade Reading Test

Kettle Moraine recognizes the importance of attendance in academic achievement. Various efforts are in place to encourage attendance. These efforts have resulted in an attendance rate that exceeds the state wide average.

Exhibit 5-31 (continued)

Attendance rate is actual days of attendance divided by possible days.

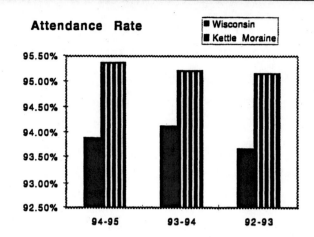

Kettle Moraine initiated several programs to identify and intercede with students who are at risk of dropping out of school. These programs have been successful in reducing the dropout rate.

Dropouts are students who stop attending class, have not graduated or completed a district approved program, and who have not been expelled.

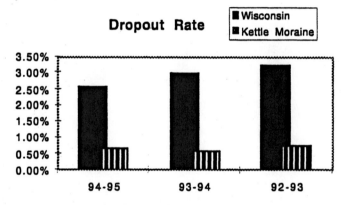

Kettle Moraine attempts to identify students who demonstrate a need for academic assistance so as to reduce the number of students retained each year. These assistance efforts have resulted in a very low retention rate each year.

The retention rate is the number of students retained by grade in the elementary and middle school, or those in the high school with a deficiency of more than 3 credits, divided by the official enrollment.

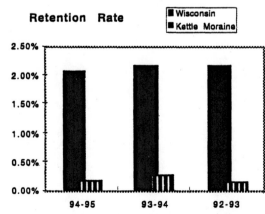

Exhibit 5-31 (continued)

As illustrated in the charts above, Kettle Moraine's performance is generally better than the state average. In 1994-95 the only measures in which the state average was better then the district's was the high school graduation rate and the average on the 8th grade knowledge test.

The above charts provide comparable data to standards of measure established by the State of Wisconsin. Locally, each school in the district prepares a report of annual highlights and establishes goals for the ensuing year. This report helps parents and other taxpayers appreciate the accomplishments of the past year and identifies the future direction of the district. The 1995-96 highlights and 1996-97 goals are reproduced in Appendix B.

Exhibit 5-32—Performance Measurements

VIII. Academic Performance

STUDENT ACHIEVEMENT

Competency in basic skills such as reading, writing and mathematics and performance on standardized achievement tests are some of the tools used to measure the quality of education provided in Jordan District schools. The statistics show most students are doing well despite Jordan District's low per-pupil expenditures in comparison to most other Utah school districts and national averages. The high test scores are especially noteworthy since Jordan District students and teachers are also coping with some of the largest class sizes in the nation.

JORDAN COMPETENCY TESTS

Minimum competency standards in basic skills are tested with Jordan Competency Tests (JCT). Students who cannot meet minimum standards in reading, writing, and mathematics are not awarded diplomas. The charts show the percentage of Jordan District students who had passed the JCT at the beginning of the 1996-97 school year.

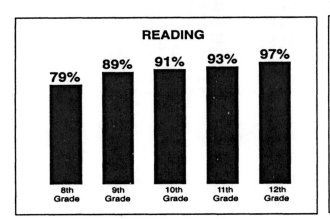

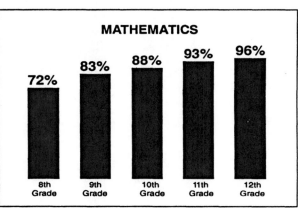

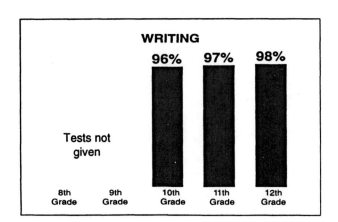

Exhibit 5-32 (continued)

STANFORD ACHIEVEMENT TESTS (SAT)

In October, 1996, over 95 percent of the students in grades 3 to 9 and grade 11 took the Stanford Achievement Test (SAT). Students in grades 5, 8, and 11 were included in a statewide testing program. The graphs show a three-year pattern of the SAT results. The national average is 50 in all grades and subject areas.

THIRD GRADE SAT SCORES

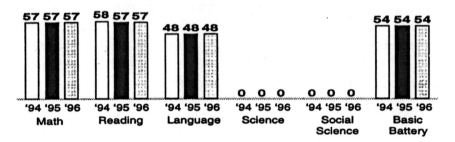

FOURTH GRADE SAT SCORES

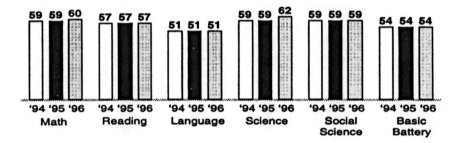

FIFTH GRADE SAT SCORES

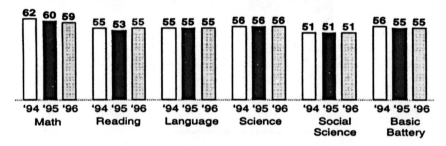

SIXTH GRADE SAT SCORES

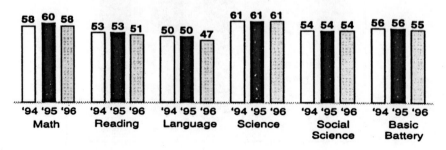

Exhibit 5-32 (continued)

SEVENTH GRADE SAT SCORES

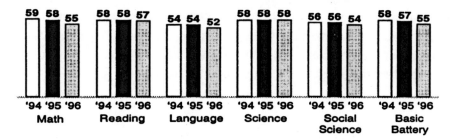

EIGHTH GRADE SAT SCORES

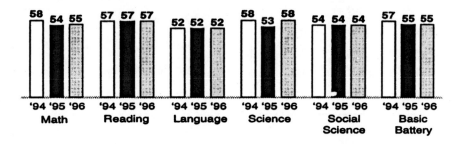

NINTH GRADE SAT SCORES

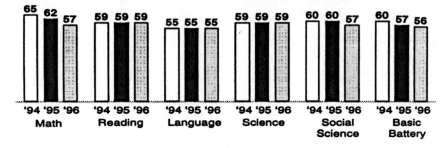

ELEVENTH GRADE SAT SCORES

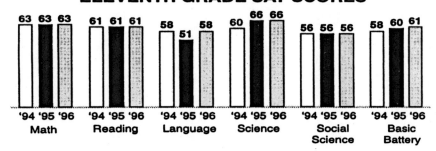

Exhibit 5-32 (continued)

AMERICAN COLLEGE TEST (ACT) and ADVANCED PLACEMENT TESTS (AP)

Students voluntarily take a variety of tests which measure academic performance against a national standard, including the American College Test (ACT) for college entrance and Advanced Placement Tests (AP) for college credit. Because students are required to pay for optional testing, there is no direct impact on the budget. The most recent standings are listed.

American College Test (ACT) (1995-96)			
	Jordan	Utah	Nation
English	21.6	21.0	20.3
Math	20.6	20.3	20.2
Reading	22.3	22.0	21.3
Science	21.9	21.7	21.1
Composite	21.7	21.4	20.9

Advanced Placement Tests (AP)
(1995-96)

AP Subjects Taught in JSD 26

AP Tests Taken 2,952

Jordan District Passing Rate 77.4%

Utah Passing Rate 69.1%

National Passing Rate.........................63.7%

OBSERVATIONS

Credit for the quality of education provided in Jordan District schools goes to a progressive Board of Education which vigorously advocates for students. Credit also goes to teachers who are professionally trained in their subject matter and who genuinely care about students. The efforts of school and district administrators who are excellent instructional leaders and competent business managers should also be recognized. Finally, credit must be awarded to those outstanding parents who send their children to school each day well-prepared to learn.

Exhibit 5-33—Performance Measurements

MSD of Washington Township, Indianapolis, Indiana
Positive Results of Our Schools
1996-97 School Year

The Metropolitan School District of Washington Township (MSDWT) celebrates a heritage of continued leadership in the education of children. The 1996-97 school year marked 40 years of service from North Central High School and 25 years from the J. Everett Light Career Center. A special **Rededication Weekend** was celebrated during Homecoming on October 11-13, 1997, and more than 12,000 residents from the community toured the newly renovated high school and career center. A newly formed North Central Alumni Association sponsored an Alumni Artsgarden Party that weekend and presented their first $1,000 scholarship to North Central senior Susan Geneice Lautz at the Senior Luncheon in June.

Greenbriar Elementary School faculty and staff invited the community to a Rededication ceremony in November to celebrate the completion of their school renovation project. The school received a facelift, remodeling of the front lobby, gymnasium and dining room, media center, and the addition of a parent and community rooms and technology to the classrooms.

MSD Washington Township moved into the spotlight when Mrs. Judy Fraps was selected as the **1997 Indiana Teacher of the Year** at a ceremony at Greenbriar Elementary School in November with State Superintendent of Public Instruction Suellen Reed and Superintendent Eugene White presiding. Mrs. Fraps has served twelve years as Title I Coordinating Mathematics Teacher for grades K-5 at Greenbriar and Nora Elementary Schools.

Another faculty member, Mr. Nathaniel Jones, principal of Allisonville Elementary School, received the **Milken National Educator Award** and $25,000 for his unrestricted personal use. This year's award to Mr. Jones makes 20 in Indiana since 1993. Allisonville Elementary School was declared a National Blue Ribbon School in May by the U.S. Department of Education, and was one of four schools selected in Indiana.

Superintendent Eugene G. White was selected as the **Outstanding Superintendent of the Year for 1997** by the Indiana Music Educators Association at their annual meeting in Indianapolis. He was selected for his promotion of the performing arts in the school district.

MSDWT received the prestigious Meritorious Budget Award from the Association of School Business Officials International both for its 1996 and 1997 Budget.

Every year staff and students receive recognition for their accomplishments for academic excellence, athletic and sports competition, and partnerships with the community. Presented below are some of the many other achievements during the 1996-97 school year.

Elementary Schools

Spring Mill Elementary School was selected an *Exemplary School* in the Indiana 1996-97 Safe and Drug-Free School Recognition Program and received an $8,500 grant.

John Strange Elementary School was one of fifteen Indianapolis-area schools earning **Four Star Schools** status from the Indiana Department of Education, and has been the proud recipient for this recognition for four consecutive years.

Exhibit 5-33 (continued)

Doris Ann Brewer, fourth grade teacher at Allisonville Elementary School, was proud recipient of the Golden Apple Awards, and $2,000.

All schools participated in the Artists-in-Residence program with Young Audiences of Indiana and Arts Partners and the MSDWT Performing Arts Commission. *Dance Kaleidoscope* performed to Grades 3 and 6 at the North Central High School Auditorium in March as a culmination of dance workshops in the schools in November.

Crooked Creek Elementary School is one of six pilot sites in the city for Arts Partners and was visited by Governor Frank O'Bannon in the spring for their "Celebration of Life" exhibits of a butterfly habitat and bird refuge and coordinating arts projects.

Harcourt Elementary School is designated as an **Indiana 2000 School** and Professional Development School.

Reading incentive programs were conducted at all schools in the district with tens of thousands of extra-curricular books read by students.

Middle Schools

An **Academics First** philosophy and team approach for academic achievement was adopted by all middle schools in MSD Washington Township.

Eastwood Middle School is an Indiana School Improvement Award winner.

Westlane Middle School is an Indiana 2000 School.

Northview has received the Hoosier School Award for advocating educational excellence.

Electronic Production Centers were established in each schools' Media Center to allow students to create desktop publishing documents, videotapes, and multi-media projects. All students have secured access to the Internet and World Wide Web for research and reference material.

North Central High School

MSD Washington Township is ranked 17th in the nation with 73% of graduating seniors pursuing college degrees in 1997. (Indiana-55.2%)

Kathryn L. Perry, North Central teacher, received the Golden Apple Award and $2,000.

NCHS graduated 597 seniors on June 4 at Market Square Arena with a successful formal commencement program.

1997 valedictorian Calvin Barnes became the first African American North Central student to achieve the distinction with a 4.95 GPA on a five-point scale.

North Central had eight (8) National Merit Scholarship Finalist, three (3) National Merit Scholarship Semifinalists, and 15 National Merit Scholarship Commended Students.

Two hundred and twenty three (223) students took 444 AP exams with 77% receiving qualifying scores.

Thirteen (13) seniors completed the rigorous International Baccalaureate (IB) Program.

North Central's SAT school average was 1,056 (Indiana-988; National-1013).

Exhibit 5-33 (continued)

Over one-fourth of the Class of 1997 graduated with a North Central or Indiana Honors Diploma.

North Central students earned over $1.5 million dollars in scholarships.

North Central had its first University of North Carolina Morehead Scholarship recipient.

North Central had three (3) students awarded the 1996 Achievement in Writing from the National Council of Teachers of English.

North Central had four (4) Prelude Competition Finalists and 11 students nominated to the Prelude Academy.

North Central had nine (9) State Winners in the National Spanish Contest.

North Central had one (1) student receive the Mayor's Volunteer Partnership Award.

North Central had three (3) students named Outstanding Mathematics Scholars in the Indiana High School Mathematics Contest.

North Central students placed first, second, and third in the 500 Festival of Art.

North Central's Men's Teams won the 1996 Sectional Baseball Championship, MIC Tennis Championship, Regional Cross Country Championship, State Soccer Championship, County Swim Championship, and Sectional Basketball Championship.

North Central's Women's Teams won the State Tennis Championship, Sectional Softball Championship, Sectional Golf Championship, Regional Cross Country Championship, County Soccer Championship, 3rd in State in Swim Championship, Sectional Basketball Championship, and State Runner-Up Gymnastics Championship.

JEL students had one (1) Commercial Art student place first in the "Artsparty" poster competition.

Fourteen (14) JEL Radio/TV students placed first, second, third and 11th in the Indiana High School Broadcasters contest.

Exhibit 5-33 (continued)

MSD of Washington Township, Indianapolis, Indiana
SAT Comparisons - North Central High School, Indiana and the Nation[1]
1992-1996

	1992	1993	1994	1995	1996
North Central Top 10% of the Class					
Verbal	531	562	571	574	627
Math	609	626	654	654	638
Total	1140	1188	1225	1228	1265
Population	61	58	57	61	58
North Central Total High School					
Verbal	436	448	438	461	530
Math	482	482	493	517	526
Total	918	930	931	978	1056
Population	469	451	451	461	453
Indiana Total					
Verbal	409	409	410	415	494
Math	459	460	466	467	494
Total	868	869	876	882	988
Nation Total					
Verbal	423	424	423	428	505
Math	476	478	474	482	508
Total	899	902	897	910	1013

[1] Source: MSD of Washington Township Department of Curriculum.

Exhibit 5-33 (continued)

MSD Washington Township, Indianapolis, Indiana
Student Information and Programs
1998 Annual Budget

Indiana Statewide Test of Educational Progress Scores
1996-97 School Year

Grade	Total Battery National Percentile	Percentage that meet State Proficiency Standards	
		Language Arts	Mathematics
3	84%	76%	78%
6	75%	68%	68%
8	75%	80%	68%
10	73%	72%	67%

The International Baccalaureate Program

The International Baccalaureate (IB) program is a rigorous two-year course of study that culminates in a battery of examinations in six subject areas. Included in this program are accelerated courses in English, mathematics, science, social studies, foreign language, music, and art.

These students also complete one hundred hours of instruction in a special course, *Theory of Knowledge*, which is the core of the IB curriculum. A 4,000 word essay is required in one of the subject areas, and the participants must contribute a minimum of one half day each week toward some cultural, aesthetic, or social service activity within the community. Attaining the IB diploma confirms that a student has achieved a standard of performance that is competitive with peers in some of the best schools throughout the world. North Central High School is the only IB school in the State of Indiana.

International Baccalaureate Diploma History

Year	Number of Diploma Candidates	Number of Diploma Candidates Earning Diploma	Percentage of Candidates Earning Diploma
1996	13	11	85
1995	13	13	100
1994	15	8	53
1993	9	8	89
1992	3	1	33
1991	7	6	86
1990	11	11	100
TOTAL	71	58	82

Exhibit 5-34—Performance Measurements

SAT
Stanford Achievement Tests

Historically, research has shown that several factors outside the classroom affect a child's performance on a norm-references test. They include: parental involvement, family income, and whether or not the child lives with both parents. These factors are beyond a school's control. To give a realistic picture of a population, one way of looking at student performance is to compare scores with those of other schools or districts with similar populations. This comparison of similar socio-economic factors is the expectancy range.

These ranges are calculated by the Utah State Office of Education, based on percentage of students receiving free lunch, A.F.D.C. (Aid to Families with Dependent Children), foster care, and food stamps.

Looking at scores in the context of expected ranges gives a picture of how students are performing on the test, considering outside influences. If scores remain fairly constant or increase while demographic factors are getting worse, district performance is considered adequate although not what the Board of Education would like it to be.

While demographics of the district is getting worse, schools are generally maintaining or improving their scores. District students, grades **5th, 8th, and 11th,** scored within the expected ranges in all categories.

**The *Total Basic Battery* includes Mathematics, Reading, and Language

Exhibit 5-34 (continued)

SALT LAKE CITY SCHOOL DISTRICT
Fiscal Year 1997-98 Budget

5th Grade District SAT SCORES
1992/1993 - 1996/1997

	1992-93	1993-94	1994-95	1995-96	1996-97
Total Reading	50	49	45	47	45
Total Math	63	57	54	53	54
Total Language	42	42	39	42	42
Science	52	48	48	48	48
Social Science	55	51	46	48	46
Basic Battery	53	50	45	45	47

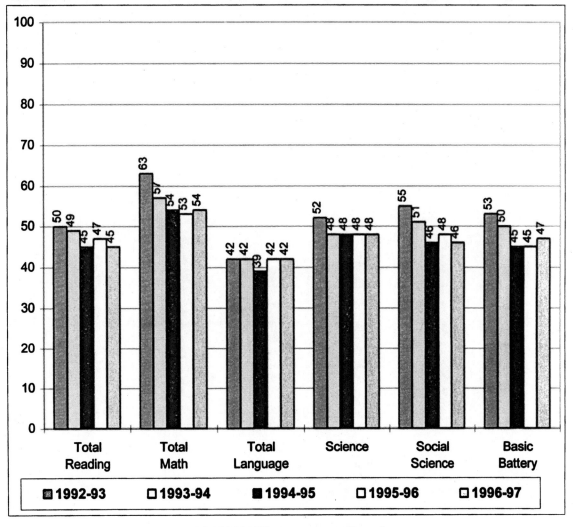

1996/1997 Expectancy Bands

Total Reading	Total Math	Total Language	Science	Social Science	Basic Battery
35----50	44----65	36----48	37----56	36---48	38----48

Exhibit 5-34 (continued)

SALT LAKE CITY SCHOOL DISTRICT
Fiscal Year 1997-98 Budget

8th Grade District SAT SCORES
1992/1993 - 1996/1997

	1992-93	1993-94	1994-95	1995-96	1996-97
Total Reading	55	51	51	49	51
Total Math	54	47	45	41	44
Total Language	41	39	41	41	39
Science	53	53	49	49	49
Social Science	54	50	50	47	50
Basic Battery	55	48	48	44	44

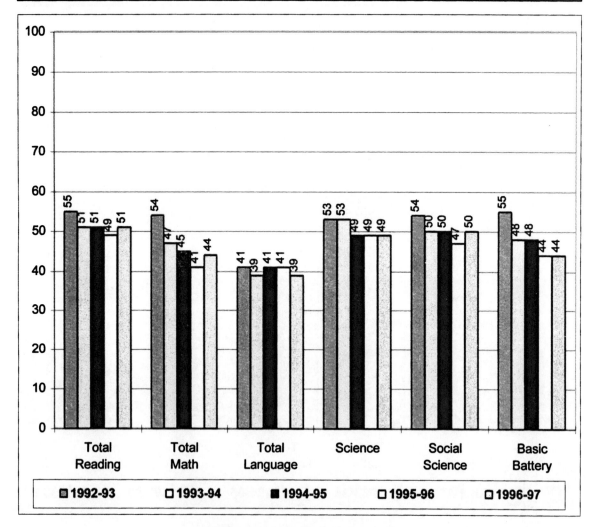

1996/1997 Expectancy Bands

Total Reading	Total Math	Total Language	Science	Social Science	Basic Battery
41-----53	37----57	32----45	36----58	32----50	37-----50

Exhibit 5-34 (continued)

SALT LAKE CITY SCHOOL DISTRICT
Fiscal Year 1997-98 Budget

11th Grade District SAT SCORES
1992/1993 - 1996/1997

	1992-93	1993-94	1994-95	1995-96	1996-97
Total Reading	61	61	65	65	61
Total Math	63	63	68	68	63
Total Language	45	45	45	45	45
Science	66	60	66	66	66
Social Science	56	51	56	51	56
Basic Batt	58	57	60	60	56

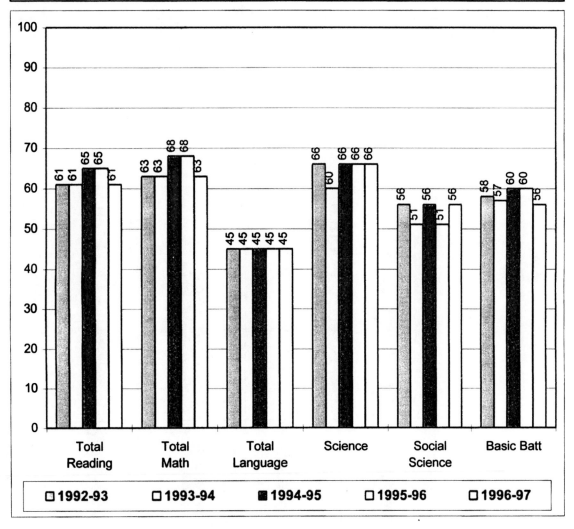

1996/1997 Expectancy Bands

Total Reading	Total Math	Total Language	Science	Social Science	Basic Battery
44---58	49---63	39---51	48---66	41---51	41---53

Exhibit 5-34 (continued)

SALT LAKE CITY SCHOOL DISTRICT
Fiscal Year 1997-98 Budget

Salt Lake City School District
ACT Scores
1993-94 to 1995-96 School Years

ACT	District 1993-94	District 1994-95	District 1995-96	State 1995-96	Nation 1995-96
Number of Students	NA	NA	767	19,483	924,663
Sub Tests					
English	20.60	21.50	21.30	21.00	20.30
Mathematics	20.50	21.10	21.30	20.30	20.20
Reading	21.80	23.10	23.00	22.00	21.30
Science Reasoning	21.10	22.00	22.50	21.70	21.10
Composite	21.20	22.00	22.20	21.40	20.90

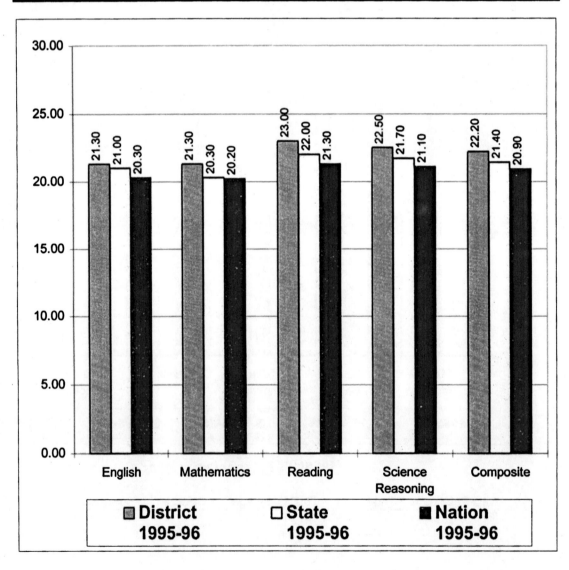

Exhibit 5-34 (continued)

Advanced Placement Results
1991-92 to 1995-96

Salt Lake's Advance Placement Program, sponsored by the College Entrance Examination Board, helps serve the needs of our academically gifted students.

The AP exams are a combination of multiple choice and essay questions, scored on a 1-5 basis with a 5 being "extremely well-qualified," and a 1 being "no recommendation." Utah colleges offer credit for scores of 3 and above. Colleges outside Utah offer differing amount of credit for different scores. Students need to be familiar with the policy of the school of their choice.

General trends from the 1995-96 school year:

- District-wide, 64% of the test taken received a 3 or above. That is down from the 1994-95 school year, but...

- There has been an increase of 21% in AP exams administered since the 1991-92 school year and an increase of 10% since the 1994-95 school year. With more students taking the tests, the usual result is a reduction in average scores. The lower scores are a result from younger students taking the test as a practice with the intent of passing it the second time taken.

Exhibit 5-34 (continued)

SALT LAKE CITY SCHOOL DISTRICT
Fiscal Year 1997-98 Budget

Advanced Placement Scores
1991/92 - 1995/96

	Number Tests Administered District	Number Exams Passed District	Percent Exams Passed District	Percent Exams Passed Utah	Percent Exams Passed **Nation/Western States
1992 Tests	820	611	75%	71%	65%
1993 Tests	786	539	69%	72%	64%
1994 Tests	836	565	68%	73%	66%
1995 Tests	934	610	65%	70%	62%
1996 Tests	1029	659	64%	69%	65%

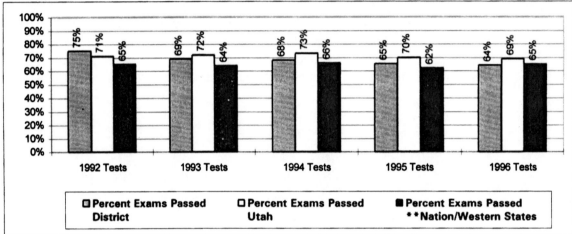

☐ **Percent Exams Passed District**   ☐ **Percent Exams Passed Utah**   ■ **Percent Exams Passed **Nation/Western States**

** Previously the Socres were compared **Nationally**.
Starting in 1995/1996, the scores were compared **Regionally**, by Western States.

Advanced Placement Results
1991/1992- 1995/1996

Salt Lake's Advance Placement Program, sponsored by the College Entrance Examination Board, helps serve the needs of our academically gifted students.

The AP exams are a combination of multiple choice and essay questions, scored on a 1-5 basis with a 5 being "extremely well-qualified," and a 1 being "no recommendation." Utah colleges offer credit for scores of 3 and above. Colleges outside Utah offer differing amount of credit for different scores. Students need to be familiar with the policy of the school of their choice.

General trends from the 1995/1996 school year:

- District-wide, 64% of the test taken received a 3 or above. That is down from the 1994/1995 school year, but...

- There has been an increase of 21% in AP exams administered since the 1991/1992 school year and an increase of 10% since the 1994/1995 school year. With more students taking the tests, the usual result is a reduction in average scores. The lower scores are a result from younger students taking the test as a practice with the intent of passing it the second time taken.

Exhibit 5-34 (continued)

Salt Lake City School District
Fiscal Year 1997-1998 Budget

Grade	1994-95 Reading Score	1995-96 Reading Score	1996-97 Reading Score
4th	2.5	2.64	2.7
6th	2.64	2.77	3.02
8th	2.74	2.85	3.1
9th	2.93	2.89	3.33

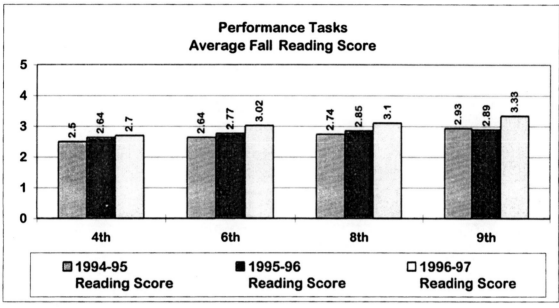

Grade	1994-95 Writing Score	1995-96 Writing Score	1996-97 Writing Score
4th	5.37	5.62	5.27
6th	5.39	5.74	6.43
8th	5.6	6.11	6.46
9th	5.61	6.06	6.8

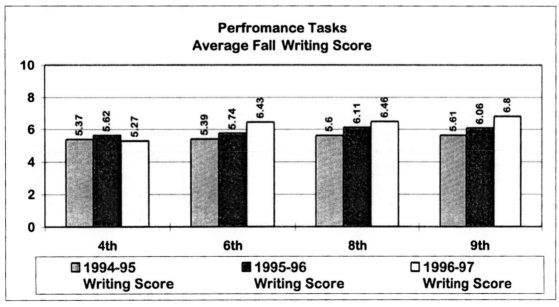

Exhibit 5-34 (continued)

Salt Lake City School District
Fiscal Year 1997-1998 Budget

Analytic Writing	5th Grade 1993-94	7th Grade 1995-96
Average Ideas	6.41	7.23
Average Organization	6.00	6.71
Average Word Choice	6.34	7.18
Average of Conventions	6.58	6.87
Number of Students With Same Scores	1259	1259

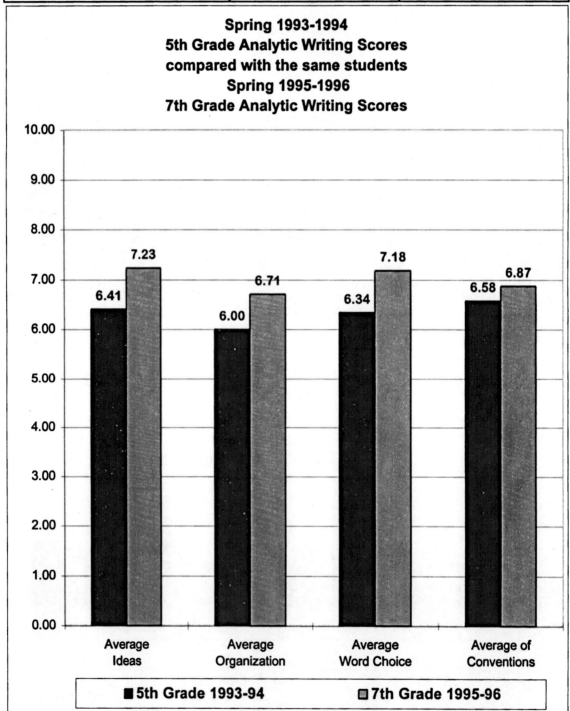

Spring 1993-1994
5th Grade Analytic Writing Scores
compared with the same students
Spring 1995-1996
7th Grade Analytic Writing Scores

Exhibit 5-34 (continued)

SALT LAKE CITY SCHOOL DISTRICT
Fiscal Year 1997-98 Budget

DROP OUT RATES

	1992-93	1993-94	1994-1995	1995-1996
% IN GRADES 7-12 Dropping Out	8%	8%	10%	10%

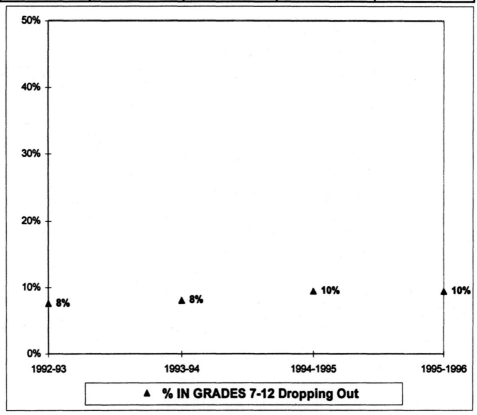

A dropout is defined as any student in grades seven through 12 as October 1 of a given year who is not enrolled in school one year later and who does not have a high school diploma.

Students who have transferred out of the district or who are enrolled in a district alternative program are not counted as dropouts. These figures are based on the spring 1995 enrollment.

To get as accurate a dropout count as possible, the district tracks students reported as dropouts by contacting other districts and private schools.

Exhibit 5-35—Performance Measurements

Chester County School Districts' Graduates for 1995-96 and Post-Secondary Education Rates

School District	Total Graduates	Two- or Four-Year College or University		Specialized Associate Degree-Granting Institution		Total College Bound		Non-Degree Granting Post-Secondary School		Total Post-Secondary Bound	
	Number	Number	Percent	Number	Percent	Number	Percent	Number	Percent	Number	Percent
Avon Grove	175	132	75.9%	0	0.0%	132	75.9%	4	2.3%	136	78.2%
Coatesville Area	411	176	42.8%	12	2.9%	188	45.7%	14	3.4%	202	49.1%
Downingtown Area	535	421	78.7	7	1.3%	428	80.0%	12	2.2%	440	82.2%
Great Valley	193	160	82.9%	5	2.6%	165	85.5%	0	0.0%	165	85.5%
Kennett Consolidated	145	94	64.8%	6	4.1%	100	69.0%	1	0.7%	101	69.7%
Octorara Area	130	73	56.2%	6	4.6%	79	60.8%	17	13.1%	96	73.8%
Owen J. Roberts	191	137	71.7%	9	4.7%	146	76.4%	10	5.2%	156	81.7%
Oxford Area	139	79	56.8%	8	5.8%	87	62.6%	8	5.8%	95	68.3%
Phoenixville Area	154	103	66.9%	6	3.9%	109	70.8%	7	4.5%	116	75.3%
Tredyffrin/Easttown	284	259	91.2%	1	0.4%	260	91.5%	2	0.7%	262	92.3%
Unionville-Chadds Ford	197	183	92.9%	0	0.0%	183	92.9%	4	2.0%	187	94.9%
West Chester Area	639	546	85.4%	3	0.5%	549	85.9%	8	1.3%	557	87.2%
County Total	3,192	2,363	74.0%	63	2.0%	2,426	76.0%	87	2.7%	2,513	78.7%

Source: Pennsylvania Department of Education, Division of Data Services

Exhibit 5-35 (continued)

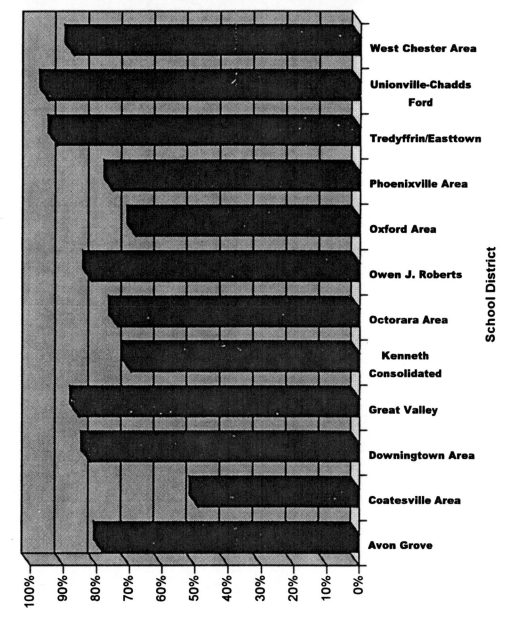

Percentage of Total Graduates Going onto Post-Secondary Education

School District

% Of Graduates Post-Secondary Bound

West Chester Area
Unionville-Chadds Ford
Tredyffrin/Easttown
Phoenixville Area
Oxford Area
Owen J. Roberts
Octorara Area
Kenneth Consolidated
Great Valley
Downingtown Area
Coatesville Area
Avon Grove

Exhibit 5-35 (continued)

Chester County School Districts' Dropout Rates for the 1995-96 School Year

School District	Enrollments Grades 7-12	Male Dropouts	Female Dropouts	Total Dropouts	Dropout Rate
Avon Grove	1,642	10	8	18	1.10%
Coatesville Area	3,359	71	48	119	3.54%
Downingtown Area	3,932	20	6	26	0.66%
Great Valley	1,350	5	4	9	0.67%
Kennett Consolidated	1,117	2	9	1 1	0.98%
Octorara Area	1,105	21	20	41	3.71%
Owen J. Roberts	1,512	10	6	16	1.06%
Oxford Area	1,151	24	11	35	3.04%
Phoenixville Area	1,279	11	6	17	1.33%
Tredyffrin/Easttown	1,961	5	1	6	0.31%
Unionville-Chadds Ford	1,468	1	2	3	0.20%
West Chester Area	4,666	24	15	39	0.84%
County Total	24,542	204	136	340	1.39%

Source: Pennsylvania Department of Education, Division of Data Services (1995-96, most recent available data)

Exhibit 5-35 (continued)

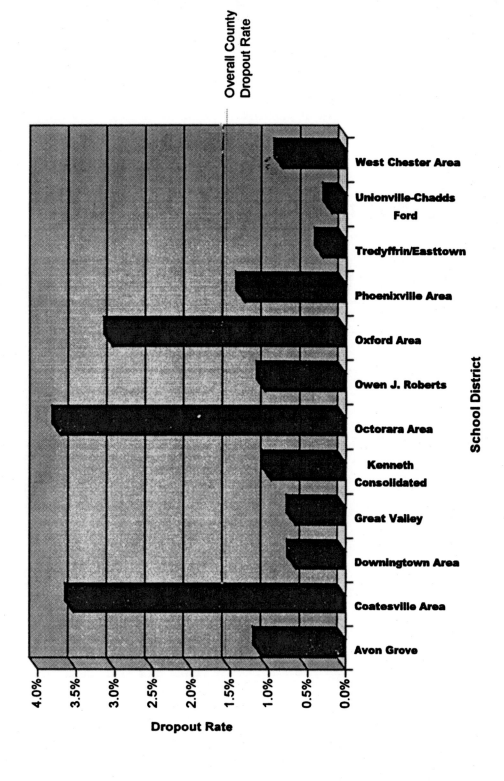

Other Useful Information

(Criterion E-11)

Exhibit 5-36

Exhibit 5-37

Exhibit 3-38

Exhibit 5-36—Other Useful Information

IV. Class Sizes

CLASS SIZE REDUCTIONS

The State Legislature is continuing to allocate funds for the specific purpose of reducing class sizes in the elementary grades. At least 50% of the money must be used in kindergarten and first and second grades. Since the class size reduction program began in 1991, Jordan District has received funding to hire 219 teachers. In 1997-98, an additional 9 teachers will be hired for class size reduction. The Teacher/Pupil Ratios will change only a fraction of a percent this year.

TEACHER/PUPIL RATIOS

	1996-97	1997-98	Change
Kindergarten	1 to 44.40	1 to 44.25	- 0.15
Grade 1	1 to 21.20	1 to ?1.05	- 0.15
Grade 2	1 to 21.50	1 to 21.35	- 0.15
Grade 3	1 to 23.00	1 to 22.85	- 0.15
Grade 4	1 to 25.10	1 to 24.95	- 0.15
Grade 5	1 to 25.10	1 to 24.95	- 0.15
Grades 6	1 to 25.10	1 to 24.95	- 0.15
Grades 7, 8, 9	1 to 26.95	1 to 26.95	none
Grades 10, 11, 12	1 to 25.30	1 to 25.30	none

NOTE: Teacher/Pupil Ratios are used for hiring staff. Actual class sizes may vary widely depending on the move-in patterns of students, etc.

PER-PUPIL EXPENDITURES

The cost of educating each student has increased steadily over the years. It now costs an estimated $3,528 per year for each student enrolled. Jordan District's per-pupil expenditures are still well below the state and national average. Several factors contribute to a lower than average per-pupil cost. For example, Jordan District operates large schools which reduces administrative costs. A high number of employees on the beginning end of the pay scale and large classes also contribute to keeping the per-pupil expenditures down.

Exhibit 5-36 (continued)

JORDAN SCHOOL DISTRICT
SCHEDULE OF TEACHER/PUPIL RATIO

CLASSROOM TEACHERS - 0050

Description	Enrollment (01-31-97) 1996-97	Staffing Teacher/Pupil Ratio 1996-97	Budget Teacher/Pupil Ratio 1996-97	Budgeted Classroom Teacher FTE 1996-97	Estimated Enrollment 1997-98	Proposed Staffing Teacher/Pupil Ratio 1997-98	Proposed Budget Teacher/Pupil Ratio 1997-98	Proposed Budgeted Classroom Teacher FTE 1997-98	Classroom Teacher FTE Increase (Decrease) 1997-98
Kindergarten	5,008	44.70	44.40	112.79	4,905	44.70	44.25	110.85	(1.94)
Elementary Schools									
Grade 1	5,313	21.50	21.20	250.61	5,212	21.50	21.05	247.60	(3.01)
Grade 2	5,278	21.80	21.50	245.49	5,434	21.80	21.35	254.52	9.03
Grade 3	5,384	23.30	23.00	234.09	5,379	23.30	22.85	235.40	1.31
Grade 4	5,361	25.40	25.10	213.59	5,440	25.40	24.95	218.04	4.45
Grade 5	5,452	25.40	25.10	217.21	5,471	25.40	24.95	219.28	2.07
Grade 6	5,457	25.40	25.10	217.41	5,601	25.40	24.95	224.49	7.08
Sub-Total 1-6	32,245			1,378.40	32,537			1,399.33	20.93
Middle Schools Grades 7-9	16,939	27.40	26.95	628.53	16,854	27.40	26.95	625.38	(3.15)
High Schools Grades 10-12	15,455	25.95	25.30	610.87	16,189	25.95	25.30	639.88	29.01
Valley High	730				712				
Youth in Custody	2				0				
Cluster	1,887				1,129				
TOTAL DISTRICT	**72,266**			**2,730.59**	**73,026**			**2,775.44**	**44.85**

Notes:

1. The teacher/pupil ratios for all grades include funds for class size reduction from the Board Leeway Levy and an amount equal to that provided by the Special Purpose Optional Program in the past.
2. The kindergarten through grade six teacher/pupil ratios include funding from the Basic School Program for class size reduction.

Exhibit 5-36 (continued)

A HISTORY OF TEACHER/PUPIL RATIOS

The teacher/pupil ratio represents the number of students that are required to hire one teacher. The actual class sizes vary. Teachers are hired at the high school level according to the number of students who are expected to be enrolled by mid-year.

1979-80
Kindergarten ....1 to 50.00
Elementary ....1 to 29.00
Middle School ....1 to 27.00
High School.......................1 to 27.00

1980-81
Kindergarten ....1 to 50.00
Elementary ....1 to 29.00
Middle School ....1 to 27.00
High School.......................1 to 27.00

1981-82
Kindergarten ....1 to 50.00
Elementary ....1 to 29.00
Middle School ....1 to 27.00
High School.......................1 to 27.00

1982-83
Kindergarten ....1 to 50.00
Elementary ....1 to 29.00
Middle School ....1 to 27.00
High School.......................1 to 27.00

1983-84
Kindergarten ....1 to 50.00
Elementary ....1 to 29.00
Middle School ....1 to 27.00
High School.......................1 to 27.00

1984-85
Kindergarten ....1 to 50.00
Elementary ....1 to 29.00
Middle School ....1 to 27.00
High School.......................1 to 27.00

1985-86
Kindergarten ....1 to 55.00
Elementary ....1 to 29.00
Middle School ....1 to 27.00
High School.......................1 to 26.00

1986-87
Kindergarten ....1 to 55.00
Elementary ....1 to 29.00
Middle School ....1 to 27.00
High School.......................1 to 26.00

1987-88
Kindergarten ....1 to 55.00
Elementary ....1 to 29.00
Middle School ....1 to 27.00
High School.......................1 to 26.00

1988-89
Kindergarten ....1 to 55.75
Elementary ....1 to 29.75
Middle School ....1 to 27.75
High School.......................1 to 26.75

1989-90
Kindergarten ....1 to 55.75
Elementary ....1 to 29.75
Middle School ....1 to 27.75
High School.......................1 to 26.75

1990-91
Kindergarten ....1 to 54.75
Elementary ....1 to 28.45
Middle School ....1 to 26.95
High School.......................1 to 25.95

1991-92
Kindergarten ....1 to 54.75
Elementary
   Grade 1 ....1 to 24.00

   Grades 2-3 ....1 to 26.50
   Grades 4-6 ....1 to 27.70
Middle School ....1 to 26.95
High School.......................1 to 25.95

1992-93
Kindergarten ....1 to 54.75
Elementary
   Grade 1 ....1 to 24.00
   Grade 2 ....1 to 24.50
   Grade 3 ....1 to 26.50
   Grades 4-6 ....1 to 27.70
Middle School ....1 to 26.95
High School ....1 to 25.95

1993-94
Kindergarten ....1 to 47.25
Elementary
   Grade 1 ....1 to 23.85
   Grade 2 ....1 to 24.50
   Grade 3 ....1 to 26.50
   Grades 4-6 ....1 to 27.70
Middle School ....1 to 26.95
High School.......................1 to 25.65

1994-95
Kindergarten ....1 to 47.25
Elementary
   Grade 1 ....1 to 23.85
   Grade 2 ....1 to 24.00
   Grade 3 ....1 to 24.50
   Grades 4-6 ....1 to 27.70
Middle School ....1 to 26.95
High School.......................1 to 25.30

1995-96
Kindergarten ....1 to 47.25
Elementary
   Grade 1 ....1 to 23.85
   Grade 2 ....1 to 24.00
   Grade 3 ....1 to 24.50
   Grade 4 ....1 to 26.40
   Grades 5-6 ....1 to 27.70
Middle School ....1 to 26.95
High School.......................1 to 25.30

1996-97
Kindergarten ....1 to 44.40
Elementary
   Grade 1 ....1 to 21.20
   rade 2 ....1 to 21.50
   Grade 3 ....1 to 23.00
   Grade 4, 5, 6 ....1 to 25.10
Middle School ....1 to 26.95
High School.......................1 to 25.30

1997-98
Kindergarten ....1 to 44.25
Elementary
   Grade 1 ....1 to 21.05
   Grade 2 ....1 to 21.35
   Grade 3 ....1 to 22.85
   Grade 4, 5, 6 ....1 to 24.95
Middle School ....1 to 26.95
High School.......................1 to 25.30

Exhibit 5-36 (continued)

PATTERN OF CLASS SIZE CHANGES OVER TIME

The graphs below show the pattern of class size changes occuring in elementary schools since 1979-80. Note: Only the years where changes were made in at least one grade are shown. The bars for each year match the tone and order shown in the key.

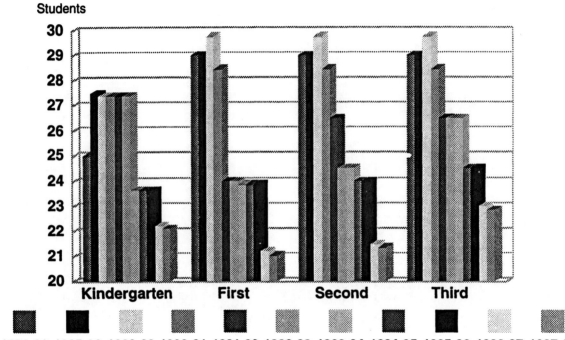

1979-80 1985-86 1988-89 1990-91 1991-92 1992-93 1993-94 1994-95 1995-96 1996-97 1997-98

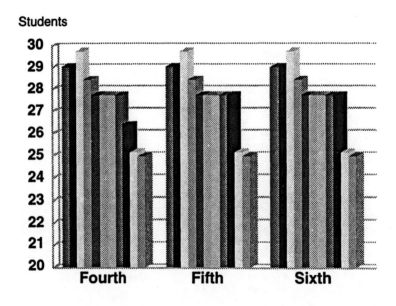

Exhibit 5-37—Other Useful Information

FISCAL YEAR 1997-98   **PRINCIPAL TAXPAYERS**

The ten largest taxpayers in the School District and the amount of 1997-98 taxes billed for each are shown below.

	Taxpayer	Type of Business	Taxes Billed
1.	Myrtle Beach Farms	Real Estate	$2,034,241
2.	General Telephone Company of the Southeast	Utility	1,515,753
3.	AVX Corporation	Manufacturer	1,053,799
4.	Horry Electric Cooperative	Utility	830,404
5.	Burroughs & Chapin	Developments	559,672
6.	Montgomery Company	Construction	489,052
7.	Carolina Equipment	Sales	484,791
8.	Combraco	Manufacturer	473,208
9.	WCI Investments	Retail Sales	425,316
10.	Justice, Inc.	Investments	418,992
	TOTAL		**$8,285,228**

Note: Taxes billed represents total taxes due for Horry County Schools, Horry County, Higher Education and Horry Georgetown Tech purposes.

Source: Horry County Finance Department

Horry County Schools

Exhibit 5-37 (continued)

Unprecedented development continues in Horry County. Development of the County's predominantly tourist-based economy has been extremely rapid. Most of the County's forty (40) miles of beaches stretching from the Georgetown County line to the North Carolina line have been developed residentially or commercially while at least 32% of the remainder of the County is yet to be developed. Thirty-two percent of the state's hotel and motel rooms are located in Horry County. Forty percent of the state's second homes are also located within the County.

Horry County ranks second in the nation in per capital housing starts, according to a "hotness index" published by U. S. Housing Markets, a Michigan research group. Woods & Poole, a Washington-based economics research group, predicted this year that Horry County will rank second in the nation over the next 20 years in job growth and population growth.

Horry County's biggest development, Carolina Forest, was opened by International Paper. Carolina Forest is approximately 17 square miles or 10,850 acres. To compare, the City of Myrtle Beach is also approximately 17 square miles or 10,700 acres. In thirty years, 50,000 to 60,000 people, twice the population of the City of Myrtle Beach, could live in Carolina Forest. There will be 37 subdivisions, eight to ten golf courses, and five million square feet of commercial space – that compares to two Restaurant Rows and North Myrtle Beaches combined. Horry County is striving to make this the County's first fully zoned and planned community. The overall concept is to intersperse houses with sidewalks, arranged by subdivisions with matching sinage, all planned around a downtown district with an old-fashioned Main Street called "Town Centre". Plans are being prepared for a precinct police department, fire stations and equipment, school construction and controlled commercial development. The population is estimated to be approximately 60 percent retirees and 40 percent younger families. The growth is expected to take place over the next 20 to 30 years. Carolina Forest is expected to be 50 percent occupied by 2005. This mass development means the County must analyze funding methods – impact fees, admissions taxes, property taxes, etc. Listed below is a partial list of infrastructure needs anticipated for Carolina Forest:

Schools:	Cost -	$54 million	Land needed – 160 acres
Fire Stations:	Cost -	$2.75 million	
		(5 stations & equipment)	
Libraries:	Cost -	$3.3 million	
County Complex:	Cost -	$3.6 million	
Public Park:	Cost -	$5.4 million	
Police:	Cost -	$5.1 million per year.	
		250 officers	
		(Budget in 2017:	
		$9.4 million)	

Horry County's Economic Development Division has committed to reorganizing the Planning Department and Commission to address the myriad of issues brought to the forefront by this community as well as by the overall development continuing throughout the County.

Horry County Schools

Exhibit 5-37 (continued)

The tourism industry is the most important industry on the Grand Strand, with more than $1.2 billion in new investment since 1994. New entertainment complexes, golf courses and accommodations will continue to occur over the next year, increasing investment and economic impact even further.

Myrtle Beach is the second biggest summer destination in America for 1996 per the Chamber of Commerce.

There were total travel expenditures of $2.3 billion in Horry County in 1995. Tourism spending exceeds thirty-seven percent of the state total. Accommodations tax collections increased 13.8 percent from $8,272,570 in fiscal year 1995 to $9,418,295 in fiscal year 1996. This constitutes 38.9 percent of the entire state's accommodations tax collections.

The beach, golf and entertainment theaters are all major attractions for the region with golf alone accounting for $287 million in expenditures in 1995. Group market sales are also an increasing part of the visitor industry for the Grand Strand.

The region now has more than 1,800 places to eat, more than 55,000 rooms available for overnight guests, 12 entertainment theaters and nearly 100 golf courses – not to mention miles of beachfront.

Retail sales, employment and construction are all intimately tied to the tourism industry. The increasing diversity of geographic origin and economic profile of tourists will help to alleviate any cyclical downturn in the national economy.

For 1997, the forecast calls for the occupancy rate to rise to an average of 59% despite an increase in available rooms. The average cost for an overnight stay is forecast to rise to $65.

Admission tax revenues are forecast to rise another 8.2% to $9.2 million.

There are many amusement attractions spanning the Grand Strand and over 100 golf courses located in the area constitute one of the largest concentrations of like facilities in the nation. By the end of 1997, the Grand Strand will have 107 courses, based on courses already open, under construction or already on the planning board. Golfers will be able to tee off any of 1,800 golf holes in the area. More than 500,000 vacationing golfers will play nearly 4.2 million rounds of golf here this year. Golf generates more than $644 million annually for the state's economy and employs more than 14,000 full time workers. The Horry County area accounts for more than 34 percent of South Carolina's golf courses with direct expenditures exceeding $30 million in 1995. This industry has been instrumental in the expansion of the tourist season, including early spring and late fall in our regular May through October season.

Horry County ranks 2nd in the state in agricultural production with more than $89.8 million in cash receipts in 1996. This adds an important component to the economic base. The County ranks high in the state in the production of crops including tobacco, soybeans and corn. The County ranks third in the state in the commercial fish landings at 1.1 million pounds. Manufacturing also provides stable employment for Horry County residents with more than one hundred seventy three (173) companies providing in excess of 6,900 jobs with payrolls greater than $154 million.

Horry County Schools

Exhibit 5-37 (continued)

FISCAL YEAR 1997-98   ECONOMIC CONDITION AND OUTLOOK

The Horry County Department of Airports, using the proceeds from bonds sold in June 1997 as well as operating revenues generated from the County airports, is completing a twenty-two million-dollar expansion and improvement program. The baggage claim area has been increased in size and expanded from two to four baggage conveyor belts, a new ticket counter was added, four new concession areas were added in the baggage claim area, and the rental car service and ready return lots have been relocated and expanded. The Airport will start a two million-dollar project in October 1997 to widen and repave the two center taxiways. This fall, the Airport should also start construction on a 3.5 million-dollar project to widen and extend the Terminal Road and curb front. The Public Benefit Conveyance of Air Force Base land should be completed by the end of FY98.

Aviation industry at the Myrtle Beach International Airport continues to bring new technical jobs to the County. Properties have been leased to an avionics repair company, an aircraft interior repair and refurbishment company, an aircraft maintenance repair company and a company that designs, manufactures, and installs aircraft parts and repairs/modifies aircraft. Prospective companies include the modification and repair of large aircraft and an aircraft painting company. The Airport is ideally suited for these industries because of the excellent facilities left by the Air Force, the quality and cost-of-living in the area and the availability of trained technicians.

A look back on some Grand Strand business highlights of 1997: House of Blues, all Star Café, Planet Hollywood, Pier One Imports and Ripley's Aquarium were a few of the national chains that debuted along the Grand Strand this year. Myrtle Beach's designation as a Metropolitan Statistical Area in the 1990 census and national media attention were credited for attracting the chains usually found in larger cities. The good news is that Horry County's unemployment dropped to an all-time low of 3.2 percent in August. The bad news is that businesses were scratching hard to find workers in the midst of a development boom. The labor shortage led some hotels to hire maids from the Caribbean and spurred efforts to get more workers bussed in from Williamsburg County, one of the state's poorest areas.

Total taxable retail sales in the Grand Strand showed a steady increase for almost 7% in 1996 over 1995 according to the preliminary figures. The increase represents real growth of about 4% after accounting for inflation.

Tourism accounts for well over half of the retail sales in the Grand Strand so a robust visitor season certainly transfers to retail sales. The golf industry is a major contributor to tourism sales with an estimated $287 million in expenditures in 1995.

Retail sales do of course show a seasonal pattern, but the first quarter of each year is the only one noticeably below the other quarters. This pattern indicates that the Grand Strand is becoming more of a year-round tourism destination than just a summer destination, although summer is still the peak.

While tourism is a vital part of retail sales, it is not the only contributor. Construction and manufacturing sectors are also important local industries that have a major contribution.

Horry County Schools

Exhibit 5-37 (continued)

FISCAL YEAR 1997-98   ECONOMIC CONDITION AND OUTLOOK

Further, as the population in the United States ages and retirees begin to look at the Grand Strand for retirement, another source of retail sales begin to emerge. Like tourists, retirees spend money in the community, but do not take up a position in the workforce.

With the large number of new projects under way or in place, such as Broadway at the Beach and Fantasy Harbour at Waccamaw, retail sales from both construction and tourism should continue to grow. The expansion of the manufacturing sector should continue to create well-paying jobs providing an income basis for even further growth in retail sales.

For 1997, forecast calls for retail sales to increase by more than inflation again to well over $5.5 billion for the first time ever.

The most significant industrial plant expansion in the County is at the AVX plant. A $20 million expansion has been started and will result in the employment of up to 250 more people and construction of an additional 100,000 square feet. The AVX Grand Strand site has been officially recognized as the manufacturer's national corporate headquarters.

Horry County and the City of Myrtle Beach agreed to build a 6000 seat baseball stadium at a cost of approximately $11 million to be completed in 1999.

In order to improve Horry County's mass transportation system, a major federal interstate I-73/I-74, which would begin in Michigan and pass through Ohio, West Virginia, Virginia, North Carolina and end in Charleston, South Carolina, after passing through the Grand Strand, is being planned by the Federal Highway Administration. The Federal Government has given South Carolina $400,000 to do a feasibility study. The U. S. House has passed a bill, the National Highway system, which contains plans for the project, which is currently underway.

In addition, the most aggressive road construction program in the history of Horry County, RIDE – Road Improvement and Development Effort was approved by Governor Beasley in September 1996. Horry County's RIDE Project is the initiation of a comprehensive solution for transportation problems which pairs significant funding from the local level with funding provided by the State of South Carolina. Horry County enacted an ordinance in the Fall of 1996 that implemented a 1.5 percent hospitality fee (accommodations, restaurants, amusements, golf and theaters) effective January 1, 1997. The purpose of this fee is to provide the financial ability for Horry County to partner with the State of South Carolina to meet the infrastructure needs of the County.

The participating parties of the RIDE project are Horry County, the South Carolina Transportation Infrastructure Bank and the South Carolina Department of Transportation. The role of the South Carolina Transportation Infrastructure Bank is to provide the necessary financing and funding for the RIDE project. It is Horry County's intent to contract with the South Carolina Department of Transportation to manage the design, construction and implementation of the RIDE project. Horry County, in addition to providing 30 percent of the overall cost of the RIDE project, will provide limited oversight to ensure that project schedules are met.

Horry County Schools

Exhibit 5-37 (continued)

The total cost of the RIDE Project is $774 million ($698 million in 1997 dollars, escalated at 4.5 percent per year over the construction period, seven years). The total debt service over the life of the proposed bonds for the RIDE project is $1.2 billion. Horry County's contribution to retire the debt is $368 million; the South Carolina Transportation infrastructure Bank is requested to fund the balance of the debt service, $859 million.

The RIDE Project includes a series of interconnected highway construction and road enhancements that will improve the overall transportation network in Horry County. These include:

♦ Conway Bypass – A fully controlled access facility from U. S. 17 (the bridge at Briarcliffe complete with interchange at U. S. 17) to U. S. 501 between Aynor and Conway; six land fill/bridging/paving between U. S. 17 and Carolina Bays Parkway, six lane fill/bridging/two-lane paving between S. C. 90 and S. C. 905, and two-lane fill/bridging/paving between S. C. 905 and U. S. 501, with temporary at-grade access allowed at U. S. 501,S. C. 319, U. S. 701, S. C. 905 and S. C. 90, the cost includes the purchase of right-of-way as originally designed.

♦ Carolina Bays Parkway – A fully controlled access facility, six-lane fill/bridging/four-lane paving from S. C. 9 to U. S. 501, including the Central Parkway connector crossing the Atlantic Intercoastal Waterway to U. S. 17 Bypass (four-lane fill/bridging/two-lane paving), the cost includes the purchase of right-of-way as originally designed.

♦ S. C. 544 – Five lanes from the U. S. 17 Bypass to U. S. 501.

♦ U. S. 501 – Frontage road system between the Atlantic Intercoastal Waterway and Forestbrook Road, intersection improvements between Forestbrook Road and the Waccamaw River, and an overpass at George Bishop Boulevard/River Oaks Drive.

♦ Central Parkway – Four lanes from the Central Parkway connector (between 48th Avenue North and 62nd Avenue North) to Harrelson Boulevard (in the vicinity of the Myrtle Beach International Airport).

♦ Fantasy Harbour Bridge Interchange – Four-lane bridge/interchange which will create the final leg of what is to be called the Metropolitan Loop, which includes Central Parkway, George Bishop Boulevard and River Oaks Drive and Extension.

♦ Conway Perimeter Road – Four lanes from U. S. 501 on the west side of Conway to U. S. 378.

♦ Intersection/Interchange Improvements – Along S. C. 90 between Conway Bypass and S. C. 9, S-31, S-66 and U. S. 17 Bypass.

SUMMARY

Horry County is continuing to experience the biggest building boom since the early 1980's. Developers see this new building boom as being healthy and substantial because it's being driven by market demands and big business investment rather than external influences such as the tax law changes of the 80's or recovery from a natural disaster. This building boom is the result of a combination of factors including a strong economy, a maturing market place and a fast-growing tourist base. Horry County recognizes this building boom and also is anticipating for the rate of build/construction/growth to stabilize within the next two to five years.

Horry County Schools

Exhibit 5-37 (continued)

Horry County is more than a bustling center of tourism and industrial activity. It is also a comfortable place in which to live, raise a family, and simply relax and enjoy life. County residents have the unique opportunity to both enjoy the pleasant tranquility of country living as well as the numerous amenities offered along the Grand Strand resort areas. Shopping opportunities are abundant in the community. A wide variety of dining choices are also available.

The outlook for the County is as exciting as the past has been. Horry is expected to grow to a permanent population approaching 200,000 by the year 2000.

Traditionally, tourism in Horry County grows at three times the national average, which is approximately 3 to 3.5%. Tourism population is projected to grow to 300,000 and the tourism season has expanded to ten months each year. This expansion of the tourism season and base are expected to provide more than 5,000 additional jobs. In addition, industrial employment is also projected to increase by 2,500 jobs by the year 2000. With projections like these, there is little doubt that the expectations for a thriving economy year round will be realized.

Exhibit 5-37 (continued)

HORRY COUNTY   POPULATION TRENDS

Year	Population	Percentage Increase
1920	32,077	
1930	39,376	23%
1940	51,951	32%
1950	59,820	15%
1960	68,247	14%
1970	69,998	3%
1980	101,419	45%
1990	144,053	42%
1996	175,500	22%
1997	187,047	7%

Source: Horry County Finance Department/Coastal Carolina University

Exhibit 5-38—Other Useful Information

MSD of Washington Township, Indianapolis, Indiana
Map of the School District
1998 Annual Budget

ASC - Administration Service Center
AV - Allisonville Elementary School
CC - Crooked Creek Elementary School
EW - Eastwood Middle School
FH - Foxhill Elementary School
GB - Greenbriar Elementary School
HC - Harcourt Elementary School
HT - Hilltop Kindergarten
JEL - J. Everett Light Career Center School
JS - John Strange Elementary School
NO - Nora Elementary School
NC - North Central High School
NV - Northview Middle School
SM - Spring Mill Elementary School
WL - Westlane Elementary School

A Glossary of Terms

(Criterion E-12)

Exhibit 5-39

Exhibit 5-39—Glossary of Terms

Mt. Lebanon School District
1997-98 Budget

GLOSSARY

This Glossary contains definitions of terms used in this guide and such additional terms as seem necessary to common understandings concerning financial accounting procedures for schools. Several terms which are not primarily financial accounting terms have been included because of their significance for school financial accounting. The glossary is arranged alphabetically with appropriate cross-referencing where necessary.

ACCOUNTING SYSTEM -- The total structure of records and procedures which discover, record, classify, and report information on the financial position and operations of a school district or any of its funds, balanced account groups and organizational components.

ACCRUAL BASIS -- The basis of accounting under which revenues are recorded when levies are made, and expenditures are recorded as soon as they result in liabilities, regardless of when the revenue is actually received or the payment is actually made. See also **ESTIMATED REVENUE** and **EXPENDITURES.**

ACCRUE -- To record revenues when earned or when levies are made, and to record expenditures as soon as they result in liabilities, regardless of when the revenue is actually received or the payment is actually made. Sometimes, the term is used in a restricted sense to denote the recording of revenues earned but not yet due, such as accrued interest on investments and the recording of expenditures which result in liabilities that are payable in another accounting period, such as accrued interest on bonds. See also **ACCRUAL BASIS.**

ACCRUED INTEREST -- Interest accumulated between interest dates but not yet due.

APPROPRIATION -- An authorization granted by a legislative body to make expenditures and to incur obligations for specific purposes. Note: An appropriation is usually limited in amount and as to the time when it may be expended.

APPROPRIATION ACCOUNT -- A budgetary account set up to record specific authorizations to spend. The account is credited with original and any supplemental appropriations and is charged with expenditures and encumbrances.

BALANCE SHEET -- A summarized statement, as of a given date, of the financial position of a local education agency per fund and/or all funds combined showing assets, liabilities, reserves, and fund balance.

Exhibit 5-39 (continued)

Mt. Lebanon School District
1997-98 Budget

GLOSSARY
(Continued)

BOARD OF SCHOOL DIRECTORS -- The elected or appointed body which has been created according to state law and vested with responsibilities for educational activities in a given geographical area.

BOND -- A written promise, generally under seal, to pay a specific sum of money, called the face value, at a fixed time in the future, called the date of maturity and carrying interest at a fixed rate, usually payable periodically. The difference between a note and a bond is that the latter usually runs for a longer period of time and requires greater legal formality. See also **SURETY BOND.**

BONDED DEBT -- The part of the school district debt which is covered by outstanding bonds of the district. Sometimes called "Funded Debt."

BONDS AUTHORIZED AND ISSUED -- The part of the school district debt which is covered by outstanding bonds of the district. Sometimes called "Funded Debt."

BONDS AUTHORIZED AND UNISSUED -- Bonds which have been legally authorized but not issued and which can be issued and sold without further authorization.

BONDS ISSUED -- Bonds sold.

BONDS PAYABLE -- The face value of bonds issued and unpaid.

BUDGET -- A plan of financial operation embodying an estimate of proposed expenditures for a given period or purpose and the proposed means of financing them.

BUDGETARY CONTROL -- The control or management of the business affairs of the school district in accordance with an approved budget with a responsibility to keep expenditures within the authorized amounts.

BUILDINGS -- A fixed asset account which reflects the acquisition value of permanent structures used to house persons and property owned by the local education agency. If buildings are purchased or constructed, this amount includes the purchase or contract price of all permanent buildings and fixtures attached to and forming a permanent part of such buildings. If buildings are acquired by gift, the account reflects their appraised value at time of acquisition.

CAPITAL BUDGET -- A plan of proposed capital outlays and the means of financing them for the current fiscal period. It is usually a part of the current budget.

CAPITAL OUTLAYS -- Expenditures which result in the acquisition of or addition to fixed assets.

Exhibit 5-39 (continued)

Mt. Lebanon School District
1997-98 Budget

GLOSSARY
(Continued)

CLASSIFICATION, FUNCTION -- As applied to expenditures, this term has reference to an activity or service aimed at accomplishing a certain purpose or end; for example. Regular instruction, special education, vocational education, or operation and maintenance of plant.

CLASSIFICATION, OBJECT -- As applied to expenditures, this term has reference to an article or service received; for example, salaries, employee benefits or supplies.

CODING -- A system of numbering, or otherwise designating, accounts, entries, invoices, vouchers, etc. in such a manner that the symbol used reveals quickly certain required information.

CONTRACTED SERVICES -- Labor, material and other costs for services rendered by personnel who are not on the payroll of the local education agency.

COST PER PUPIL -- See **CURRENT EXPENDITURES PER PUPIL**.

CURRENT EXPENDITURES PER PUPIL -- Current expenditures for a given period of time divided by a pupil unit of measure.

DEBT -- An obligation resulting from the borrowing of money or from the purchase of goods and services. Debts of local education agencies include bonds, warrants and notes, etc.

DEBT LIMIT -- The maximum amount of gross or net debt which is legally permitted.

DEBT SERVICE -- Expenditures for the retirement of debt and expenditures for interest on debt.

ENCUMBRANCE ACCOUNTING -- A system or procedure which involves giving recognition in the accounting budgetary expenditure control records for the issuance of purchase orders, statements, or other commitments chargeable to an appropriation in advance of any liability or payment.

ENCUMBRANCES -- Purchase orders, contracts, and/or other commitments which are chargeable to an appropriation and for which a part of the appropriation is reserved. They cease to be encumbrances when paid, as in accounts payable, or when actual liability is established or when cancelled.

EQUIPMENT -- Those moveable items used for school operation that are of a non-expendable and mechanical nature, i.e. perform an operation. Typewriters, projectors, vacuum cleaners, accounting machines, computers, lathes, clocks, machinery, and vehicles, etc. are classified as equipment. (Heating and air conditioning systems, lighting fixtures and similar items permanently fixed to or within a building are considered as part of the building.)

Exhibit 5-39 (continued)

Mt. Lebanon School District
1997-98 Budget

GLOSSARY
(Continued)

ESTIMATED REVENUE -- When the accounts are kept on an accrual basis, this term designates the amount of revenue estimated to accrue during a given period regardless of whether or not it is all to be collected during the period.

EXPENDITURES -- This includes total charges incurred, whether paid or unpaid, for current costs, capital outlay, and debt service. (Transfers between funds, encumbrances, exchanges of cash for other current assets such as the purchase investments in U.S. bonds and payments of cash in settlement of liabilities already accounted as expenditures.)

FISCAL PERIOD -- Any period at the end of which a local education agency determines its financial position and the results of its operations. The period may be a month, a quarter, or a year, depending upon the scope of operation a requirements for managerial control and reporting. The fiscal year of Mt. Lebanon School District begins July 1, and ends June 30.

FUND -- A sum of money or other resources set aside for specific activities of a school district. The fund accounts constitute a complete entity and all of the financial transactions for the particular fund are recorded in them.

FUND BALANCE -- The excess of assets of a fund over its liabilities and reserves. During the fiscal year prior to closing, it represents the excess of the fund's assets and estimated revenues for the period over its liabilities, reserves and appropriations for the period.

FUND BALANCE; UNDESIGNATED -- That portion of the excess funds which has no legal commitments or formal designations by the board of school directors for future funding needs.

FUND, GENERAL -- The fund used to finance the ordinary operations of the local education agency. It is available for a legally authorized purpose and consists of money not specifically designated for some other particular purpose.

INSTRUCTION -- The activities dealing directly with the teaching of students or improving the quality of teaching.

LEVY -- (Verb) To impose taxes or special assessments. (Noun) The total of taxes or special assessments imposed by a governmental unit.

MAINTENANCE, PLANT (PLANT REPAIRS AND REPAIRS AND REPLACEMENTS OF EQUIPMENT) -Those activities which are concerned with keeping the grounds, buildings, and equipment at their original condition of completeness or efficiency, either through repairs or by replacements of property (anything less than replacement of a total building).

PCPs (PROGRAM CHANGE PROPOSALS) -- The annual list of program enhancements presented to the board for funding consideration.

Exhibit 5-39 (continued)

Mt. Lebanon School District
1997-98 Budget

GLOSSARY
(Continued)

PERSONNEL, ADMINISTRATIVE -- Personnel on the school payroll who are primarily engaged in activities which have as their purpose the general regulation, direction, and control of the affairs of the school district.

PERSONNEL, CLERICAL -- Personnel occupying positions which have as their major responsibilities the preparing, transferring, transcribing, systematizing, or preserving of written communications and records. This includes classroom aides.

PERSONNEL, HEALTH -- Persons in the field of physical and mental health such as physicians, psychologists, school nurses, and dentists whose services are directed primarily to students, although sometimes used for group activities.

PERSONNEL, INSTRUCTIONAL -- Those who render services dealing directly with the instruction of pupils.

PERSONNEL, MAINTENANCE -- Personnel on the school payroll who are primarily engaged in the repairing and upkeep of grounds, buildings, and equipment.

PROGRAM -- The definition of an effort to accomplish a specific objective or objectives consistent with funds or resources available. Budgets and actual revenue and expenditure records may be maintained per program.

PROGRAM BUDGET -- A budget wherein expenditures are based primarily on programs of work and secondarily on character and object. A program budget further defines function to subject area when necessary.

PUBLIC SCHOOL CODE OF 1949 -- The primary State law which governs school districts.

RECEIPTS, NONREVENUE -- Amounts received which either incur an obligation that must be met at some future date or change the form of an asset from property to cash and therefore decrease the amount and value of school property. Money received from loans, sale of bonds, sale of property purchased from capital funds, and proceeds from insurance loss settlements constitute most of the nonrevenue receipts.

RECEIPTS, REVENUE -- Additions to assets which do not incur an obligation that must be met at some future date and do not represent exchanges of property for money.

SCHOOL -- A division of the school system consisting of a group of pupils composed of one or more teachers to give instruction of a defined type, and housed in a school plant of one or more buildings. More than one school may be housed in one school plant, as is the case when the elementary and secondary programs are housed in the same school plant.

Exhibit 5-39 (continued)

Mt. Lebanon School District
1997-98 Budget

GLOSSARY
(Continued)

SCHOOL, ELEMENTARY -- A school classified as elementary by State and local practice and composed of any span of grades not above grade six. This term includes kindergartens if they are under the control of the local school board of education. Mt. Lebanon's grade structure currently includes students in grades K thru 6.

SCHOOL, JUNIOR HIGH -- A separately organized secondary school intermediate between elementary and senior high school. Mt. Lebanon's grade structure currently includes students in grades 7 and 8.

SCHOOL, MIDDLE -- A school offering education to students spanning both elementary and secondary levels. Mt. Lebanon is planning to move to a 6-8 grade configuration.

SCHOOL, SENIOR HIGH -- A school offering the final years of high school work necessary for graduation; invariably preceded by a junior high school in the same system. Mt. Lebanon's grade structure currently includes students in grades 9 through 12.

SCHOOL, SUMMER -- The name applied to the school session carried on during the period between the end of the regular school term and the beginning of the next regular school term. Tuition is charged to participants of a summer school program.

SCHOOL, VOCATIONAL -- A secondary school which is separately organized under a principal for the purpose of offering training in one or more skilled or semi-skilled trades or occupations.

SCHOOL PLANT -- The site, buildings, and equipment constituting the physical facilities used by a single school or by two or more schools sharing the use of common facilities.

SCHOOL SITE -- The land and all improvements to the site, other than structures, such as grading, drainage, drives, parking areas, walks, plantings and playgrounds, and playfields.

STUDENT-BODY ACTIVITIES -- Services for public school pupils, such as interscholastic athletics, entertainments, publications, clubs, band, and orchestra, that are managed or operated by the student body under the guidance and direction of an adult, and are not part of the regular instructional program.

SURETY BOND -- A written promise to pay damages or to indemnify against losses caused by the party or parties named in the document, through nonperformance or through defalcation; for example, a surety bond given by a contractor or by an official handling cash or securities.

TAXES -- Compulsory charges levied by a governmental unit for the purpose of financing services performed for the common benefit.

Association of School Business Officials International
11401 North Shore Drive
Reston, VA 20190-4200

MERITORIOUS BUDGET AWARDS CRITERIA

A. GENERAL

1. The cover of the budget must contain the title "Budget", include the full name of the school entity, the city/county and state/province in which the entity is located, and the budget year covered.

2. The document should be divided by major sections with consecutive page numbers. A Table of Contents should precede the *Introductory Section* which identifies all the major sections.

3. A cover letter should identify any information required by the criteria that is not relevant to the school entity and therefore not included in the budget presentation. For example, for some dependent school districts, assessed and market value of taxable property and tax rates may not be information relevant to their budgets.

4. Submitters must respond to the previous review team recommendations regarding not meeting criteria in a separate letter.

5. The use of graphs and charts is encouraged in all sections of the budget document to facilitate the understanding of the presentation.

6. The budget document should be technically well prepared, easy to read, information should flow in a logical sequence, narratives should be clear and understandable, and the document should be free of spelling or grammar errors.

7. Budgets must meet all criteria to be eligible for the *Meritorious Budget Award*.

B. INTRODUCTORY SECTION

1. The document should include an *Executive Summary* which is liftable and which presents the budget in narrative, numeric and graphic form. The *Executive Summary* should present, in an integrated and summary form, the following components of the budget:

   a. An *Organizational Summary Component* which includes a discussion of the major goals and objectives, a brief summary of the budget process, a description of significant changes in the budget process and/or budget policies, and an explanation of how human/financial resources are allocated to achieve significant goals and objectives.

b.   A *Financial Summary Component* which presents an overview of revenues and expenses/expenditures for all funds, budget comparisons of at least the current year to the budget year, a discussion of significant trends, events and` initiatives, and an explanation of significant financial and demographic changes. The use of charts and graphs is strongly encouraged.

c.   An *Informational Summary Component* which presents important data and information in which there is a high level of public interest.

2.   The document should include a copy of the *Meritorious Budget Award* certificate if received for the prior year.

3.   The document should also include a listing of members of the school board and first-level administrative personnel.

C. ORGANIZATIONAL SECTION

1.   The document should provide an explanation of the school entity which includes the following:
- Legal autonomy, fiscal independence/dependence
- Level of education (type of service) provided (elementary, secondary, intermediate unit, community college)
- Geographic area served
- Number of students and number of schools
- Number of funds and fund types and titles (governmental, proprietary, fiduciary)
- An explanation of the classification of revenues/expenditures
- An explanation of the measurement basis for budget revenues and expenditures (GAAP, cash, modified accrual, or some other basis)

2.   The document should include a discussion of significant budget and financial policies, procedures, rules, and regulations at the legal, board and administrative levels. Such policies discussions may include, among others, legal, board or administrative requirements on fund balance, encumbrances, reserves and debt management.

3.   The document should include an organizational chart which includes the administrative staff by position or title.

4.   The document should include a coherent statement of the mission of the school entity.

5.   The document should set forth the major goals and objectives for the school entity. If the cost of a goal or objective is significant and measurable it is suggested, but not required, that the cost be included.

6.   The document should describe the budget development process including the capital budget development process.

7.   The document should describe the budget administration and management process.

D. FINANCIAL SECTION

1. The document should include a presentation of the budgets for all governmental and proprietary funds of the school entity at the legal level required by state/provincial laws and/or the level at which the budget is adopted by the governing body of the school entity. The presentation should include revenues by source and expenditures by function and object. Budgets may also be presented by program, location and/or by administrative unit. In addition to the minimum level of presentation required above, budgets may also be presented in greater detail.

2. The presentation of the budgets should use a pyramid approach which begins with a summary of all funds and then presents individual funds. These presentations may be followed by optional program, location and/or administrative unit budgets.

3. The presentation of the budgets should include fund balances, revenues, expenditures and other financing sources/uses, for the current year budget and/or the estimated current year actual and the proposed budget year. The presentation of three years of actual data is preferred in this *Financial Section*. However, at the option of the preparer/submitter, this information may be presented in the *Informational Section* in a form and format which is comparable to the current year and proposed budget year data presented in this section.

4. The document should include budgeted capital expenditures and list major capital projects for the budget year, whether authorized in the operating budget or in a separate capital budget.

5. The document should describe if and to what extent capital improvements or other major capital spending will affect the school entity's current and future operating budgets. The focus should be on reasonably quantifiable additional costs and savings (direct and indirect) or other service impacts that result from capital spending.

6. The document should include financial data on current debt obligation, describe the relationship between current debt levels and legal debt limits, and explain the effects of existing debt levels on current and future budgets.

E. INFORMATIONAL SECTION

1. The document should describe major revenue sources, explain the underlying assumptions for the revenue estimates, and discuss significant revenue trends. Some explanation of the state/local funding structure and regulations may be necessary to complete this explanation.

2. The document should present the assessed and market value of taxable property of the school entity for a minimum of three years actual, current year budget and/or estimated current year, and the proposed budget year.

3. The document should include the property tax rates and collections for a minimum of three years actual, current year budget and/or estimated current year, and the proposed budget year. The document should describe whether the tax rate is a rate per ($100) of taxable value or on some other form of rate.

4.	The document should include an analysis of the budget's effect on taxpayers (tax burden on citizens) for a minimum of three years actual, current year budget and/or estimated current year, and the proposed budget year.

5.	The document should provide a five-year summary comparison of revenues and expenditures for the three prior years actual, current year budget and/or estimated current year actual, and proposed budget year for all governmental funds. Presentation of similar data for other funds is optional. If the preparer/submitter opted to include three years of actual data with the presentation of the current year and proposed budget year in the *Financial Section*, this requirement was met in the *Financial Section* and to present the information again in the *Informational Section* is redundant and unnecessary. The five-year summary if presented in the *Informational Section* must be in a form and format that is comparable to the data presented for the current year and proposed budget year in the *Financial Section*.

6.	The document should present a minimum of three years of budget forecasts beyond the proposed budget year, which include beginning and ending fund balance, and revenue and expenditures for all governmental funds.

7.	The document should present a minimum of three years of actual student enrollment history, the current budget and/or estimated current year enrollment, the proposed budget year enrollment and a minimum of three years of enrollment projections. Forecasting methodology and techniques must also be discussed as part of the presentation on enrollment projections.

8.	The document should present personnel resource allocations of the school entity for a minimum of three prior years actual, current year budget and/or estimated current year actual, and proposed budget year.

9.	The document should include the bond amortization schedule(s) of the school entity.

10.	The document should provide performance measures (quantitative and/or qualitative measurement of results) for a minimum of three prior years. Such performance measures may include standardized test scores, drop-out rates, accomplishment of goals and objectives, parent/student satisfaction surveys and/or other performance measures.

11.	The document should include other information that would help the reader understand the past and future directions of the school entity.

12.	The document should include a glossary of terms to improve understanding.

Association of School Business Officials International
Meritorious Budget Awards Program Application

APPLICANT INFORMATION

Full Name of School System _____
(This name will appear on all Meritorious Budget Award announcements and the award plaque.)

Street Address _____

City _____ State/Province _____ Zip/Postal Code _____

☐ Ms. ☐ Mrs. ☐ Mr.   ☐ Ph.D. ☐ Ed.D.   ☐ RSBA   ☐ RSBO   ☐ RSBS

Name of Submitting School Official _____

Title _____

Phone Number _____ Fax Number _____ E-mail _____

Are you an ASBO International member? ☐ Yes   ☐ No   Member # _____

SCHOOL SYSTEM INFORMATION

Fiscal/Calendar year beginning _____ Fiscal/Calendar year ended _____

Date budget was legally adopted _____

Size of budget (total of budgets, all governmental funds) _____

Is this your school system's first application to the program? ☐ Yes   ☐ No

Federal Employer Identification Number (FEIN) _____
(This is your school system's unique identification in ASBO International's database.)

FEE INFORMATION

Check the appropriate fee category and include payment with your application. All fees must be in U.S. dollars.

Total Revenue, All Funds	Member Fees	Non-Member Fees
Less than $10 million	$ 525	$ 675
$10 to $50 million	$ 675	$ 825
Greater than $50 million	$ 900	$1,025

Method of payment:

☐ Check or Money order enclosed

Charge: ☐ MasterCard   ☐ VISA

Account number _____ Expires _____

Signature _____

MBABK

MEMBERSHIP APPLICATION/RENEWAL

A school business official or a school system may become a member or renew membership with ASBO International with this application. All membership publications and correspondence will be mailed to the official designated below.

☐ Ms.   ☐ Mrs.   ☐ Mr.   ☐ Ph.D.   ☐ Ed.D.   ☐ RSBA   ☐ RSBO   ☐ RSBS

Name of Submitting School Official _____

Title _____

School System _____

Street Address _____

City _____ State/Province _____ Zip/Postal Code _____

Phone Number _____ Fax Number _____ E-mail _____

Membership Choices:

       ☐ Active Individual (voting privileges and non-transferable) $125
       ☐ Active School (voting privileges and transferrable) $125
       ☐ Publications Only (non-voting) $ 68

Dues are for a twelve-month period. Dues include a $50 subscription to *School Business Affairs* magazine and a $20 subscription to *ASBO Accents* newsletter.

AWARD ANNOUNCEMENT

If you would like others to be notified of your accomplishment, please list these persons.

☐ Ms.   ☐ Mrs.   ☐ Mr.   ☐ Ph.D.   ☐ Ed.D.

Name _____

Title _____

Organization _____

Street Address _____

City _____ State/Province _____ Zip/Postal Code _____

☐ Ms.   ☐ Mrs.   ☐ Mr.   ☐ Ph.D.   ☐ Ed.D.

Name _____

Title _____

Organization _____

Street Address _____

City _____ State/Province _____ Zip/Postal Code _____

APPLICATION MATERIALS

Your application must include:

- 1 copy of a completed application form
- 4 copies of the school system's budget
- 4 copies of the completed Criteria Location Checklist
- 4 copies of the school system's responses to last year's comments (if applicable)
- 4 copies of a transmittal letter indicating any Meritorious Budget Award Criteria that do not apply to the school system because of legal requirements (if applicable)
- Appropriate payment

If four complete sets of materials are not forwarded, processing will be delayed.

The application must be postmarked within ninety (90) days of the legal adoption of the budget. The application, with materials and payment, should be forwarded to:

ASBO International
Meritorious Budget Awards Program
11401 North Shore Drive
Reston, VA 20190-4200

A typical review requires at least 12-16 weeks to process.

APPEALS PROCEDURE

If a school system is denied a Meritorious Budget Award, the decision may be appealed. Within 30 days of the receipt of a denial letter, the school system should resubmit to ASBO International three copies of its budget, three copies of the original Criteria Location Checklist, and a letter requesting an appeal and addressing why the school system believes the denial is inappropriate.

ASBO International staff will send the resubmitted budget to an Appeals Review Team. The Appeals Review Team will review the budget and decide to award or deny the Meritorious Budget Award. The decision of the Appeals Review Team is final.

Association of School Business Officials International
Meritorious Budget Awards Program

Criteria Location Checklist

me of Entity: _____   State/Province: _____

e purpose of this checklist is to ensure applicants have met the requirements of the Meritorious Budget Awards
program criteria and Reviewers are able to locate examples in the budget document that meet the criteria.

A. GENERAL REQUIREMENTS	APPLICANT USE List all pages of budget document where examples can be found.	REVIEWER USE EC = Exceeds Criteria MC = Meets Criteria DN = Does Not Meet Criteria
1. The cover contains: • The title "Budget" • Full name of the entity • City/County of the entity* • State/Province of the entity* • Budget year covered *Provide City/County and State/Province that is used in the entity's formal address.		
2a. The document should be divided into major sections.		
2b. The pages of the document should be numbered consecutively from page 1 to __.		
2c. A Table of Contents precedes the Introductory Section.		
2d. The Table of Contents identifies all major sections.		
3. A cover letter identifies any information required by the criteria that is not relevant to the school entity.		
4. A response to the previous review team recommendations has been provided by this school entity in a separate letter.		
5. The use of graphs and charts is used to enhance communication.		
6. The budget document should: • Be technically well prepared • Be easy to read • Flow in a logical sequence • Be clear and understandable in narration • Be free of spelling and grammar errors	Note: Entire budget document should meet this requirement of the Meritorious Budget Awards Program. Listing of page numbers is unnecessary.	

REVIEWER COMMENTS:

B. INTRODUCTORY SECTION	APPLICANT USE List all pages of budget document where examples can be found.	REVIEWER USE EC = Exceeds Criteria MC = Meets Criteria DN = Does Not Meet Criteria
1a. The document includes an Executive Summary.		
1b. The Executive Summary is liftable (liftable means that the Executive Summary presents a comprehensive summary of required information in each section of the budget and could be presented separate from the budget document).		
1c. The Executive Summary tells the budget story in narrative, numeric and graphic form.		
1d. The Executive Summary presents in an integrated and summary form the following components of the budget: (A) The Organizational component • Major goals and objectives • Budget process • Significant changes in the budget process and/or budget policies • Explanation of allocation of human and financial resources to achieve goals and objectives		
(B) The Financial component • Overview of revenues and expenses/expenditures for all funds • Budget comparisons of at least the current year to the budget year • Discussion of significant trends, events and initiatives • Explanation of significant financial and demographic changes •Use of charts and graphs		
(C) The Informational component • Budget forecast • Student enrollment trends • Tax base and rate trends • Personnel resource changes • Changes in debt of the school entity • Performance results		
2. The document includes the Meritorious Budget Award certificate if received for the prior year.		
3. The document includes a listing of members of the School Board. The document includes a listing of first-level administrative personnel.		

REVIEWER COMMENTS:

C. ORGANIZATIONAL SECTION	APPLICANT USE List all pages of budget document where examples can be found.	REVIEWER USE EC = Exceeds Criteria MC = Meets Criteria DN = Does Not Meet Criteria

1. The document should provide an explanation of the school entity which includes the following:
    • Legal autonomy, fiscal independence/dependence
    • Level of education provided
    • Geographic area served
    • Number of students and number of schools
    • Number of funds and fund types and titles
    • Explanation of the classification of revenues/expenditures
    • Explanation of the measurement basis for budget revenues/expenditures		

2. A discussion of significant budget and financial:
    • Policies
    • Procedures
    • Regulations which govern the budget process		

3. An organizational chart which includes the administrative staff by position or title.		
4. A coherent statement of the mission of the school entity.		
5. The major goals and objectives for the school entity. *If the cost of a goal or objective is significant and measurable, it is suggested that the cost be included.*		
6. Describe the budget development process. • Include the capital budget development process		
7. Describe the budget administration and management process.		

© 1994

REVIEWER COMMENTS:

D. FINANCIAL SECTION	APPLICANT USE List all pages of budget document where examples can be found.	REVIEWER USE EC = Exceeds Criteria MC = Meets Criteria DN = Does Not Meet Criteria
1. A presentation of the budgets includes: • All governmental funds • All proprietary funds • Level of detail required by law or adopted by the governing body • Revenues by source • Expenditures by function and object *Optional: Budgets may also be presented by program, location and/or administrative unit.*		
2. A pyramid approach should be used (summary of all funds, followed with the presentation of individual funds). *Optional: The presentation may be followed by program, location, and/or administrative unit budgets.*		
3. The budget presentation includes: • Fund balances • Revenues • Expenditures • Other financing sources/uses • The current year budget or estimated current year actual • The proposed budget year *The presentation of three prior years of actual data is preferred in the Financial Section. At the option of the preparer, the information may be presented in the Informational Section in a form and format which is comparable to the current year and proposed year.*		
4. The document should include: • Budgeted capital expenditures • Major capital projects for the budget year (whether authorized in the operating budget or in a separate capital budget)		
5. Describe to what extent capital improvements or other major capital spending will affect the school entity's current and future operating budgets. *The focus should be on reasonably quantifiable additional costs and savings (direct and indirect) or other service impacts that result from capital spending.*		
6. The document should: • Include financial data on current debt obligations • Describe the relationship between current debt levels and legal debt limits • Explain the effects of existing debt levels on current and future budgets		

REVIEWER COMMENTS:

E. Informational Section	Applicant Use List all pages of budget document where examples can be found.	Reviewer Use EC = Exceeds Criteria MC = Meets Criteria DN = Does Not Meet Criteria

1. The document should:
  • Describe major revenue sources
  • Explain underlying assumptions for each major revenue estimates
  • Discuss significant trends for each major revenue
 	
Some explanation of the state/local funding structure may be necessary.		

2. Present the assessed value of taxable property and the market value of taxable property for:
  • A minimum of three years actual
  • The current year budget and/or estimated current year actual
  • The proposed budget year		

3. Include property tax rates and collections for:
  • A minimum of three years actual
  • The current year budget and/or estimated current year actual
  • The proposed budget year
 	
Describe whether the tax rate is per $100 of taxable value or on some other form of rate		

4. Include an analysis of the budget's effect on taxpayers for:
  • A minimum of three years actual
  • The current year budget and/or estimated current year actual
  • The proposed budget year		

5. The document should provide a:
  • Five-year summary comparison of revenues and expenditures (three prior years actual, current year budget and/or estimated actual, and the proposed budget year. If the three prior years actual data is presented in the Financial Section, this presentation is not required.) All years must be presented in a comparable form and format, whether presented in the Financial or Informational Section.
  • Five-year summary should be presented for all governmental funds. (Presentation of similar data for other funds is optional.)		

6. Present a minimum of three years of budget forecasts beyond the proposed budget year.
  • Include beginning and ending fund balance
  • Revenue
  • Expenditures
 	
The three years of budget forecasts is for each governmental fund. Forecasts for other funds is optional.		

Continued on back.

E. Informational Section	Applicant Use List all pages of budget document where examples can be found.	Reviewer Use EC = Exceeds Criteria MC = Meets Criteria DN = Does Not Meet Criteria
7. The document should present: • A minimum of three years of actual student enrollment history • Current budget and/or estimated current year enrollment • Proposed budget year enrollment • A minimum of three years of enrollment projections • Forecasting methodology and techniques		
8. Present personnel resource allocations for: • A minimum of three prior years actual • The current year budget and/or estimated current year actual • The proposed budget year		
9. Include the bond amortization schedule(s) of the school entity.		
10. Provide performance measures for three prior years. • Standardized test scores • Drop-out rates • Accomplishment of goals and objectives • Parent/student satisfaction surveys • Other performance measures		
11. Include other information to help the reader understand the past and future directions of the school entity.		
12. Include a glossary of terms.		

Reviewer Comments:

SUMMARY OF CRITERIA	REVIEWER USE EC = Exceeds Criteria MC = Meets Criteria DN = Does Not Meet Criteria
A. GENERAL REQUIREMENTS	
B. INTRODUCTORY SECTION	
C. ORGANIZATIONAL SECTION	
D. FINANCIAL SECTION	
E. INFORMATIONAL SECTION	
BUDGET PRESENTATION	

REVIEWER COMMENTS:

REVIEWER AWARD CONCLUSION:

☐ Award Meritorious Budget Award   ☐ Deny Meritorious Budget Award

Reviewer Signature _____   Date _____

CPSIA information can be obtained at www.ICGtesting.com
Printed in the USA
BVOW04s1449300715

410797BV00024B/36/P